The Way We Vote

The Way We Vote

The Local Dimension
of American Suffrage

Alec C. Ewald

Vanderbilt University Press

Nashville

© 2009 by Vanderbilt University Press
Nashville, Tennessee 37235
All rights reserved

13 12 11 10 09 1 2 3 4 5

This book is printed on acid-free paper
made from 30% post-consumer recycled content.
Manufactured in the United States of America

Library of Congress Cataloging-in-Publication Data

Ewald, Alec C., 1970–
The way we vote : The local dimension of American
suffrage / Alec C. Ewald.
p. cm.
Includes bibliographical references and index.
ISBN 978-0-8265-1653-4 (cloth : alk. paper)
ISBN 978-0-8265-1654-1 (pbk. : alk. paper)
1. Suffrage—United States—History. 2. Voting—United
States—History. 3. Election officials—United States—History.
4. United States—Politics and government. I. Title.
JK1846.E94 2009
324.6'20973—dc22
2008035572

Contents

Acknowledgments

There is a convention of thanking one's spouse or partner last, presumably for dramatic effect. I would prefer to remove any doubt that my first and last debt is to my wife, Emily. Thank you.

Though it stings to know I am forgetting many important people, it is still a great pleasure to acknowledge here those who have helped in the writing of this book. John Brigham provided invaluable guidance in the project's early life, as did his colleagues at the University of Massachusetts, Sheldon Goldman and Ray LaRaja. At Vanderbilt University Press, Michael Ames has provided an ideal mix of patience, close reading, and critical prodding. The comments of three anonymous reviewers made the book much better (I hope). Several people read parts of the manuscript and offered key suggestions, questions, and criticisms: John Dinan, Heather Gerken, Rick Hasen, Brian Pinaire, Rick Valelly, and Avital Rosenberg. Naturally, I bear responsibility for those factual errors and interpretive flaws that I somehow snuck past these readers. Many others offered timely research suggestions, including Peter Argersinger, Keith Bybee, Doug Chapin, William Gillespie, John Mark Hansen, Jeffery Jenkins, Dan Katz, Brian Landsberg, Marc Mauer, Lori Minnite, Becky Morton, Spencer Overton, Rick Pildes, Tim Ryan, Scott Schaffer, and Jessica Trounstine. For inspiration, support, and conversations that helped clarify important concepts, thanks to Jim Biancolo, Alyson Ewald, Rich and Gaelen Ewald, Ian Finseth, Lisa Holmes, Dustin Howes, Garrison Nelson, Greg Petrow, John Roberts, Adam Schiffer, Peter VonDoepp, and Alex Zakaras.

This book is dedicated to my teachers.

Introduction

The right to vote is protected in more than the
initial allocation of the franchise. Equal protection
applies as well to the manner of its exercise.
    Bush v. Gore (2000)

The texts of the law must be made socially
real: enacted, implemented, imposed.
    Sally Engle Merry (2000)

In the long and roiled wake of the 2000 election, Americans are still fight-
ing over the way we vote. Voter registration, ballot design and technology,
polling-place selection, who should pay for elections (and how much), how
to count (and recount) votes, the process for "purging" voters—all once
lumped under the unglamorous title of "election administration" and widely
ignored—are now hotly disputed in courts, legislatures, op-ed pages, weblogs,
and the academy. The study of voting was once called *psephology*, a term derived from the Greek word for "pebble," which also came to mean "ballot"
or "vote" since Greeks dropped pebbles into vessels to decide some public
contests. American voters now tap screens instead of tossing small stones, but
psephology is back with a vengeance. Each day brings a new think-tank study,
book, academic article, or media exposé on the trials and tribulations of exercising the franchise in the United States.

One structural feature of American voting stands out in the ongoing re-
discovery of electoral practices, and has survived the tumultuous years since
2000: the crucial role of local officials in American voting. *Bush v. Gore*, the
signature voting-rights decision of our constitutional moment, is a case about
counting votes—not the extent of the formal franchise, but "the manner of its
exercise," as the Supreme Court's majority put it.[1] It is also a decision about
counties. To a degree unique among democracies, the United States has always
placed responsibility for running national and state elections in the hands of

city, town, and county officials. The power and discretion wielded by local staff has been trimmed by state and federal law since 2000, but local authority remains substantial. In its account of the 2008 U.S. elections, which it formally observed, the Organization for Security and Cooperation in Europe (OSCE) notes that "consistent with the U.S. political system, the legal framework for elections is highly decentralized."[2]

Whether or not they approve of *Bush v. Gore*, many observers of American elections have taken a cue from the Court's willingness to scrutinize how Americans exercise the right to vote. As the National Museum of American History explained in a 2004 exhibit titled "The Machinery of Democracy," voting methods and electoral practices in the United States "are as varied as the individual states and their local election districts," and how we vote is "as important as who votes."[3] Any lingering doubt about the truth of that assessment was laid to rest by the presidential election of 2004, in which congressional Democrats officially challenged the ritual certification of electoral votes because of locally patterned problems such as long lines at the polls, poor distribution of voting machines, and the lack of uniformity in handling provisional ballots in Ohio.[4] In the 2006 congressional elections, the Republican candidate in Florida's 13th Congressional District prevailed by fewer than four hundred votes, while more than eighteen thousand voters in a heavily Democratic part of the district somehow failed to enter a vote at all for congressional representative. Because their ballots were electronic, there was no paper trail to check. (In a stranger-than-fiction twist, the district was previously represented by Katherine Harris, who had won the seat partly because of her starring role as Florida's secretary of state in the 2000 election dispute.) Though all 2006 victory margins exceeded what election-law wags call the "margin of litigation," within a few weeks election watchers reported serious problems that had affected tens of thousands of voters across the country, ranging from long lines to glitchy machines.[5]

Close and constant bipartisan attention to electoral mechanics characterized the late stages of the presidential campaign of 2008. The *Wall Street Journal* featured a dueling pair of "Will This Election Be Stolen?" op-eds three days before the election, with a Democrat and a Republican each arguing that the other side was committing fraud, "purging" voters unlawfully, deploying hackable and error-prone machines, or otherwise engaging in suffrage chicanery.[6] In the event, while long lines again plagued many polling places across the country, serious problems were few. Barack Obama's sizable victory margin obviated close scrutiny of presidential balloting, though Minnesota's senatorial race and other scattered close congressional contests did force recounts. Advocates, policy makers, and scholars rejoined a spirited debate over election reform in the weeks after the election.[7]

Americans sometimes observe that "the Constitution means what the Supreme Court says it means."[8] Yet when it comes to the right to vote, in some ways the Constitution means what your county elections board says it means. Of course, federal and state constitutional and statutory law governs most aspects of elections. But as the Supreme Court acknowledged in 1992, the rules regarding electoral mechanics leave states and localities a great deal of administrative leeway.[9] All along the serial voting process, many of the institutions that administer those rules are located in cities, counties, and towns, and they often have a considerable amount of practical autonomy. Indeed, in American suffrage, many of the civil servants who "run the Constitution" are local officials.[10] Many important aspects of U.S. election law are formally directed by states rather than the national government, such as ballot access rules for candidates, the availability of absentee ballots for voters, and the eligibility of people with criminal convictions. In the parlance of American government, these policies can be said to be "federalized," in that rulemaking authority is held by subnational units rather than the central government. Practical control of suffrage practices, meanwhile, is still further decentralized, or *hyper*federalized. American voting, we might say, has been franchised out to local affiliates.

On the long list of today's most contentious voting-rights topics—registration rules, voter identification, the availability of early and satellite voting, help for those with poor literacy or English-language skills, use of provisional ballots, and who pays for it all—most involve some blend of national, state, and local responsibility.[11] Registering voters and keeping lists of those eligible to vote is of course essential, and federal legislation and a series of Supreme Court decisions have together helped change the process of registering to vote in important ways over the past forty years. But at the dawn of the twenty-first century, with very few exceptions, states did not keep any lists of voters: counties, cities, and towns did. Voter rolls were still "maintained in the separate files of the nearly 13,000 local election jurisdictions of the United States," as the 2002 report of the National Commission on Federal Election Reform observed.[12] And while the Help America Vote Act of 2002 (HAVA) mandates statewide voter rolls, local officials still help manage them, adding and removing names under varying levels of state supervision. This way of registering voters is highly unusual: more than one hundred countries have some form of national system.[13]

Or consider funding. Prior to HAVA, Congress had never provided money to states to help them administer elections; many states, in turn, have left the burden of election financing on localities.[14] Indeed, because many counties' and towns' election-related expenditures are too low to meet Census reporting requirements, we do not know how much the United States spends on elections.[15] And despite HAVA's allocation, which is quite limited, states and localities continue to shoulder most of the financial weight of paying for elections. .

Then there is the matter of election observers. Particularly since 2000, partisans, good-government groups, and academics alike have taken new interest in watching people vote, for various reasons. But there is no national law regarding observers, and most states lack legislation spelling out when and how to allow election observers (partisan, academic, or otherwise) at the polls—meaning that the practical authority to make those decisions rests with local officials, as the OSCE found when it tried to observe the 2006 elections.[16] Indeed, so uncertain is U.S. law in this area that under the current patchwork of state rules, attorneys helping out at election time could be subject to prosecution for "unauthorized practice of law."[17] By contrast, in most Western European democracies, "tenured civil servants specializing in electoral questions" manage elections and arbitrate disputes.[18]

The physical act of voting, certainly, remains a deeply local activity, as most Americans still vote in local public institutions—typically schools, town halls, and fire stations. But local officials may choose almost any place they think will be convenient for voters (and, after HAVA, "accessible to individuals with disabilities"). Thus, in many towns across the country voting takes place in residences, businesses, and churches. (Recent unsuccessful lawsuits have challenged that practice in Massachusetts, where sixty towns used churches as of 2003, and Florida, where a Jewish man objected to voting in a Palm Beach Catholic church in 2006.)[19] We now visualize local variation as part of American voting: maps in the most authoritative post-2000 study of American voting depict U.S. electoral machinery not by state but by county, and post-election photos in the national press routinely feature unusual polling places.[20]

Even fundamental matters of formal franchise inclusion rest on the decisions of local officials. For example, the voting rights of the millions of Americans with criminal convictions vary by state. But until HAVA required statewide voter lists, county elections officials were almost entirely responsible for enforcing such bans. Local officials also essentially determine the voting rights of another large and growing group of citizens: people with degenerative cognitive ailments such as dementia. Almost a third of all states have no

laws governing the electoral rights of this population; another third bar voting by those under guardianship or declared non compos mentis but do not
precisely define those terms; and the final third determine who cannot vote
based on an individualized judgment of incompetence.[21] With precious little
case law and almost no statutory guidance, "poll workers and nursing home
operators are deciding which patients are competent to vote."[22] In 2007, a
case challenging Missouri law revealed that some county elections officials
have ordered individual assessments of people who want to vote but are under guardianship for "mental incapacity," but it is not clear whether state law
invests them with the authority to do so.[23] "That is a very, very gray area,"
said a North Carolina official involved in designing a new law to help nursing-
home patients vote.[24]

As Americans have grasped the fact of local variation in suffrage practices,
their reactions have been mostly critical. While a few scholars have penned
thoughtful defenses of our localized suffrage institutions, the typical response
has been similar to that of the prominent political scientist who remarked
that the effects of locally administered U.S. elections ranged "from amusing to
appalling."[25] "Scandalous" is the preferred description, as when the *New York
Times* called locally maintained registration records "a national scandal."[26]
Historian Jack Rakove said the same of substandard voting machinery, which
he called "the dirty little secret of the ballot booth" and "a corruption of the
fundamental ritual of democracy."[27] Federal Elections Commission chairman
Michael Toner told a 2006 conference that "the state of election administration in this country has been an embarrassment," and law professor Heather
Gerken argued in 2007 that our election system "is in scandalous shape."[28]
A public-opinion poll conducted after the 2000 election concluded that
substantial majorities of Americans would favor uniform rules for voting in
presidential elections, while another taken after the 2004 election found that
more than a quarter of Americans worried that the presidential vote count
was unfair.[29]

Even once the heat of crisis cools, perhaps many of us share the sentiment voiced by Supreme Court Justice Robert Jackson in a 1943 free-speech
case. Writing for the Court, Justice Jackson worried that "small and local authority may feel less sense of responsibility to the Constitution."[30] After all,
we conceive the right to vote as a *national* right: it is the essential attribute
of membership in the national community, enshrined in federal statutes, Supreme Court decisions, and the Constitution itself. Perhaps it is not wise, the
reasoning goes, to entrust the protection of such a right to mere "small and
local authority."

But before 2000, those authorities had been controlling the suffrage for a long time. As a leading election-law text acknowledges, "Until the controversy surrounding the results in Florida in the 2000 presidential elections, few people probably ever thought about how election administrators counted (or failed to count) ballots."[31] Even among election lawyers, few understood just how important and controversial election administration could be prior to 2000. As federal judge and law professor Richard A. Posner points out, "The acquaintance of the professional commentators with the actual administration of elections" was limited.[32] But in 2000, "forms of law became exposed to an intense nationwide scrutiny," and that scrutiny has not abated since.[33]

Indeed, in the first years after 2000, it appeared that the end might be near for localism. Having come to light and proved faulty, our patchwork voting practices were to be homogenized, particularly through new federal legislation. Responding directly to the election of 2000, the federal HAVA statute held out the prospect of a new level of uniformity and centralization in American suffrage. HAVA offered federal funds for election administration and required states to create computerized voter-registration lists, make polling places accessible to people with disabilities, improve voting machines, and allow for provisional voting by those of uncertain registration status.[34] The *New York Times* trumpeted HAVA's passage with headlines noting its intent to "Clean Up [the] Election System" and "End Voting Disputes."[35] For the first time, the United States would have a federal body concerned with election administration: the Election Assistance Commission (EAC), established by HAVA.

But a funny thing has happened on the way to uniformity. Put simply, local administration of elections has proved far more durable than many reformers suspected. Consider a few snapshots of American suffrage since HAVA:

• In the spring of 2005, the first chairman of the HAVA-created EAC, DeForest Soaries, resigned. Soaries made no secret of his discontent with both Congress and the White House; in a post-resignation interview, he called running the EAC "probably the worst experience of my life" and said he had learned "how pitiful and perhaps how hopeless Washington is." The EAC had received so little support that, remarkably, Soaries never had office space. More substantively, the EAC had only advisory authority, and even that rankled many state officials. In February 2005, the National Association of Secretaries of State formally requested that Congress let the EAC die after the 2006 congressional election; that request was not granted, however, and the EAC was still very much in business after the 2008 election (and the secretaries' organization had not withdrawn its suggestion).[36] As late as 2007, a quarter of HAVA's initial appropriation had not been allocated.[37]

- Prior to the 2004 election, many Florida counties refused to purge from the rolls those voters who were listed by the state as having a felony conviction. Even before media accounts revealed the list's inaccuracies, county elections officials said they would leave the state's "potential felons" on the rolls. "I have no desire to move forward quickly," Pinellas County Supervisor of Elections Deborah Clark told a reporter in May. "I'm really erring on the [side of] the right to vote, there being something considerable before denying that right," said Hillsborough County official Buddy Johnson. "The supervisors are going to go very slow in doing their research," said Orange County Supervisor of Elections Bill Cowles. The state eventually scrapped the list, but in 2006, this dispute over the formal portals of the franchise repeated itself—with a twist. This time, some county officials believed the state was being too *lenient*. "They're overstepping their authority," said Pasco County's Kurt Browning. "They are not turning out felons quickly enough for us."[38]

- When Republican Dino Rossi lost the 2004 Washington gubernatorial election by 129 votes to Democrat Christine Gregoire, Republicans were unable to get access to all of the previously rejected ballots they wanted to recount—because *county* canvassing boards refused Republican calls to rerun their ballot counts.[39]

- Nineteen states missed HAVA's January 1, 2006, deadline for completion of statewide voter lists. Even in states where HAVA's voter-list requirements have now been fully met, local officials still handle additions and corrections to lists of registered voters. "We still have to rely on the counties to do the footwork, the investigative work at the local level," said Steve Excell, Washington's assistant secretary of state.[40]

- In Arizona, state and federal officials fought over how local officials should determine the citizenship of would-be voters. Arizona's Proposition 200, enacted in 2004, required voters to show proof of U.S. citizenship in order to register. But the EAC advised Arizona that voters had to be allowed to use a federal registration form, which requires only that the voter attest to being a citizen. Secretary of State Jan Brewer told county officials to ignore the EAC's interpretation of federal law, which she called "inconsistent, unlawful, and without merit."[41]

- In Pennsylvania in 2006, it became unlawful to use homes and other private buildings as polling places unless they met new accessibility standards. In Philadelphia, where some large neighborhoods include few public buildings and at least ninety private establishments have long been used for voting—including St. Monica's Bowling Lanes, Wright's Barber Shop, and the Church of God of Prophecy Kitchen—some officials were angry.[42] "Maybe they're going to build us some sort of municipal building in every voting division—what are the chances of that happening?" asked City Commissioner Edgar Howard sarcastically.

- When the federal government sued the state of Missouri for failing to enforce the 1993 National Voter Registration Act (NVRA) because several counties had failed to keep accurate voter lists, a federal court ruled against the Department of Justice. U.S. District Judge Nanette Laughrey ruled in the spring of 2007 that Missouri officials are not legally responsible for mistakes on voter-registration rolls, because the state's 116 local elections jurisdictions keep those lists. As Judge Laughrey noted, Missouri law had given voter-registration authority to localities "long before the NVRA was conceived, and the allocation is consistent with the American tradition of dividing power between myriad elected officials to maintain checks and balances."[43] The NVRA was not intended to make states restructure their governments, the judge ruled in 2007, "and the state of Missouri should be able to continue its tradition of decentralized elections."[44]

These stories illustrate the sheer complexity of U.S. election law, and the intimate connection between the formal and mechanical components of the right to vote. They stand as evidence of the intriguing fact that our national, state, and local governments continue to share authority over American voting, despite the traumatic elections of the new century. Some readers will see these incidents (and scores more like them) as evidence of the dangers posed and the damage done by our hyperfederalized franchise. In some measure, they are right: there are strong voices in the chorus now denouncing local administration of American elections. But the record of localism's origins, character, and impact is mixed and complex. By emphasizing the historically grounded, constitutive, and potentially redemptive qualities of our decentralized suffrage system, this book tries to counter the prevailing assumption that local variation is either a toxin or simply an embarrassment.

The Right to Vote as a Practice

Sparked by professional curiosity, partisan interest, and the surprises of recent elections, a burgeoning scholarly and popular literature touches on the practical elements of American suffrage.[45] Keeping up with the election-reform news today is like "drinking from a fire hose," writes Doug Chapin of

Electionline.org.[46] Just in the past few years, countless academic articles, media accounts, weblog posts, and books, such as Spencer Overton's *Stealing Democracy* (2006), Roy Saltman's *The History and Politics of Voting Technology* (2006), and Ronald Hayduk's *Gatekeepers to the Franchise: Shaping Election Administration in New York* (2005), have analyzed what Overton calls "the matrix" of institutions through which Americans express their electoral preferences. Much of this body of work accepts Overton's core premise that "there is no 'right' to vote outside of the terms, conditions, hurdles, and boundaries set by the matrix."[47] Another important account chooses a different metaphor, describing American election-administration structures as an "ecosystem," where changes in one area are sure to affect activities elsewhere.[48]

Regardless of what side these recent works have taken concerning certain details—paper trails, early voting—most have focused on practical, what-now questions faced by legislatures and courts. Some savvy observers have already lost faith in reform, convinced that excess partisanship has poisoned the waters, but others believe strong new federal election legislation remains possible and desirable.[49]

This book tries to fill what I see as a gap in this rich and growing literature, focusing squarely on the autonomy of local officials and institutions in conducting national elections—the local dimension of American suffrage. The book is a work of synthesis, touching on many historical, legal, theoretical, and empirical questions in order to analyze the historical construction of our locally administered electoral regime and its connection to American ideas about popular sovereignty and fairness. Our hyperfederalized franchise presents vital questions about the design of democratic institutions, and the book focuses on what I believe are the three reasons we care so much about voting-rights questions in the first place: their ability to illuminate change and continuity in American history and political development; their theoretical and practical impact on the exercise of self-rule, or popular sovereignty; and their intimate connections to the forces of exclusion and inequality.

My arguments are built on a theoretical premise that in the United States, the right to vote is a practice constituted by local administrative control of elections. In calling the right to vote a *practice*, I mean that it is a social convention, subject to rules, which creates and carries social meaning. While important components of the suffrage live in constitutions and courts, there is an aspect of the right to vote that is "visibly present in everyday life."[50] And to a degree unique in the democratic world, that visible, practical dimension of American voting rights varies across counties and towns.

When I say that the practice of suffrage is *constituted* by local administrative authority—and by locally patterned variation accompanying that

authority—I mean that the American right to vote is defined by its local dimension. Thinking of our electoral localism simply as an embarrassment—a
historical accident to be rectified as quickly and as totally as possible by robust application of legal doctrine—cheats us out of an inquiry into the meaning of American suffrage. For good or ill, the precious thing Americans call
"the right to vote" cannot be separated from the institutional context in which
it is exercised. Local practices *are* that thing—they form it and help create its
meaning. Though the scope of county clerks' authority is narrower now than
it was just ten years ago (let alone a century ago), the American right to vote
still carries its local texture. Understanding this phenomenon yields a fuller
picture of the relationship between the national and the local in American
law and politics. I focus more on how we got here and what it means than on
where we should go next, hoping to sidestep the adversarial and increasingly
partisan nature of many current disputes over American voting. Certainly,
localism should be held to account for its past and present flaws. Seen one
way, there is a kind of gap between our nationalized conceptions of the right
to vote and our localized electoral practices. But I hope to show that localism
is neither atavistic nor altogether without merit.

The book has two core purposes, the first of which concerns historical explanation. How did the United States come to enter the twenty-first century
with so much voting variation, and so much practical authority exercised by
county, city, and town officials in running national elections? In the first three
chapters, I show not only that local suffrage variation has endured through
dramatic changes in political and constitutional structure but also that such
variation is the product of a clear, repeated developmental pattern, not of
simple neglect, ignorance, or the famed "fit of absence of mind" in which the
British supposedly built their empire. Juxtaposed alongside consistent local
control is a record of recurrent federal intervention in electoral mechanics.
Federal statutes, the records of contested congressional elections, and many
Supreme Court decisions tell us that national lawmakers have long understood perfectly well that a certain level of disorder characterizes U.S. national
elections. For its part, Congress has responded by exercising its own authority over suffrage practices—but only in limited, even halting steps, over
time effectively helping to construct our triply governed electoral system. I
offer new accounts of two landmarks in the development of American electoral law—the Jacksonian conventions of the early nineteenth century and
the Australian-ballot reforms of the end of that century. Both help illustrate
the paradox of de jure state and national authority alongside de facto local
responsibility for U.S. elections. Ultimately, even if we criticize local variation

today, we must appreciate that modern differences in how Americans vote are dwarfed by those that existed for most of our past.

The book's second purpose is to assess the effects of our voting practices on American popular sovereignty (Chapter 4) and on our polity's old and continuing struggle with exclusion (Chapter 5). In both areas, the conventional wisdom takes a dim view of local variation, but I argue that the full picture is more complex. In fact, the American way of voting fits coherently, even comfortably, into our conceptions of popular sovereignty. Popular self-rule in the United States has always been understood as *mediated*, by federalism, parties, and interest groups, and running elections locally is consistent with that understanding in important ways. Taking a holistic view of the American political system, I argue that uniformity—the central concern of much reform advocacy today—simply has not been a fundamental value in the shaping of American electoral structures. Certainly, local variation can threaten both the *instrumental* and *constitutive* aspects of popular sovereignty, and I sketch a simple framework to help clarify that question. But local administration of elections can also enhance self-rule, particularly to the extent that it gives Americans more ownership of the voting process, more room for experimentation and innovation, and a structural way to minimize the effects of partisanship and error.

Many critics of our localized suffrage system contend that while uniformity may not be a central value of American electoral law, equality certainly is. Chapter 5 challenges the view that localism is inextricably linked to noxious forms of exclusion and inequality in voting. Local administration of elections certainly did play a role in some dark discriminatory episodes in the history of the American right to vote, and those periods are part of a full picture of local variation's impact on American democracy. I show, however, that while local control may have facilitated those exclusions, they were driven by national and state political elites, rather than by local officials. Second, I show that local administration of elections has been a vector of inclusion in American citizenship law. In different ways, men without property, women, and people who were not yet citizens were enabled to vote by the locally varying architecture of American elections. Third, I explore the impact of local administration on two areas of current controversy: criminal-disenfranchisement law, and policies requiring would-be voters to show state-issued photo identification. Criminal disenfranchisement is a particularly important case, because it demonstrates local officials' continuing role in shaping even fundamental policies related to voter qualifications. In addition to being erratically administered by our hyperfederalized electoral regime, disenfranchisement laws are themselves in some ways relics of long-discredited ideas. And although we still know little about the implementation of new photo-ID requirements, early evidence suggests that their administration may also be uneven and have exclusionary effects. But these new laws also show that the greater threat to electoral fairness today may well come from state and national governments rather than local officials. I do not want to overstate the argument here; in some ways further centralization and standardization would enhance equality in American elections. But to a degree that is insufficiently recognized, the relationship between exclusion and localism in American suffrage has always been complex and multifaceted. Local variation has advanced the cause of equality in U.S. elections, and it could do so again.

Our new awareness of the importance of the local dimension of the right to vote demands a reassessment of these essential topics, the things that are ultimately at stake when we talk about voting—history, popular sovereignty, and exclusion. In general, I have chosen not to wade too deeply into current disputes over particular voting reforms, concluding that I can best inform those debates by presenting the developmental and normative argument sketched above. My hope is that where my normative claims are not persuasive, the book at least demonstrates that approaching suffrage as a practice helps clarify these problems, and that my historical and theoretical analysis provides useful context and resources for contemporary reform debates.

Antecedents and Influences

A generation ago, political scientist Stuart Scheingold pointed out that the idea of a "right" can be "a myth that spreads coherence over a very uneven field of practices." Something similar has been going on with American suffrage. Of course, concepts like "the right to vote" and "the American voter" are not mythical in important senses of the term: they are real things with meaningful consequences, things people fight over. But to some degree, they have achieved "catchphrase" status. Some words and phrases become "more than a name for a thing"—they begin to "form . . . the very fields to which [they] only seem to refer."[51] A catchphrase captures meaning, but it can also ensnare those who use the term.

This book examines the right to vote, but here that right is defined primarily as a practice rather than as a legally enforceable guarantee. I hope to exploit both the "low" and "high" senses of the word *practice*. The common use simply refers to how, where, when, and under what kinds of governmental supervision people vote: the behaviors of the franchise, as it were. A more sophisticated use of the term anchors several scholarly fields. One is the sociology of law. Unsatisfied with theoretical and textual accounts of what the law is, does, and means, sociolegal scholars wrestle with the way people, settings, and institutions constitute law. What constitutions and courts say about the right to vote matters a great deal, but so do the institutions and physical settings in which that right is exercised. As legal anthropologist Sally Engle Merry says in explaining how law helped colonize the islands of Hawaii, "The texts of the law must be made socially real: enacted, implemented, imposed."[52] In terms of voting rights, local institutions are "the places where law matters," in John Brigham's words.[53] And voting rights acquire meaning through our shared exercise of the suffrage—"by the repeated acts of citizens using those conventions," as Michael McCann writes in his study of workplace rights.[54]

Of course, courts and legislatures are "places where law matters" too, and constitutions and statutes can also be interpreted as institutions and conventions. Each has powerfully shaped American suffrage. But until quite recently, they have dominated our conceptions of the right to vote, to the exclusion of attention to local practices—and to our detriment. Local elections officials are part of what political scientists call the "interpretive community" that gives the Constitution its meaning.[55] County clerks may not argue explicitly over the Constitution in their daily work, but it is through their labors that the text is made real.

Another scholarly stream informing my conception of suffrage comes from historically oriented political science, particularly the school examining American political development. Here, "institutions" rather than "practices" are the watchword. An emphasis on institutions, argues a leading text in the field, "locates [ideas] in the setting where, politically speaking, they count most."[56] Another scholar, Daniel Wirls, paraphrases Harold Lasswell's famous definition of politics, noting that electoral structures determine who gets to *vote* for what, when, and how. Wirls notes that although the "who" has always gotten the lion's share of scholarly attention, "the 'how' and 'for what' of voting have also played crucial, though perhaps less understood, roles in the politics of democratization."[57] While our understanding of the development of American electoral institutions has improved considerably in recent years, however, little new scholarship has dealt directly with the local dimension of American suffrage. One important exception is Richard F. Bensel's *The American Ballot Box in the Mid-Nineteenth Century* (2004), probably our first full-dress analysis of voting practices. Studying records of contested elections from 1850 to 1868, Bensel defines the polling place as a key locus of American citizenship. He notes that there has been a "void in both American political historiography and general democratic theory" regarding the "actual practice of elections."[58] *The American Ballot Box* begins to fill that void by probing deep into a short time period; I draw on Bensel's discoveries in various places, while pursuing a broader synthesis and presenting original research into crucial periods.

Those seeking to shape the law are in turn influenced by the way they understand the law,[59] and the way scholars have studied American suffrage helps explain why the importance of the local dimension has eluded us for so long. Until the butterfly ballot left chaos in its wake, students of American voting generally divided theory and practice. Political science, law, and related fields have produced superb work on voting rights, elections, and parties, but our understanding of electoral "behavior" has been limited in a few key ways. In thinking about what voters do, scholars have focused on the instrumental motivations of voters, on the kinds of variation that most clearly shape aggregate outcomes, and on the formalistic, even binary attributes of the right to vote. My approach to suffrage as a practice, then, builds on work in the sociology of law, political theory, and institutionally oriented political science, and also responds to what I see as gaps in these literatures on American voting.

Behavioral political science has long sought to understand the American voter "in a highly aggregated sense," and election procedures have mattered "mainly as they relate to outcomes."[60] And that is why the locally patterned nature of American suffrage has finally begun to draw the attention of behavioral political science. Local variation did the one thing guaranteed to catch the behavioral eye: it showed that it can *affect outcomes*. After all, as one prominent article demonstrated, Palm Beach County's confusing ballot gave Patrick Buchanan thousands of votes he should not have received, effectively depriving Al Gore of victory in the 2000 presidential election.[61]

The balloting inequities of 2000 bring us back to the courts, and to scholars interested in the "right to vote" in its strictly legal or formal sense. Courts and legal disputation have played an essential role in constructing the political identity of the American voter, particularly in relation to race, community, and the meaning of "the people."[62] But our close attention to the formal, justiciable dimension of the right to vote may have both constructed and constricted our understanding of the suffrage. Before 2000, analysis of the right to vote was usually driven by the assumption that what matters most is an enforceable guarantee of participation (or, of course, its absence). Judith Shklar, for example, argued in her influential book *American Citizenship* that the most important thing about the right to vote is its possession, regardless of whether it is employed as a means to an end—or, by extension, whether it is employed in any particular context or fashion.[63] Certainly, theoretical and doctrinal questions regarding the formal right to vote—to be included in the franchise as a matter of law—are worthy topics for inquiry. (At least I hope so, since I have participated in that work myself.[64]) But particularly when combined with its corollary—an emphasis on the federal courts, at the expense of other places and actors—this interest in the formal, even binary aspect of the right to vote seems to have obstructed our vision of the practices and institutions that make suffrage real.[65]

The right to vote's numerous paradoxes and puzzles have long seduced scholars in law, political science, and history. The U.S. Constitution itself contains plenty of them. As one text puts it, when it comes to election law, the Constitution "is a curious amalgam of textual silences, archaic assumptions that subsequent developments quickly undermined, and a small number of narrowly targeted more recent amendments that reflect more modern conceptions of politics."[66] Indeed, despite its deep historical, philosophical, and constitutional significance, the right to vote in American law is a difficult thing to pin down. It is "slippery and confusing," as one of the people who understands it best wrote in 2007, and as a result, the Supreme Court has been unable to find any clear theory of democracy in the Constitution.[67] Responding to such complexities, Pamela S. Karlan concludes that the right to vote is not a single thing but rather a "nested constellation of concepts."[68]

Judicially oriented equal-protection analysis is an essential tool for understanding the local dimension of American suffrage. I draw on its concepts in places and direct the reader toward important recent work. This book, however, is not built around the doctrine of equal protection nor focused exclusively on the work of courts. What judges have said figures large in this tale, but I take a cue from recent work emphasizing the "profound role that non-judicial actors play in shaping constitutional values," and this book's center of gravity lies in other institutions.[69] At least since Karl Llewellyn famously argued in 1934 that practices "legitimize" constitutional words and not vice versa, some constitutional scholars have been talking about the importance of "practices," and research has shown that prominent decisions like *Engel v. Vitale* and *Brown v. Board* had far less impact on local practices than is commonly thought.[70] But until recently, very little attention had been paid to local institutions and local variation, despite their essential role in the practice of American suffrage.

In 1887, Albert Shaw wrote that the American "lives in one world of theory and in another world of practice."[71] After the election of 2000, a simple and, to some, appealing vision took hold: get rid of local variation, and wrench the practices of suffrage into line with our nationalized theories of voting rights and voter behavior. Continuing a secular trend in U.S. political history, today the scope of county, city, town, and parish authority is indeed more limited than it was eight years ago. But traditions so deeply rooted do not make sudden leaps, and the local dimension of American suffrage has proved durable. While casting votes at St. Monica's Bowling Lanes may no longer be allowed, Americans continue to conduct their central democratic ritual just as they always have—in local settings, with the assistance and supervision of local officials.[72] This book tries to shed light on the meaning of that ritual, and to draw more closely together our theories of the right to vote and the practices that make American democracy real.

1

"Times, Places, and Manner":
Early American Voting

Whereas yow . . . are appointed and betrusted ffor the
opening the Proxies sent in by the Freemen, and receiving
sorting and numbering the Votes for the choice of Gou'nor[,]
Deputy Gou'nor, Assistants and other public Officers of this
Jurisdiction to be Chosen on the ellection Day yow doe now
sweare by the Name of Almighty God that yow will deale
truely and uprightly therein as also that you will not either
directly or indirectly discouer either persons or number
of Votes until the Election is ended. So help you God.
> Oath to be administered to those that sort and number
> votes, Massachusetts Bay Colony (1679–1680)

Each and every sheriff . . . in said territory, shall
cause to be held the election prescribed by this act
. . . under the penalty of one thousand dollars.
> An act to extend the right of suffrage in
> the Indiana Territory (1811)

The conventional history of the American right to vote is straightforward,
its landmarks familiar. The state constitutions of the early nineteenth century largely did away with property tests, moving toward suffrage for all
white males. During Reconstruction, the Union Army and the Republican-
controlled Congress collaborated to enfranchise African Americans; the
Fifteenth Amendment explicitly banned exclusion on the basis of race. State
constitutional, statutory, and partisan change, particularly in the South, led to
the subsequent disenfranchisement of those same African American citizens.
In the twentieth century, the passage of the Nineteenth Amendment banned
discrimination on the basis of sex in national elections. The Warren Court
and the Voting Rights Act together finally made good on century-old racial

promises, while further amendments to the national Constitution guaranteed the right to vote to those who could not pay a poll tax and to people over eighteen.

Our new appreciation of the local texture of the American right to vote offers an opportunity to revisit that history. It is not that the narrative sketched above is incorrect, but that its emphasis on the formal ability to participate obscures significant aspects of the history of our electoral institutions. As Henry Glassie said, "History is a map of the past . . . drawn to be useful to the modern traveler."[1] For this modern traveler and student of American constitutional and political development, the most fascinating thing about the right to vote today is our distinctive mix of national, state, and local authority, spread over a great many steps in the serial voting process. And the central historical question is what particular events, forces, and ideas have constructed that system.

For most of U.S. history, voting in national elections has employed a diversity of practices that far outstrips anything we see today. Through political, partisan, and constitutional change, one constant has been a great deal of local responsibility for running elections. While the United States has seen a secular trend toward centralization and uniformity in voting, this process has been very gradual and uneven, set against the remarkable continuity of local control. But local variation and local administrative authority have not glided through two centuries unseen and undisturbed by state and national lawmakers. Indeed, a second central characteristic of the history of American voting practices is the long list of federal and state interventions in voting mechanics and electoral institutions: this is not a record of inaction, but one of construction.

Whether written by historians, political scientists, or legal scholars, most previous work concerned with the practices and procedures of American suffrage has focused on a single period, institution, or even county (or two). I have profited (and borrowed) a great deal from such research, and do not for a moment question its merit. My premise is that a more synthetic vantage can also help us understand behavior in its institutional setting, discern patterns across time, and draw conclusions about the nature of political authority and political change.

These are the central concerns of scholars working in the interdisciplinary field known as "American political development." For many people in this field, it is vitally important to identify those events that constitute significant *development*, as opposed to those that are merely the normal fluctuations of *change*. Attempting to nail down that difference, Karen Orren and Stephen Skowronek argue that only "a durable shift in governing authority" constitutes meaningful development. Political development, they insist, "is, in effect, zero-sum: for politics to develop, it is necessary that authority be moved from one location to another."[2] While this standard is meant to apply to various policy arenas, Orren and Skowronek choose the field of election law for one of their first illustrations of the concept. The 1870 enactment of the Fifteenth Amendment was, on its face, a clear elevation of national authority to set voting qualifications—but to Orren and Skowronek, passage of the Fifteenth Amendment is actually a prime example of *non*-development. Historians such as Alexander Keyssar have argued that southern restrictions on black voting after 1890 "reversed" the "signal achievements of Reconstruction."[3] But Orren and Skowronek reject the "reversal" account, arguing that southern black suffrage during Reconstruction was "extraordinary, precarious, and fleeting," its legitimacy not accepted by other institutions.[4]

This conception of development as a zero-sum "durable shift in governing authority" has already begun to take hold among scholars. Several have quoted it approvingly in published work, with one calling it an "elegant definition of what constitutes political development."[5] It is an exacting, limiting conception, and purposefully so: it means to impart rigor and focus to the study of change and political power. And it has helped guide my inquiry into the history of voting rights in practice—that is, how, where, when, for whom, and under what kinds of supervision Americans have voted in national elections. I hoped to locate those cut-points, those moments where zero-sum transfers of authority from one institution or level of government to another occurred.

But the definition's parsimony proves to be too much of a good thing, at least in terms of the development of American suffrage. As I will show, the history of American voting mechanics amply supports other aspects of Orren and Skowronek's theoretical framework. But one searches in vain for discrete, durable, zero-sum transfers of legally enforceable power over election practices. From the first, those exercising the right to vote in U.S. national elections have been subject to multiple and overlapping authority. The development of American suffrage practices has been layered and repetitive, even halting, as a durable system of mixed authority has persisted through centuries of ideological, partisan, and formal constitutional change.

This is a complex and paradoxical story. To a degree that is not sufficiently understood, Congress in fact has a long and extensive record of wielding authority over voting practices. Asserting a national interest in addressing a particular problem, Congress acts to supervise or direct voting practices—but constrained by federalism, lack of capacity, the Constitution, and partisanship, it repeatedly does so in ways that are limited temporally, spatially, or substantively. As a result, each federal action leaves considerable authority in state and local hands, ultimately reinforcing the primacy of state and local institutions. State governments, meanwhile, forcefully asserted their authority over voter qualifications in the constitutional conventions of the Jacksonian era, and over close details of the voting act itself during the Australian-ballot reforms of the century's end (which I discuss in Chapter 2). But in doing so, state lawmakers made it clear that local authorities would remain in charge of elections.

As the Introduction argues, the work of local officials in running American elections should be understood as part of the process by which constitutional meaning is constructed. But what if the performances of local officials in this setting are not *visible to*, and broadly understood by, other constitutional actors? Today's media coverage of voting problems often implies as much, suggesting with a breathless, exposé tone that county and town staff have been making and counting ballots in the dead of night, politically speaking. If that were true historically, it would be harder to argue that local practices have helped shape the public meaning of constitutional rights. But in fact, the record shows that throughout U.S. history, state and national lawmakers have understood full well that voting practices vary dramatically from one place to another. To be sure, they have often been quite critical of what they see, sometimes overturning elections or making new rules with an eye to constraining variation, correcting past errors, and preventing future problems. But local administrative control over the suffrage has been well-understood throughout U.S. political history.

This history is not presented as evidence for a particular position in contemporary debates. However, the record does challenge a few terms bandied about in the election-reform discussion today. For example, some prominent voices have called balloting flaws a "dirty little secret" or "the Family Secret."[6] The record does not support that language, unless "family" and "secret" are defined very broadly indeed. And one outstanding recent book on American voting refers to the "chaotic" nature of American elections before the Australian ballot.[7] But chaos is in the eye of the beholder. There was great diversity of practice, and even disorder. But where disorder is clearly perceived and normatively accepted, it is not "chaos."

One of our wisest voting-rights scholars wrote recently that the United States is only now "reverse-engineering" itself out of "the pathological decentralization of American elections."[8] If the localized franchise is indeed a pathology, those seeking to treat it can only benefit by knowing how deeply lodged it is in the American polity.

The Mechanics of Suffrage, 1620–1787

In the beginning, all voting was local. During the colonial era and into the early national period, virtually every substantive aspect of voting was under local control and varied considerably from one place to the next. Some used ballots, others voted aloud; some voted silently in church, others did so drunkenly in taverns; some submitted party tickets, others wrote down names; some voted on a single spring day, others voted over a three-day period in the fall. Counties and towns alone implemented whatever state-level qualifications existed, either using locally maintained property, taxation, and residency records or making do without the aid of any records at all. Early American voting was governed by a fully decentralized, even fragmented institutional order. Obviously, the broader nature of citizenship (and the meaning of those votes) changed enormously between the early seventeenth century and the middle of the nineteenth. But in terms of local control, the creation of the national state may have brought less change than we would assume. This period started American suffrage down a developmental path that helps explain where we are today.

Before independence, Americans voted for many local and colonial offices. Elections were held at widely varying and uncertain intervals; many were essentially uncontested, and voting itself was entirely public, usually conducted out loud, or viva voce.[9] The voter declared his choice, and probably then enjoyed a glass of rum punch at the expense of the man he had voted for. Even when it was contested, an election was no place for serious conflict, and served to reaffirm the social hierarchy of the community; elections were occasions "for eating, drinking, and being merry at the expense of the candidates."[10] In England, merriment was so widespread that rum prices often rose sharply at election time.[11]

American ideas and practices alike emerged from seventeenth- and eighteenth-century English electoral politics, and local variation was part of that colonial continuity. In fifteenth-century England, ownership of a church pew was one way to satisfy the property qualification for shire elections, and in the seventeenth-century English colonies, churches continued to play an important role.[12] For example, by a Massachusetts law of 1631, the franchise was limited to full members of the church, so that about one in five adult males were enfranchised.[13] The best way to provide notice of an upcoming election was through postings on the church door—an appropriate site, because there "men would discuss the shortcomings of the present government along with those of the minister."[14] The first use of a written ballot in English North

America may have been in a Salem church's choice of a minister, on July 20, 1629.[15]

The dignity of paper, however, did not spread immediately. Paper was used to choose the governor and deputy of the Massachusetts Bay colony in 1634, but a Massachusetts Bay statute of 1648 ordered that "for the yearly choosing of Assistants . . . the freemen shall use Indian Corn and Beans, the Indian Corn to manifest Election, the Beanes contrary."[16] (This was not such an unusual arrangement, since later voting systems derived from James Harrington's 1656 *Oceana*—a republican manifesto dressed in utopian clothing—often required voters to cast ballots not just *for* one candidate, but *against* others.) Beans were also used in Pennsylvania in 1689, when black and white legumes were placed into a hat, and balls made of some substance were used in 1676 in West Jersey.[17] Massachusetts was using paper ballots regularly as early as the 1680s, and a secret ballot of one kind or another generally prevailed in colonial New England.[18] Nevertheless, colonial areas employing written ballots used widely varying practices concerning confidentiality, counting measures, and responding to fraud.[19] Most southern elections were viva voce.[20] What we now call "absentee" voting was generally not allowed, though Massachusetts in 1635 permitted frontier freemen to "stay home for the safety of their towne" and send in a kind of proxy vote.[21]

Even regional generalizations are hard to make, for the most striking features of the history of balloting in late colonial America—and later, the young United States—are its variation and nonlinear development. North Carolina, for example, changed its voting methods four times in the eighteenth century.[22] South Carolina voters used secret ballots until 1766, then apparently reverted to viva voce methods. Pennsylvania, Connecticut, and Massachusetts all permitted but did not require the use of ballots, meaning that one town might vote aloud while others did so privately in writing. In Rhode Island, ballots for county elections had to be signed by the voter, though votes for town offices could be secret. New Jersey required that voters be listed, and that their choices be compiled and occasionally published.[23]

In the eighteenth century, many people believed voting aloud *encouraged* honesty and integrity, both on the part of the individual and the electoral system. After all, the ballot box could not be stuffed, and individual votes could not be disputed, so deception and corruption were all but impossible. By contrast, the secret ballot would "destroy that noble generous openess that is characteristick of an Englishman, and . . . introduce a Vile Venetian Juggle and Cunning," as South Carolina governor James Glen argued in 1748.[24] (Harrington and others had taken an interest in the secret ballot after learning of its use in Venice.) In New York in 1769, opponents of reform argued successfully that ballots would allow more coercion and corruption than viva voce selection, because ballots allowed some illiterate voters (including the infamous Germans of Pennsylvania) to cast prepared tickets in complete ignorance of their content, enabling partisans to bribe and intimidate voters more efficiently and effectively.[25] Some pointed to authorities like Montesquieu and Blackstone, both of whom argued that the secret ballot had failed the ancient world.[26] Montesquieu, later cited more than any other authority in the debate over the Constitution, contended that after the basic question of who was qualified to vote, *the manner of voting* was the most important decision facing practical statesmen."[27]

Americans imitated the "medley of voting qualifications" that England's franchise featured, but the most fundamental idea Americans adopted from English elections was geographic representation: the belief that sending delegates from *places* was the best way to represent both people and interests.[28] Local conditions in the colonies quickly strained some inherited ideas about voting, such as the English notion of "virtual representation." Almost immediately, Americans wanted a closer fit, even in selecting colonial assemblies. Massachusetts established a system of assembly delegates for every hundred voters, but residents of small towns protested: "might as well share a soul with other individuals," as James Morone imagines their response.[29]

Many colonies did not put in place formal age, sex, or residency restrictions, leaving a good deal of discretion in the hands of local officials.[30] Meanwhile, eighteenth-century Americans actually lived with several different franchises, since the voter qualifications for colony elections often differed from those held in a town, city, or county.[31] Naturalization (toward English citizenship, of course) was in local hands in some places: South Carolina put justices of the peace in charge of administering the required oaths after 1704.[32] For a full generation before the Revolution, Pennsylvania Germans apparently voted and even held office, regardless of whether they were ever naturalized.[33] (A few Pennsylvania communities printed electoral material in Dutch as early as 1742.) Property tests, meanwhile, were usually based on towns' lists of assessable property.[34] Some colonies did attempt to bring a measure of regularity to franchise rules, even before independence. For example, in 1742 Massachusetts limited the suffrage to owners of twenty pounds' worth of real estate and required assessors to provide the town clerk with a copy of land records "for use in connection with elections."[35]

Between independence and the Constitution, terms of office were regularized and states established election dates—some in the fall, others in the spring. Where towns were small, as in New England, elections lasted only one day. But in New York, polls were open for up to five days; a three-day election in New York was common into the nineteenth century, as in Virginia, where state law allowed sheriffs to extend elections for up to three days if either the turnout or the rains were heavy.[36] All this helps explain why scholars struggle to derive firm estimates of the percentage of American adults enfranchised at the nation's founding. It is not just the absence of firm population data that stands in our way but suffrage's local variation, based on property ownership, officials' discretion, and the type of election being held.[37]

The Early Path and the Right to Vote in the Founding Era

American elections had been locally managed for generations before the formal founding of the United States. Localism in the suffrage was consistent with a political philosophy emphasizing decentralization, and with English theories of representation emphasizing specific geographic places. This developmental path was well-marked and well-trodden by 1787, and it would guide late-eighteenth-century American political thinkers.

Meanwhile, because suffrage among white men and public engagement with lawmaking were both quite broad, Americans effectively enjoyed "democracy before bureaucracy," as a relatively inclusive democratic politics flowered before the growth of state administrative capacity.[38] This sequence contrasts with that of most Western European democracies, where broad suffrage was generally won only *after* the expansion of the state enabled electoral processes to be centrally directed.[39] American town officials were best positioned to manage elections, and they continued to do so even as the wealth, expertise, and authority of state and national governments grew, and even as voting-rights protections were clarified in state and national law. As Stephen Skowronek observes, this was part of a "broad diffusion of power among the localities" that led nineteenth-century foreign observers to feel a "sense of statelessness" in America.[40] Skowronek follows Samuel P. Huntington, who in the 1960s called the early American political order "essentially Tudor and . . . significantly medieval."[41] Elements of that "medieval" constitution in America included "the vitality of local governmental authorities." "American political institutions are unique," Huntington famously concluded, "if only because they are so antique."[42] Earlier, historians including Charles Beard had reasoned that local administration in various settings "gave rise to an assumption that liberty was promoted by local autonomy," an idea brought to America by English emigrants.[43]

David Brian Robertson has criticized this "Tudor polity" theory of American political development, noting that major differences did exist between Constitution-era America and England.[44] For example, colonial assemblies represented public opinion much more effectively than their British predecessors, and male freeholders shaped state policy making in ways never seen in England. While that is true, suffrage *practices* were indeed highly localized, as in England. Here Huntington and Skowronek are correct. In part because the United States experienced a relatively democratic politics before the growth of concentrated governing capacity, the country built a tradition of locally run elections, and that tradition has powerfully influenced subsequent events.

For those who regard fragmentation in modern American voting as a serious democratic flaw, this story is ironic. But it is also consistent with what we know about institutional development and the path-dependent nature of policy making. As Robert C. Lieberman puts it, "institutionalized, taken-for-granted understandings" of political arrangements constrain policy makers, "limiting the range of policies that are considered rational."[45] Americans arrived in the early national period via a particular set of experiences, and ideas born of those experiences shaped and defined their policy choices. At the same time, part of the messiness of democratic lawmaking is that it can build on prior policies and institutional arrangements without clearing them away.[46] That is what occurred with American voting. Even as local institutions retained their central role, the new national government began to assert its own authority over suffrage practices.

The country's formal founding had important, paradoxical effects on American voting practices. Political leaders shaped by the war for independence and Constitutional ratification believed the right of suffrage was essential to democracy, and worthy of inclusion in written constitutions. The phrase "consent of the governed" in the Declaration of Independence signals the foundational importance of voting in American political thought, and numerous public writers and speakers of the late 1770s spoke of the "right of free suffrage" as "the greatest right of freemen."[47] Despite their exclusionary aspects, it is also true that virtually every state constitution protected the right to vote in one way or another.[48] Advocating ratification of the new Constitution, Madison wrote in *Federalist* 52 that "the definition of the right of suffrage is very justly regarded as a fundamental article of republican government," and suggested that it would have been better "to define and establish this right in the Constitution" than to leave it to the states, as the Constitution did.[49]

Juxtaposed alongside that belief in suffrage's importance was a clear-eyed understanding of the very diverse ways Americans voted. From a modern perspective, of course, their right to vote was a limited one, in that a great many adults did not share it. But the founders had little difficulty accepting a great range of voting practices among those who *could* vote. What today feels like a tension, gap, or outright conflict was for them simply the order of things, one of those "taken-for-granted understandings" that structure politics. The founding generation accepted the vote's importance, in a context of widely varying electoral practices.

Historian Jack Rakove writes that the Philadelphia framers faced questions such as "how, literally, were citizens to give their votes: by voicing their preference to the sheriff, who would then record their vote in a poll book, or by secret ballot; at a raucous public fete, with people gathered from miles around for the closest approximation to carnival a Protestant society could produce, or in widely separated polling places, with a decorum more suited to republican manners?"[50] Rakove has the list of options right, but he errs by phrasing these as *questions* faced by the framers. The Constitution's authors *knew* about these phenomena, of course, since virtually all of them had long been active in politics and would have participated in and been selected by such gatherings many times. (Thirty-nine of the fifty-five delegates to the Constitutional Convention had served in Congress, and seven had been governors.)[51] But they did not believe they had to *answer* these questions: they quite pointedly left them unresolved, and did not discuss them much. Instead, the founders took for granted that the answers would come from state and local authorities.

What the Constitution Wrought

The colonial path had established basic understandings and limits. Now, the Constitution empowered the national government to regulate voting practices, and it did so in a complex and uncertain way that has heavily influenced the mixed political order that still endures. From the start, federal regulatory authority to define and shape American voting has been part of the triply divided nature of American electoral institutions. The national government has repeatedly exercised its power over voting practices, but in a piecemeal, even fragmentary fashion. Moreover, Congress has long understood just how much local variation exists in American voting, and has seen firsthand the occasionally serious costs of running national elections locally.

Given that the framers did not resolve the basic question of whether geography or demography should structure national representation, perhaps it is no surprise that they also failed to come together on a single method or standard for electing members of the central government. The president would be chosen by special electors, whom state legislatures could appoint in any manner, while senators would come two from each state, "chosen by the legislature thereof." For congressmen, the framers settled for language *linking* state and national suffrage, while making clear that states set the boundaries: "The Electors in each State shall have the Qualifications requisite for Electors of the most numerous Branch of the State Legislature."[52]

A similar linkage is present in the Elections Clause, which effectively divides responsibility for defining American suffrage between Congress and the states.[53] I discuss what this clause tells us about Madisonian theories of popular sovereignty in Chapter 4. What is important here is to identify the Elections Clause as a key moment in the development of mixed, shared election-mechanics authority. Article I, section 4, says this: "The Times, Places and Manner of holding Elections for Senators and Representatives shall be prescribed in each State by the Legislature thereof; but the Congress may at any time by law make or alter such Regulations, except as to the Place of Chusing Senators."[54] As a federal court interpreted the clause in 2007, it "gives the States the initial authority to determine how federal elections are to be run, and that authority is curtailed only when the United States Congress so provides."[55] Congress reserved the ability to set the rules for federal elections, and over time it has repeatedly done so. But it left the work of running elections and the burden of paying for them to state and local governments. Indeed, two prominent scholars of election administration recently called running federal elections "the country's oldest unfunded mandate."[56]

At the time it changed nothing specific, but the Elections Clause was a significant development, a meaningful enlargement of the potential federal power to supervise voting practices. Opponents of the new Constitution certainly saw the clause that way. One author envisioned it as key to the withering away of states that was allegedly sought by the Federalists: "When the state legislatures drop out of sight ... then Congress are to provide for the election and appointment of representatives and senators."[57] Patrick Henry denounced the clause: "What can be more defective than the clause concerning elections? The control given to Congress over the time, place, and manner of holding elections, will totally destroy the end of suffrage. The elections may be held at one place, and the most inconvenient in the State; or they may be at remote distances from those who have a right of suffrage."[58] Previously, election rules had been entirely in the hands of states and localities. Now, a new *national* power over balloting had been established.

So where does the Elections Clause figure in our search for zero-sum "durable shifts" of enforceable authority over election mechanics? On one hand, the clause certainly represents an official statement of ultimate national power relating to voting practices. A leading scholar wrote recently that the Court now treats the clause as "a grant of essentially plenary authority."[59] And in 1995, the Supreme Court said that "the Framers understood the Elections Clause as a grant of authority to issue procedural regulations."[60] It is unsatisfying, however, simply to define constitutional ratification as the developmental moment when full federal authority over suffrage practices was firmly established, when in fact such an extraordinary amount of local variation survived it. Moreover, Congress did not actually *do* anything with that authority until it required district election of congressmen in 1842 (more on that later). Subsequent interventions—always limited, and usually explicitly deferential to states—made abundantly clear that Congress believed *states* still properly controlled most election laws and voting practices. States, in turn, for a long time left most decisions in the hands of localities.

Without a doubt, the clause has provided a resource for the national government to draw on in later years, and it has done so repeatedly. But as we will see, the use and enforcement of Congress's Elections Clause power has an uneven history—as befits its central place in the larger evolution of suffrage practices.

"To Extend the Right of Suffrage": Defining Voter Qualifications in Federal Territories, 1787–1814

The Constitution grants Congress plenary power over nonstate territories, and federal statutes governing elections in federal territories are part of our story here.[61] First, they help demonstrate the partial, idiosyncratic ways in which the U.S. national government governed directly the voting rights and practices of American citizens in the first half of the nineteenth century. Second, these statutes show that the federal government actually helped write into law the close connection between local institutions and national suffrage.

Prior to the Spanish-American War, all U.S. territories were understood to be moving inevitably toward full statehood. But territorial possessions by definition are not yet states, and from the first years of the country's existence, Congress has used its power over territories to structure their elections. Indeed, the federal government's first intervention in voting rights actually came prior to the Constitution's creation, when the Northwest Ordinance of 1787 defined formal suffrage qualifications by imposing both durational residency and property tests.[62] In requiring a fifty-acre freehold for voters, the Ordinance set a higher property threshold than most states would employ in the first U.S. elections.[63] The Ordinance allowed noncitizens to vote but required them to have longer residence in the territory than citizens needed to qualify.[64]

Congress shaped suffrage qualifications in the territories one at a time. In 1808, Congress declared that any free white male twenty-one or older who "holds in his own right a town lot at the value of one hundred dollars" was entitled to vote for representatives to Indiana's territorial assembly.[65] Three years later, new legislation "to extend the right of suffrage in the Indiana Territory" made payment of "a county or territorial tax," rather than ownership of a "town lot," the threshold. Now free white males who met that standard could vote for the legislative council, the territorial legislature, and the territory's delegate to the U.S. Congress.[66] Mississippi saw similar changes. Federal legislation passed in 1808 stated that any free white man over twenty-one owning fifty acres or "hold[ing] in his own right a town lot of the value of one hundred dollars" was entitled to vote for the Mississippi territorial assembly and for a territorial delegate to the U.S. Congress.[67] Three years later, Congress extended the Mississippi franchise to any free white men over twenty-one who paid "a county or territorial tax."[68] Residents of the Illinois Territory, which was part of the Indiana Territory until 1809, apparently tried and failed to win a similar broadening of the suffrage.[69]

These federal statutes made clear that local property records and taxes ("a town lot," "a county tax") were key to territorial voting. Moreover, the 1809 and 1811 Indiana statutes explicitly placed responsibility for running elections in local hands. Initially, Congress required county sheriffs to transmit copies of township voting returns to the secretary of the territory.[70] In 1811, it added a penalty for those who failed to do so: "Each and every sheriff . . . in said territory, shall cause to be held the election prescribed by this act . . . under the penalty of one thousand dollars."[71] Of course, Congress did not set such rules for elections in the states proper, and when these territories became states, they made their own voting rules. Thus, although the national government wielded real authority over federal suffrage in the territories, by citizens and noncitizens alike, it later yielded that authority to the new states formed in those lands.

One extraordinary early case reversed that sequence. In February 1801, Congress effectively and totally disenfranchised the citizens of parts of two states when it passed legislation assuming jurisdiction over parts of Maryland and Virginia and creating the City and County of Washington, D.C.[72] Inhabitants of this land had been residents of Maryland and Virginia, and voted there, through December of 1800. But thereafter, they no longer were provided any right to vote, either by statute or by the federal Constitution, since they were now residents of federal territory, and no state.[73] Congress understood that the 1801 statute would disenfranchise residents of the new federal district. One congressman worried that D.C. residents would be "reduced to the state of subjects, and deprived of their political rights." Another said that because they would no longer be subject to state taxation, "it could not be expected that the States would permit them, without being taxed, to be represented." A third congressman recommended that the bill stipulate that D.C. residents retained the right to vote in Maryland and Virginia.[74] But the majority apparently concluded that politicians would absorb and act on behalf of the interests of the citizens of the nation's capital simply because of their "contiguity to, and residence among" those citizens.[75] Here Congress's intervention went beyond practices or structures and stripped about fourteen thousand American citizens of the right to vote altogether.[76]

Initially, the national government controlled voting-rights qualifications in federal territories out of simple necessity: to enable the formation of territorial government, some group of participants had to be specified. These exercises of authority appear to have been uncontroversial, but Congress did exercise some agency in its choice of qualifications.[77] If the 1787 Ordinance placed voting rights in the territories slightly behind then-prevailing norms, by enacting a more demanding property test than most states would employ, the moves toward a taxpayer test in 1808–1814 put the territories slightly ahead, since most states would shift to taxpayer tests only decades later. Each act enlarging the franchise referred to "the *right* of suffrage"—relatively early uses of that phrase. Most important, even as it chose broad, affirmative language articulating voting rights, Congress compelled local officials to enforce those rights.

Voting in the Early National Period

Neither independence from Great Britain nor the establishment of new state constitutions changed the fact of broad local administrative discretion for a full generation after independence. Indeed, as the 2002 National Commission on Federal Election Reform noted in a revealing and accurate judgment, it was not until the early nineteenth century that state governments "established that they, not municipal governments, were the final arbiters of who could vote in the state."[78]

Even where formal voter-qualification requirements were followed, they were locally adjudicated and implemented. Property records were kept by county, city, or town officials, and most taxes were assessed locally as well.

Some states did employ statewide taxation as early as the 1790s—since payment of a "state tax" met their suffrage qualification—but at least as many others declared that payment of any "county tax" met the standard.[79] In Pennsylvania, no direct state tax was collected until 1832; voters met the state's taxpayer qualification by paying a county tax, levied six months before the election. In 1825, the New York state senate wrestled with one of the difficulties created by the taxpaying requirement for lessors and lessees: where the *tenant* paid the taxes, the *landlord* could lose his right to vote, and vice versa. Similar phenomena extended to noneconomic qualifications: two years earlier, hundreds of New York men apparently lost their suffrage rights because instead of doing militia duty, they served on volunteer fire departments.[80]

How and *where* people voted remained matters of great diversity. Independence did not alter the character of southern elections, which retained their carnival air—"barbecued oxen, kegs of rum, and everybody roaring drunk."[81] There was a general shift to paper beginning in the 1770s, but Virginia and Maryland retained viva voce elections, and at least half a dozen states adopted voice voting after that time.[82] Kentucky went back to viva voce in 1799 and did not formally adopt paper again for state elections until almost a century later.[83] In the Ohio territory, viva voce voting was required by law in 1794.[84] Voice voting would hold sway in most of the South until after the Civil War.[85]

Even paper voting was a far cry from the activity we know today. One difference was that before the development of party-produced tickets, voters often had to write down the name of their preferred candidates. In Massachusetts, it was not until 1829, when the state's highest court sided with a voter whose pre-printed ticket had been rejected, that voters officially won the right to use printed ballots. Maine, Vermont, and Connecticut would officially authorize the use of printed ballots in the 1830s and 1840s, either by statute or constitutional amendment.[86] At any rate, the written ballot was not at all necessarily a secret ballot, and it appears that for at least the first several decades of U.S. elections, relatively few voters cast written votes in private. In 1782, New Jersey abolished the secret ballot in a brazen effort "to intimidate the Tory vote," then restored it in 1783—but only in some counties.[87] Wealthy New York Federalist Stephen Van Rensselaer openly offered his tenants significant reductions in their fees if they would vote as directed, and sent colleagues to make sure they did so. New York established a secret ballot for city elections in 1804 and town elections in 1809.[88]

In sharp contrast to modern practice, federal courts played virtually no role in regulating suffrage or elections during the pre–Civil War period. The most high-profile example of the Supreme Court's pre–Civil War reluctance to involve itself in elections came in *Luther v. Borden*, the 1849 decision holding that even the most momentous matters of elections and representation were "political questions" unfit for judicial resolution.[89] As the courts remained on the sidelines, political parties moved to the heart of American voting through the nineteenth century. Parties were national in scope and closely connected to state governments, but they were built on local foundations.[90] Local officials continued to supervise elections: town selectmen, local judges or election inspectors in New England, and sheriffs or parish church wardens in the South. Increasingly, these officials were members of the locally dominant political party, and their impartiality was often called into question.[91]

Once the parties developed an electoral infrastructure, public voting could be exploited in earnest. Peter Argersinger concludes that the total absence of secrecy in voting was the single biggest reason why early nineteenth-century parties enjoyed so much influence. Voters carried their tickets to a window or table, often on the street, courthouse steps, or a public porch, announced their identity, and passed their ballot to an official. When producing the ballots, parties had every incentive to design tickets distinctive in color, size, and design.[92] Sometimes they were deceptive, listing one party's names but featuring the image of another party's standard-bearer to trick illiterates.[93] Later laws required ballots to be white, but because the parties used different shades of "white," poll watchers could easily tell for whom a person had voted.[94]

A final important change in the early national period involved the location of polling places. The long distances colonial voters had traveled became unacceptable in the new republic, and across the country electoral districts became smaller, making it easier for rural voters to get to the polls.[95] As early as the 1790s, voters in New York, Maryland, and New Jersey were calling for an increase in polling places. "True principles of Republicanism and of genuine Liberty," one advocate of township polling in New Jersey argued in 1793, "requires [*sic*] that elections should be brought as near to every Man's Door as possible so that the genuine voice of the People may be taken."[96] Commenting on New Jersey's election-reform law of 1788, which allowed polls to move from town to town, one author argues that the "bringing of the poll closer to the voters was, possibly, as important an event as the prior abandonment of the freehold qualification for voting."[97] Notably, it was *state* governments that multiplied the number of polling places, adding more taverns, mills, and churches to go with the county courthouses and schools that already hosted elections.[98] It is one small yet significant way in which state governments helped build the localized American suffrage system.

"The Main Object of Producing Uniformity": Mandating Districts and Simultaneity (Sort Of)

It took fifty years to do so, but Congress finally exerted its ability to shape national electoral practices and institutions in the years before the Civil War. Though districting questions fall outside the bounds of "election administration" as the phrase is typically used today, the nineteenth-century origins of single-member districts and election timing offer important illustrations of the layered, overlapping nature of American election authority. Moreover, in different ways, both the use of single-member districts and the practice of simultaneity in voting are very much contested in twenty-first-century U.S. elections, so it is worth revisiting their history briefly here.[99]

The district-election system traces its lineage not only to English political theory but also to mid-nineteenth-century congressional enactments. As elsewhere in the history of American election law, here Congress's work has been repetitive, uneven, and halting. Congress first mandated the use of single-member districts in an 1842 statute, but since then it has repeatedly allowed apportionment and districting requirements to lapse, resurrected them, and only ineffectually used its constitutional ability to "make or alter" states' congressional districts.[100] In fact, except for a few years after 1842, there was no firm requirement that representatives come from single-member districts until the current law was enacted in 1967.[101]

And that 1842 law was not all it appeared. Initially slow to interfere in states' power to choose their congressmen, Congress seemed in the 1842 law to do so decisively, requiring that representatives be "elected by districts of contiguous territory . . . [with] no district electing more than one representative."[102] Twenty-two states used single-member districts as of 1842; four (New Hampshire, Georgia, Mississippi, and Missouri) did not.[103] On its surface, then, the June 1842 act would seem a decisive shift in authority. President Tyler expressed doubts as to the power of Congress to force states to alter their electoral regulations, but he signed the bill.[104] Congressional debate over the measure appears to have been lively. Early on, Connecticut lodged a formal protest resolution "denying the right of Congress to dictate to the States the mode in which they shall elect their Representatives in Congress." Such regulation, Connecticut lawmakers argued, was "a palpable and dangerous violation of rights of Legislatures and people of the States."[105] When an amendment proposed "leaving it optional with the States to adopt either the district or general-ticket system," Kentucky Senator John Crittenden protested, arguing that such a choice "paralyzed *the main object of producing uniformity*, as it left it optional with the States of taking either the district system or the general-ticket system." Crittenden believed that "the only true and fair mode of obtaining a just representation, was by the local district system."[106] Reformers today would like to see "uniformity" in more areas than Crittenden and his 1842 colleagues did, of course, but it is important to understand that such language has long been part of debates over American voting. And Crittenden saw the legislation as quite consequential, even transformational, believing that "it would be utterly impossible to retrace this step."

In this belief he was mistaken. Crittenden won the debate, but Congress's control over this crucial dimension of suffrage proved weak. New Hampshire, Georgia, Mississippi, and Missouri simply flouted the law, continuing to use the "general-ticket system" to elect congressmen. Their action did not go unnoticed: the elections of all twenty-one congressmen chosen from those states were formally contested, and much of Congress's next session was consumed with debating the matter. In the end, the men retained their seats.[107] Congress considered a bill suspending the toothless law temporarily, but it could not even manage to pass legislation doing that much. In 1850, new legislation regarding apportionment simply deleted the reference to districts.[108] And though the 1842 law would figure in the younger Justice John Marshall Harlan's apportionment dissents more than a century later, for many years the Supreme Court did not even mention it.[109]

The act of June 25, 1842, represented Congress's first effort to fundamentally structure American elections on a national scale. In the eyes of some congressmen, the act's demand for single-member districts was a defining step that shaped federalism, representation, and the nature of American democracy. Yet the act posed only briefly as a durable shift in authority relations, then lapsed into something different and weaker—a development, to be sure, but one that was somewhat latent and incomplete. As we will see, this kind of tale is not at all unusual in the history of American suffrage.

Also in the 1840s, presidential elections forced the beginning of electoral simultaneity. Popular selection of presidential electors had spread slowly: nine of the twenty-four states still chose electors in their state legislatures in 1820, and there seem to have been no popular-vote tallies for a quarter of the states in the 1824 presidential election.[110] As popular selection spread, states held presidential elections on different days within a thirty-four-day window set by Congress in a 1792 statute.[111] This was the beginning of the era of mass parties, and in some parts of the country, both parties organized "gangs of voters" who went from one state to another, voting again and again in the same presidential election.[112] Responding to this problem, Congress passed legislation in 1845 establishing the Tuesday after the first Monday in November as the date when electors should be appointed in each state.[113]

Congressional supporters of the measure argued not only that they had the power to set a date "but that it was their duty to do it."[114] The ensuing debate revealed a number of fascinating aspects of presidential suffrage in the 1840s. For example, Representative Samuel Chilton noted that since Virginians voted viva voce and the state was "mountainous and intersected by large streams of water," "it frequently happened that all the voters were not polled in one day."[115] He urged that the bill "obviate any difficulty of this kind," and he got the flexibility he asked for. The law declared that "when any state shall have held an election for the purpose of choosing electors, and shall fail to make a choice on the day aforesaid, then the electors may be appointed on a subsequent day in such manner as the State shall by law provide." With only slight alterations, this law is still in place today.[116]

Was enactment of the 1845 measure a sharp shift of suffrage-supervisory authority from state to national government? On the one hand, that statute forms the foundation on which current law rests, and Congress did consider it a substantial limitation on state power. Moreover, the measure did serve as a precedent for post–Civil War statutes requiring senators and congressmen to be chosen on uniform dates. Yet, on the other hand, its limits as a zero-sum developmental shift in institutional authority are equally obvious: in setting an election day, Congress explicitly declared that states which did not comply with Congress's mandate could simply appoint electors later.

Congress's pre–Civil War pushes toward uniformity in how Americans would choose their representatives and presidential electors illustrate both the reach and the limitations of congressional power. Congress saw differences in congressional selection and the timing of state presidential elections as problems and acted to address them. But the national government was respectful of state authority—indeed, almost submissive to it—and left states and localities still in charge of virtually every other aspect of suffrage.

Their Own Qualifications:
The Clue in Contested Elections

The simultaneity statute returns us to the question of visibility. I have argued above that even where local officials are not consciously interpreting the Constitution in their election-administration work, we should understand them as part of the interpretive community that constructs constitutional meaning. Evidence that members of other influential institutions, particularly Congress and the courts, have a clear and certain understanding of local variation and its consequences strengthens that claim. And some of the best evidence to that effect comes from contested-election records, particularly for congressional elections but also for presidential contests.

The history of high-stakes election-administration questions in U.S. national contests goes back nearly to the beginning of the nation. Since Washington was chosen twice virtually by acclamation, the elections of 1796 and 1800 represent the first two presidential tilts involving genuine competition for the office. Both featured potentially decisive conflicts over the validity of votes. In the 1796 contest between Adams and Jefferson, the validity of Vermont's four electoral votes was under suspicion. The specific allegation related not to popular vote-casting (Vermont held no popular vote for president that year) but to the state law setting up the selection of presidential electors. As a letter in the Boston *Centinel* in early December 1796 put it, "We have good authority to believe the election of electors in Vermont is invalid— being grounded on a *Resolve* of the Legislature, not a law."[117]

The claim appears to have been baseless, but the rumor spread.[118] Jefferson and Madison exchanged letters about the matter, with Madison commenting that Adams would win "unless the Vermont election" proved to "contain some fatal vice."[119] By the time electors' votes were to be counted in Congress, Adams had a three-vote lead. If Vermont's four votes were thrown out, Jefferson would prevail. The controversy was prominent enough that when Vice President Adams, presiding over the official count as president of the Senate, formally opened the ballots in Congress, he paused and provided Republicans an opportunity to challenge them before declaring himself the winner.[120] There was no challenge, and Adams became president.

Four years later, the tables were turned, and Jefferson won despite flaws in Georgia's electoral-vote certificate. Bruce Ackerman and David Fontana have concluded that the Georgia ballot opened by Vice President Jefferson in Congress was defective, and that Jefferson probably knew it. Presiding over the official count (again, as president of the Senate), Jefferson counted Georgia's four votes into the Republican column anyway, a crucial step in his eventual elevation to the presidency.[121]

Because of the 1796 and 1800 presidential elections, U.S. national political leaders knew from very early on that allowing voting rules and procedures to vary among states could present problems. But these presidential battles are the tip of the proverbial iceberg when it comes to the visibility of early election irregularities. For sheer quantity, and for extended attention to local variation in voting practices, we must turn to the records of formally contested congressional elections. These contests are the fruit of the language in Article I, section 5, allowing congressmen and senators to judge the "Election and Qualifications" of their members. Scholars have recently exploited the official records of these contests to produce innovative and fascinating work, but the cases remain insufficiently understood as an essential part of the history of American election administration.[122]

The point I want to make is simple: from the beginning, Congress has known perfectly well that our national elections are run locally and that voting conditions vary a great deal from one place to the next. In fact, Congress has again and again witnessed these facts not in such neutral terms but as *serious problems*, as election after election laid bare just how much room for error our hyperfederalized system has, and just how high the stakes are. Congress after Congress, in decade after decade, has been brought face-to-face with confusion, incompetence, and corruption, alleged and real, in American election administration. While the contexts and partisan effects of these challenges have varied, Congress's institutional response has been consistent: it has limited itself to the work of error correction and left the underlying system in place. The proceedings of these contests stand as quintessential examples of Congress's pervasive yet deeply limited engagement with election administration.

From registration through checking voter eligibility and counting ballots, Congress has faced every item in the contemporary catalogue of election-administration challenges, most of them many times. In fact, the overwhelming majority of these contests concerned matters such as voting irregularities, polling-place fraud, improper ballots, and wrongly counted votes. While the many Reconstruction contests are most famous—desperate to hold southern seats in the face of resurgent white Democrats, Republicans used contests as a partisan measure—election contests came consistently and relentlessly both before and after that time. Between 1789 and 1830, twenty challenges alleged fraud or corruption, six focused on various nonfraudulent irregularities, and two had to do with the improper counting of votes. From 1830 to the Civil War, twenty-one contests involved nonfraudulent irregularities, while seven concerned fraud or corruption. This chapter's focus is the pre–Civil War period, but contested elections continued unabated afterward. From the Civil War through the end of the nineteenth century, many challenges concerned Reconstruction conflicts, but certainly not all—dozens occurred in northern and western states and dealt with fraud, nonfraudulent irregularities, and improperly counted ballots. From 1900 to the New Deal, forty-three contests dealt with fraud, seventeen with irregularities, and fifteen with improperly counted ballots. From the New Deal to 1960, twenty-one contests dealt with fraud, while seven dealt with general irregularities and eight with improperly counted votes. Some contested elections occurred in the territories, where non-voting delegates were selected and where Congress's powers were unfettered. But the great majority took place in the states proper.[123]

The Committee on Elections was the first standing committee appointed by the House, and hundreds of elections, to both the House and the Senate, have been formally contested in their respective houses since the United States was founded.[124] These hearings were often controversial, colorful, and remarkably detailed. Proceedings run to hundreds or even thousands of pages: fourteen contested elections for House seats between 1851 and 1860, for example, produced a total of 5,985 pages of evidence and debate, or about 428 pages per election.[125] The number and importance of these cases can be startling to the modern reader, probably because we have seen so few recent contests. Until the 1950s, every decade saw at least eleven House elections contested, and some periods saw many times that: twenty-three in the 1850s, eighty-seven in the 1890s.[126] The House has heard a total of 601 contested election cases, the Senate 132. More than once, partisan control of a chamber turned on the results. In the House, the candidate who won the original count (that is, the contestee) has prevailed about two-thirds of the time, leaving a full third in which either the seat was vacated or the result reversed outright. Similar results have occurred in Senate contests, with the exception that the Senate prefers vacating a seat to installing a challenger in it.[127]

The early challenges show how immediately and intimately Congress became acquainted with our hyperfederalized electoral system. The first contested election relating to what we'd now call "election administration" (rather than, say, candidate eligibility) dealt with a battle between James Jackson and Anthony Wayne for a seat from Georgia, heard in the Second Congress following the 1790 election. Jackson, who lost, laid out a list of charges familiar to the modern eye: only one election observer in Effingham County was a justice of the peace, though under the law all three should have been; nine more votes were given than there were qualified voters in that county; elsewhere, votes were mistabulated, and counted from people who were not present; and Camden County had not correctly used its tax returns, which were "the only check upon persons offering to vote."[128] The House declared the seat vacant.

The next Congress heard a case dealing with differing interpretations of state ballot law, which required a voter to "deliver in writing, on one piece of paper, the names of two persons . . . one of whom, at least, shall not be an inhabitant of the same county with himself." Officials in some counties thought that meant that one of the listed candidates *had* to be from the voter's own county; the House rejected that interpretation, overturned the election, and seated the losing candidate. Another case dealt with a ballot box that had temporarily been unlocked in New York, in violation of the law, and with an excess of votes. A third dealt with sheriffs who had adjourned voting for a day and with soldiers intimidating would-be voters at a polling place in Virginia.[129] True, witnesses said, a justice of the peace was knocked down at the polls—but he was drunk himself, and threw the first punch.[130]

The record marches on, decade after decade, with almost every Congress hearing challenges dealing with how, where, on what kinds of ballots, and under what supervision Americans voted. Congress in the 1790s saw contests dealing with invalid military votes in Pennsylvania, a Vermont election of which several towns were not notified, and allegations of illegal proxy voting in Massachusetts.[131] Elections officers refused to take a required oath in Maryland, and Georgia's governor certified an election before returns came in from three counties—they had been delayed by a hurricane.[132] A Massachusetts candidate lost in 1808 because some voters wrote "Charles Turner, Jr.," while others wrote "Charles Turner, Esq." Despite the fact that he was the only "Charles Turner" running (or eligible to run) in the district, the official tally in some towns split the vote, and Turner lost. (The House later heard *four* similar contests from New York alone. "Junior" seems to have been a real problem in American election law in the early nineteenth century.)[133] In 1801, Congress looked to Virginia "land lists" for help in determining whether ineligible votes had been cast.[134] The same two candidates faced off two years later, and again the result was contested—in part because some counties tabulated votes in separate columns, while others used one column or made marks next to candidates' names.[135] Inspectors tallied votes incorrectly in New York; a Virginia city mayor adjourned an election, which only county sheriffs could do under state law; and Kentucky sheriffs disagreed over signing poll books in 1832. In North Carolina in 1834, voters put ballots in the wrong boxes, and election judges moved them to the right ones.[136] These are but a tiny fraction of the whole record.

Self-interest is a powerful motivator for any politician, and partisanship is an excellent predictor of how contests turn out in Congress.[137] What is striking about the history of contested elections is that the parties and states have paid a real price for leaving election administration in local hands. Both major parties repeatedly lost seats, and almost every state has been affected, quite often losing a voting representative entirely. Only four states have never seen a House election officially contested, and just eight states have never had an election for a Senate seat contested.[138] Yet neither the parties nor the states ever led a major push for centralized, harmonized balloting procedures. As argued by the sitting member in a debate over Vermont vote-counting in 1818 (according to a summary by Chester H. Rowell), the House's power "must be exercised in subordination to the State laws prescribing the manner of those elections and returns, until such time as Congress should by law alter the laws of the States."[139] As another analysis puts it, both houses of Congress try to re-solve contested elections "in a manner that recognizes the evolution and gen-eral reliability of state election procedures" while fulfilling their constitutional power and obligation to be the final judge of their members' elections.[140]

In sum, not only were the diverse voting methods employed in U.S. na-tional elections perfectly visible to Congress at its inception, but they were immediately and consistently *problematized*, understood as serious and po-tentially very consequential phenomena. Congress as an institution knows that our national elections have always been loose affairs with a good deal of play in the joints, and it has not hesitated to investigate and judge the work of state and local officials in running elections and to overturn what it regards as fatally flawed contests. But what Congress repeatedly has *not* done—that is, respond to these contests by asserting its Elections Clause authority to erect national rules or a national election-administration bureaucracy—is equally important here. Congress wants to ensure that its members are chosen law-fully and democratically, but it also believes in leaving election management in state and local hands—even in the face of some high costs.

Voting Practices in the State Constitutional Conventions of the Jacksonian Era

In contested congressional elections, we see the national government stepping in to assert its ultimate authority over American voting but leaving state law and local practices in charge of ongoing operations. An analogous develop-ment occurred in the state constitutional conventions of the Jacksonian era. These conventions helped bring about important shifts in voter qualifications and franchise membership, and they are conventionally examined for chang-ing ideas about *who* should vote. While their inclusionary legacy is mixed, these conventions remain landmarks in the history of American suffrage and popular sovereignty.[141] I revisited records of conventions in Massachu-setts (1820–1821), Virginia (1829–1830), New York (1821), North Carolina (1835), and Iowa (1844), exploring what they tell us about *how* Americans voted.[142] Reading debates about voting and elections, I looked for awareness of local administrative control, judgment about local variation, and actions changing that arrangement.

These records reveal that even as they engaged in what remain some of the most searching, contentious disputes over the nature and purpose of voting in the country's history, American political elites did not seriously consider removing control of suffrage practices from local hands. The importance of electoral mechanics had become clear, and local variation and the difficulties of running elections were frequently described, examined, and criticized. Yet in none of these states were statewide election-administration systems even mentioned. By asserting state authority to make voting rules, discussing local variation, and then leaving county and town officials in charge of elections, the Jacksonian conventions ultimately helped *reinforce* local control.

One of the central questions facing Massachusetts constitution-drafters in the fall and winter of 1820 was whether to maintain, alter, or scrap the state's current freehold qualification, which allowed those owning property worth two hundred dollars to vote.[143] Once debate began, the very first comment dealt with "difficulties" in administering the test and the conversations that resulted at the polls: "What property have you? Have you the tools of any trade? Yes. What else? A pair of steers my father gave me."[144] The freehold test "tended to throw suspicion of unfairness on the municipal authority," since hardworking laborers and seamen were supposed to be excluded unless they owned physical property worth two hundred dollars (which most did not). That meant that "an honest poor man who paid his debts" would be excluded while "a fraudulent man . . . who owed more than he was worth" could vote.[145] Another delegate said the test "had been frequently the means of raising ill blood and producing confusion."[146] A kind of press release published after the convention declared that the new taxpayer test would "relieve Selectmen from much perplexity, and . . . enable them easily to distinguish between those who have a right to vote and those who do not."[147] Selectmen had previously determined who was qualified, and the new rule meant they would continue to do so.

It is worth reiterating that key property and tax records were at this time usually kept locally, not by any state office. An early motion in the Massachusetts convention proposed "that every citizen of the Commonwealth who is subject to pay and does pay taxes *in the town where he resides* . . . shall have the right to vote in the election of public officers of this Commonwealth."[148] In later debate, delegates quarreled over whether the qualifying tax had to be paid in the same town "where the vote was offered."[149] Some state taxes were levied at this time, and Daniel Webster was among those who argued that a tax paid "to the Commonwealth" should be the standard.[150] But others expressed the hope that "we should not always have to pay a Commonwealth tax," and the final version settles on "any state or county tax," assessed "in any town or district of this Commonwealth."[151] (A similar debate took place in New York, where one delegate said that defining the franchise by payment of a state tax was risky, since "there might be a time when no state tax would be necessary," perhaps "when the great canal was finished." He continued, "Would gentlemen have no voters in such halcyon days?")[152]

The residency requirement would also be administered by local officials, and this too occasioned a good deal of debate, set in a close understanding of local governance. Residence, opined Mr. Leland of Roxbury, "would be a question of fact to be determined by the selectmen"; a short, six-month standard would be easiest for them, since they could simply use records of "the taxes assessed in May."[153] A delegate from Dracut argued that farm workers often came into the state in spring for a six-month period and "were taxed in May for the whole year," and should therefore be allowed to vote.[154] But a Mr. Saltonstall disagreed, pointing to "the evil" known in those towns where "hundreds of men" came from New Hampshire in the spring to "vot[e] in our elections, just after they have voted in the elections in their own state."[155]

Delegates responded to lax administration of the property test by eliminating it—a fascinating development in American electoral history, and one I discuss further in Chapter 5. But despite the difficulties that taxpaying and residency requirements clearly posed to local officials (and despite the absence of privacy in voting, which troubled several delegates), no new state supervision was established. Running Massachusetts elections remained a local job.

Even by the standards of prolixity established by its peers, the New York convention of 1821 was remarkable. Focusing mostly on property and race, delegates argued over voting for entire afternoons. Their resolution was a complex half step toward universal male suffrage that allowed white men to qualify by either paying a state or county tax, performing militia or fireman duty, or working on the highways, provided they met residency tests—which, in turn, varied depending on the method by which a man earned the franchise. A property test survived for black men alone.[156]

Delegates clearly understood and regularly remarked upon variations and problems in election administration. The property qualification, one argued, "had always been an odious feature in the constitution"; abolishing it would "bear away with it a vast proportion of the perjuries, slanders, &c. that had often disgraced our elections."[157] As in Massachusetts, those "perjuries" appear to have been the oaths regarding property value that electors swore to local officials. Also as in Massachusetts, New Yorkers assumed that even written votes were not secret.[158] (Only "road masters and fence viewers" were still chosen viva voce.)[159]

Local variation did not survive this period accidentally, unseen and underfoot. Locally compiled voter-registration lists were proposed: the New

York legislature would be mandated to require "each town and ward" to make "a register of all citizens entitled to the right of suffrage."[160] Debate was intense. One delegate noted that local officials commonly lacked any kind of list to help them determine who was qualified: "entering them in a register," he argued, would make us "able to test the qualification of electors, without resorting to the multiplication of oaths, which under the present constitution had grown into a most corrupting and alarming evil."[161] Another urged the measure as conducive to "peace and quietness at the polls" and argued that it would counteract "those scenes of iniquity and perjury that had been often witnessed with pain, and which had a powerful tendency to sap the foundation of morals, and the principles of justice." Opponents, however, argued that the "tribunal" compiling such a list would effect "a modification of the elective franchise," something beyond the power of any official.[162] While fragmentary—the proposal disappears from view after surviving an early vote—the debate is striking. Delegates were quite aware of local variations in the interpretation and application of suffrage law; at least some regarded that uncertainty and variation not only as a problem, but as a problem that could "sap the foundation of morals." And the proposed solution was to be implemented not by state government but by *local* officials. Nevertheless, no action was taken, and it remained up to New York localities whether to even compile a list of eligible voters.

The voluble New Yorkers met their match in Virginia's 1829–1830 convention, which featured lengthy debates about rights and privileges, representation, and the philosophy of self-rule, as one might expect from a convention featuring James Madison, John Marshall, and John Randolph, among other luminaries. Virginia's eastern landowning elite held disproportionate political power in the state, and westerners hoping to expand their influence sought a new constitution. But new suffrage requirements lowering the property threshold tended to help easterners most, and westerners got little that they hoped for in apportionment reform.[163]

What Merrill Peterson called "an exhibition of political theory in the thick context of practical political life," however, did not include much discussion of local electoral contexts or suffrage administration. Delegates quote Shakespeare and Alexander Pope; invoke "the genius of Locke, and Sydney, and Milton"; and refer to Solon, classical Athens, the Roman republic, and Caesar.[164] But there is relatively little about how elections were run or what people actually *did* when they voted. To be sure, the context is vivid, the conflicts sometimes quite personal. (Randolph mocks Jefferson's authority by telling the story of how Jefferson designed an elegant plow, lovely to look at and honored by the French as the "mould-board of least resistance"—but no good to plow with.)[165] But voting debates were dominated by apportionment, social class, regional identity, and, occasionally, references to that part of the population "in bondage."[166]

County governance was strong, and eastern elites like Randolph considered the county courts one of the "pillars in the ancient edifice of our State Constitution."[167] But counties appear in voting disputes most often as pawns in apportionment battles.[168] As elsewhere, taxes were key to voting, and the Virginia debates show that relevant taxes were collected locally. This emerges in a disparaging speech against a taxpayer test, as a delegate mocks the idea that a man who pays "four cents upon a horse" or "a poor rate and county levy" has shown any "interest in the community."[169] Another delegate remarks on the range and complexity of different kinds of state and county taxes—on auctions, salt, and carriages (referring to a recent Supreme Court ruling, presumably the landmark 1796 case *Hylton v. United States*).[170]

Virginia's 1776 Bill of Rights had made no mention of *how* votes were to be cast. But the new constitution adopted in 1830 changed that: "In all elections in this Commonwealth . . . the votes shall be given openly, or *viva voce*, and not by ballot."[171] Several delegates had launched spirited defenses of voice voting, which was often described as particularly compatible with limited suffrage.[172] A decade earlier, New York had required ballots in all elections, but among Virginians there does not seem to have been serious interest in using paper—or in enabling voters to shield their votes from the ears and eyes of their neighbors.

As in Virginia, North Carolina's 1835 convention was sparked by western calls for more political influence, but here too westerners generally did not get what they sought.[173] Also as in Virginia, we find in the convention's records little direct discussion of election administration. North Carolina delegates fought heated debates over breaking the state into small electoral units but apparently had no interest in interfering with how localities actually ran elections.[174] The nexus between local taxes and elections surfaces again, here in a debate over how population and taxation together should determine a district's level of apportionment.[175] Another glimpse into ideas about voting practices comes from a debate over whether to compel the Assembly to vote viva voce on certain matters. Some speakers restricted their analysis to voting in the legislature, but others argued more generally that the ballot protected voters from "fear of the merchant's books," or that secrecy "was productive of prevarication and deception," since one could not ascertain another's vote with certainty. The motion succeeded, but North Carolinians outside the Assembly continued to use ballots.[176]

Iowa held two conventions, in 1844 and 1846. The first was necessary to get Iowa into the Union, but the proposed constitution was defeated by popular vote in 1845, mostly because Congress reduced the territory's size in offering it statehood.[177] The latter convention made only minor changes prior to resubmitting the constitution to popular vote, which this time succeeded. Voting was clearly an important topic in 1844, and the debate yields several interesting insights with regard to election administration and governmental authority.

An early motion that elections be held viva voce failed, and the convention declared that all elections "shall be by ballot."[178] Next, a delegate named O'Brien explained that in his county, unnaturalized men had been subject to a poll tax and had therefore asked for the ballot. O'Brien proposed that any "foreigners" who had lived in Iowa for three years and declared their intention to become citizens be permitted to vote—but only for county officers and state representatives.[179] White male immigrants in Illinois, he pointed out, could vote after living there for only six months, as long as they swore an oath pledging their intention to remain and to become citizens, and the same should suffice in Iowa. Intriguingly, opponents worried about violating the *national* Constitution, which stipulated that those who voted for "the most numerous branch of the state legislature" must be allowed to vote in national elections as well. In fact, a provision allowing noncitizens to vote in all elections would have violated no federal law, but the motion failed.[180]

The 1844 convention moved the general elections from August (harvest time) to October, despite the arguments of those who called October a "time of sickness."[181] Weeks later, a discussion of "County Organization" took place that offers an intriguing glimpse into the conduct of elections. The relevant committee had urged that sheriffs be limited to two terms, and some objected along familiar let-the-people-vote lines. But one advocate of the restriction "thought that the patronage and influence of the Sheriff might become such as to interfere with the freedom of elections."[182] The delegate did not elaborate, but he could well have meant that election administration, and not just voters' choices, would be distorted. Sheriffs ran elections in many parts of the country; recall that Congress had required them to do so in the Indiana Territory.

Finally, one comment in an 1845 speech to the Territorial Legislature on resubmitting the constitution for popular ratification reveals unequivocally that such a vote would be locally administered. One representative asked rhetorically, "Have we a right to order polls to be opened in the different counties, townships and precincts, and compel the judges of said election there to receive votes 'for' and 'against the constitution'[?]" He then affirmed, "We have not only the right, but . . . it is perfectly clear and apparent as a sunbeam."[183] The speaker was focusing not on a controversy over whether the state could order localities to hold elections but on the question of *resub-mitting* the constitution for popular ratification. Nevertheless, his specific description of how the vote would be held is meaningful, and he repeats it later.[184] The infrastructure of voting was local, and that fact was as plain and unobjectionable to Iowa lawmakers as sunlight.

The modern reader will find in the Jacksonian conventions virtually no specific discussion about why election administration stayed in local hands. While that can be frustrating, some absences are telling. Delegates clearly understood that local contexts and local officials mattered, and many believed that local authority and local variation caused problems. These conventions asserted state control over formal franchise qualifications loud and clear. But aside from debates over paper versus voice voting, I find not a single instance in which delegates seriously considered stripping local officials of the responsibility to decide how, when, and where American ballots would be cast and counted.

In the very act of drafting new rules for who could vote, the Jacksonian conventions gave new life to local administration: when delegates in Massachusetts and North Carolina acknowledged the importance of towns and counties in assessing taxes and determining residency, when New Yorkers allowed service as a fireman or highway worker to qualify a man to vote, when the Iowans discussed "causing polls to be opened in each township or precinct," and when New Yorkers considered requiring "each town and ward" to compile a list of qualified voters. In all of these actions, we see a kind of endorsement of locally run elections. State-level actors in the Jacksonian conventions believed that they, not county and town officials, held the ultimate authority to determine membership in the franchise. But there was no consideration of statewide administration, and very little by way of basic standards—just an effort to help the locals. Even as they declared state control over formal franchise qualifications, then, constitution drafters renewed and reasserted local responsibility for running the voting process.

Conclusion

As the Civil War approached, most procedural aspects of American voting varied from one county to the next, and even the most fundamental matters were left to the states. Shaped by the colonial experience, American political thinkers had little difficulty combining a powerful theory of the importance of the suffrage with an understanding that it would be exercised in different ways in different places. The national government began to see nonuniform election practices as a problem, but despite its textually clear constitutional authority to change the "Times, Places, and Manner" of elections, it acted only in limited ways, establishing a weak requirement for single-member districts, a common day for presidential elections (with exceptions for any states that needed them), and regular contested-election hearings that revealed every wart and dysfunction a locally administered suffrage system could have—yet left that system in place. The states, for their part, asserted their de jure authority over qualifications in the Jacksonian conventions, but aside from new laws requiring voting to be either by ballot or by voice, they left localities to answer virtually every procedural question relating to elections. This is a story of supervision and intervention by the national and state governments, not neglect. Yet each suffrage intervention was partial, a shift in degree rather than kind, a continuing construction of mixed and overlapping authority.

War and Reconstruction would test the durability of this institutional arrangement. But well before the Civil War, a fundamental pattern was established. That the national government had the power to intervene in election mechanics was undisputed. Yet in practice, national authority penetrated only occasionally, even erratically, into a deeply decentralized electoral regime controlled almost entirely by states and localities.

2

"Who Shall Create the Voter":
The Late Nineteenth Century

The problem of purifying the ballot-box and securing an honest
expression of the popular will is very difficult of solution,
especially in a great City like ours, but it is one which must
speedily be solved or our political fabric will be ruined.
"Purity of the Ballot Box," *New York Times* (1870)

This is a radical change in the practice, and the statute
which creates it should be explicit in its terms.
United States v. Reese (1876), referring to the
federal Enforcement Acts of 1870

It is commonly assumed that our current debates mark the first time the national and state governments, the courts, and reformers have engaged in sustained examination of American election administration.[1] In fact, the period
between the Civil War and the turn of the century amounted to a decades-
long running debate over how Americans voted, and recovering the political
and legal language of that debate is crucial to understanding the history of
the local dimension of American suffrage.[2] This era saw two essential developments. The first was the passage of *national* laws erecting what amounted
to a federal election-administration supervisory regime in 1870 and 1871,
the endorsement of those laws by the federal courts, and their subsequent
demise. The second occurred among the states, where Australian-ballot laws
spread in a few short years at the close of the nineteenth century, forcefully
asserting *state* authority to regulate the minutiae of voting practices. Both reduced the scope of local variation and administrative discretion, and both far
outstripped the many pre–Civil War changes. Local election-administration
authority was diminished in this period, leading the *Reese* Court to describe
one federal statute as having brought about "a radical change in the practice"
of suffrage.[3] Yet paradoxically, each of these signal developments would ulti-

mately preserve and even reinforce local government's vital role in shaping the practice of American voting.

Reconstruction

The Civil War altered American suffrage in direct and immediate ways. During the war, Republican-controlled state legislatures made it easier than ever for soldiers to vote, either as an absentee or in temporary precincts. Democrats encouraged noncitizens, who were generally hostile to the war, to vote; Republicans met these voters at the polls and, as they registered, added their names to the list of those eligible to be drafted into military service. Border states employed new loyalty oaths. And in many northern and border areas, Union soldiers and state militia appeared at the polls, ostensibly to defend against Confederate attack but in reality helping impose de facto loyalty tests.[4] Some southern and border states would temporarily discontinue viva voce polling during the war and its immediate aftermath, fearing the practice would enable traditional elites to reassert control.[5]

In the longer term, the war would mark the beginning of a considerable expansion of federal authority over the conduct of voting in America. Those changes were of a piece with the war's broader effects on constitutional development: as Akhil Amar writes, after the war "liberty would no longer be automatically associated with localism, as it had been for the generation of Americans who lived through the Revolutionary War."[6] Increasingly, Americans would see the national government as the best guarantor of liberty and equality, a view that carried powerful implications for election law. Before the Civil War, local officials exercised sweeping authority over voting practices, shaped only intermittently by federal and state action. As we have seen, Congress intervened to scrutinize contested elections, require the use of districts, and mandate simultaneity in presidential balloting, while states clarified their authority over formal qualifications in the Jacksonian conventions. From the first, the Elections Clause had provided an explicit constitutional warrant for federal action to "make or alter" any law relating to the time, place, or manner of voting. But relatively little such action occurred. Localities kept virtually all records relevant to the franchise and, together with the parties, were generally undisturbed in their management of the casting and counting of votes. That began to change after the Civil War, as the scope and volume of federal engagement with voting practices increased considerably.

With the Reconstruction Amendments, the Constitution finally began to speak directly of the "right to vote." This occurred first with the Fourteenth

Amendment—though not with its most famous language, the guarantee of "the equal protection of the laws" embedded in the amendment's first section. While the Equal Protection Clause is essential to voting-rights law today, that development came about primarily as a result of twentieth-century political thought and jurisprudence.[7] Instead, it was the amendment's second section that dealt explicitly with voting rights. In 1868, even Radical Republicans were reluctant to assert federal control over suffrage qualification and directly confront northern racism, so they decided *not* to use the Fourteenth Amendment to explicitly bar racial discrimination in voting. Instead, they included in section 2 of the amendment a formula meant to allow resurgent southern whites to bar black men (or anyone else) from exercising the right to vote, but also to firmly penalize states that did so by reducing their representation in the national government proportionally.[8] This representation-reduction aspect of section 2 was never employed, and the enactment of the Fifteenth Amendment just two years later essentially negated it.[9] The federal courts have regarded its disenfranchisement-endorsing aspect as a dead letter, with one major exception: in 1974, the Supreme Court ruled that state criminal-disenfranchisement laws receive explicit constitutional approval from the phrase "except for rebellion, or other crime" in section 2 of the Fourteenth Amendment.[10] (I discuss these policies in more detail in Chapter 5.)

The Fifteenth Amendment's direct regulation of state voter qualifications was a major change in the American constitutional order. At issue, as one senator argued, was not just who would be allowed to vote but who *decided* such questions: "Not who shall be the voter, but who shall create the voter."[11] Despite the constitutional linkage between the state and national franchise, states had always held that ultimate authority: recall that the original Constitution declared that states had to allow everyone who could vote for "the most numerous branch of the state legislature" to vote for congressional representative at the national level. Now, the Constitution had declared that the right of U.S. citizens to vote "shall not be denied or abridged by the United States or by any State on account of race, color, or previous condition of servitude."

But this dramatic change did not stick. The text, purpose, and spirit of the Fifteenth Amendment were quickly and flagrantly violated by the white primary, poll taxes, literacy tests, the grandfather clause, and racially targeted criminal-disenfranchisement laws, as well as extralegal intimidation and violence. So although the Reconstruction Amendments do represent the national Constitution's first formal definition of the franchise, their direct effects on voting practices were altogether temporary. That is the challenge of characterizing these amendments as developmental events. Today, localities and states must act in accordance with court interpretations of the Equal Protection Clause in administering elections—but that was not so until the 1960s. Meanwhile, the second section of the Fifteenth Amendment, by authorizing congressional enforcement, provided a foundation for some of the nation's most consequential legislation—but it too would not become a "vehicle for transformation" until a full century after its enactment.[12] Great institutional, partisan, and regional conflict characterized the drafting and ratification of the Reconstruction Amendments, and I do not mean to minimize their colossal importance to constitutional theory and American history. But if we ask *when* the Reconstruction Amendments actually brought about lasting change in the practices of American suffrage, we see again what the Elections Clause illustrated before. Constitutional text is a powerful resource in political conflict, and it can plant seeds that sprout later into more durable transformation. But the practical, developmental impact of constitutional text is defined by other institutions.[13]

National intervention in electoral practices after the Civil War was not limited to formal constitutional change. Partisan politics and new confidence in national power led to several election-law statutes. First, in 1865, Congress banned federal troops from appearing at voting sites, "unless it shall be necessary to repel the armed enemies of the United States, or to keep the peace at the polls." (Today's law to this effect is based on 1948 and 1909 codifications of the 1865 statute.)[14] Then, the Military Reconstruction Act of 1867 was passed, allowing former Confederate states to be readmitted to the Union only if they adopted new state constitutions putting in place universal male suffrage. And in 1872, Congress mandated that congressional representatives be chosen on a single day, the Tuesday after the first Monday in November— another law that still stands.[15] As the Supreme Court would observe in 1884, Congress took this step "to remedy more than one evil arising from the election of members of Congress occurring at different times in the different States."[16] Fraudulent repeat voting by partisans may have been among those evils, but as the Court noted in 1997, the original bill's sponsor emphasized that publicized results from early states might distort voting in later states, and that the need to vote on two different days in presidential election years was a burden on voters.[17] The rule was less than airtight, effectively exempting from the simultaneity requirement any state whose constitution required an amendment to change the day of election. (When Congress required in 1914 that senators be chosen on a single day, it again used language deferential to state authority.)[18] The 1872 statute did more than just establish a simultaneity requirement; it also stated that congressmen should be "elected by districts composed of contiguous territory," and repeated the language of the Fourteenth Amendment's section 2 regarding apportionment.

These were important statutes. But from the perspective of national authority, election administration, and the scope of local control, the greatest developmental event of the immediate postwar period—indeed, one of the most important in all of U.S. history—was the passage and enforcement of laws enacted in 1870 and 1871.

Erecting an Election-Administration Supervisory Regime, 1870–1871

The Enforcement Acts of the early 1870s were not merely Reconstruction legislation, putting teeth in the Fifteenth Amendment and protecting black voters in the South. The 1870 Enforcement Act did bar racial discrimination in election administration, clearly anticipating discriminatory obstructions to the franchise in the South. But it was not solely a racial and regional measure. Among the statute's twenty-three detailed sections were several pertaining to election administration generally—part of why the *New York Times* editorialized in favor of the 1870 law. "We are quite sure," said the *Times*, "that the Federal Courts, with the assistance, if need be, of the authorities at Washington, will enforce all the penalties of the law against fraudulent registration, double voting, false canvassing, and attempted violence or intimidation at the polls." The *Times* denounced partisan Democrats for abusing the suffrage and urged "Republican Committees" to use the new census and its ward counts in checking false registrations.[19]

On paper, the 1870 act wrought a real transformation in the structure of American suffrage, shifting authority away from states and localities and toward the national government. As the Supreme Court put it in the 1876 case *United States v. Reese*, "The statute contemplates a most important change in the election laws. Previous to its adoption, the States, as a general rule, regulated in their own way all the details of all elections. They prescribed the qualifications of voters, and the manner in which those offering to vote at an election should make known their qualifications to the officers in charge. This act interferes with this practice. . . . *This is a radical change in the practice*, and the statute which creates it should be explicit in its terms."[20] The 1870 law enlarged the scope of federal authority by criminalizing interference with the right to vote.

The next year, Congress went a step further, placing the federal government in an oversight role. While not well known outside election-law circles, the Enforcement Act of February 28, 1871, represents one of the most substantial developmental steps in the history of American voting. Writing in

1970, one scholar called the act's tenure "the longest run to date of national supervision of elections."[21] Remarkable in detail, complexity, and length, the act is nothing less than a blueprint for federal supervision of every stage of elections—registering voters, checking voter qualifications, monitoring the casting of votes ("personally inspect and scrutinize, from time to time, and on the day of the election, the manner in which the voting is done"), tallying the results, and punishing those who interfere with any part of the process. The 1871 measure directly involved the federal government in election administration in cities across the country, establishing "a uniform system of supervision and enforcement at national elections."[22] It belongs in a class with the Voting Rights Act of 1965—both acts constitute major legislative interventions in voting practices that, despite their limitations, transformed the existing blend of federal, state, and local authority over the exercise of the right to vote.

Both the 1870 and 1871 acts were in large part responses to Democratic Party shenanigans in northern cities in the 1868 and 1870 elections.[23] Northerners like John Sherman called election fraud "a national evil so great, so dangerous, and so alarming in character" that it was "of greater magnitude even than denial of [the] right to vote to colored people." Of course, partisanship and principle mixed freely in these judgments, since Sherman, a Republican, was obviously concerned about fraudulent Democratic votes.[24] Most Republicans supported the acts, but some joined Democrats in opposing the 1870 law on the ground that it violated states' right to regulate the suffrage.[25] Democrats saw the statute as pure partisanship—and as an excessive enlargement of federal power. Senator George Vickers of Maryland contended that "the extension of suffrage to the African race was not intended to enlarge the power of Congress over the white race."[26]

The 1871 measure barred impersonation, repeat voting, intimidation, or bribery of voters in congressional elections or in registration for those elections. Its first section dealt with voter registration, and its rules extended to registration procedures used for state or local elections if the voter-registration records from those elections could later be used for a national election. This section's coverage was national, but most of the law applied initially only to cities with more than twenty thousand inhabitants; an 1872 amendment applied the law to smaller cities.

Two different types of federal officials oversaw elections under the law, and each type had very different connections to partisan politics. First, there were supervisors, appointed by federal district courts at citizen request. Minority parties—Republicans in most northern cities, Democrats in Philadelphia—usually requested supervisors. If it believed supervisors were warranted, the federal court would appoint two supervisors per district, and the supervisors had to be of different parties. Supervisors could challenge registration, inspect voting processes, count ballots, and issue election certificates. The second type of official authorized by the 1871 law were deputy U.S. marshals, who did *not* have to be of different parties. The marshals were appointed in particular locations at the discretion of the (usually Republican) president, which gave a distinctly Republican cast to election administration and law enforcement in the 1870s and 1880s. As Peter Argersinger writes, it seemed to some "that the presence of armed federal election officials was intended to intimidate Democratic voters, particularly in certain ethnic neighborhoods."[27] Thousands of such deputies were authorized over the life of the law. There is a great deal of evidence that Republican deputies aided corruption, sometimes flagrantly; in fact, the marshals sometimes arrested Democratic elections officials and ran the polls themselves.[28]

Enforcement of the 1871 act was costly—expenses for supervisors and marshals ran to hundreds of thousands of dollars in some years, and total expenditures on enforcement over the law's twenty-three-year history came to more than four and a half million dollars.[29] The Supreme Court upheld the 1870 and 1871 laws and their complicated, state-by-state enforcement in two 1880 cases, *Ex parte Clark* and *Ex parte Siebold*, departing considerably from the narrow view of the 1870 statute taken in the *Reese* and *Cruikshank* decisions just four years earlier.[30] (I will say more about these cases in the next section of this chapter.)

The Enforcement Act of 1871 changed the authority structure supervising U.S. voting, but it did so only for about two decades. After Massachusetts Republican Senator George Frisbie Hoar led his party in a failed 1890–1891 effort to pass new federal legislation protecting African American voting rights, Democrats made big gains in the 1892 elections. Alarmed by the expansion of national authority that Hoar had proposed and almost enacted, Democrats struck back, repealing the 1871 election law almost in its entirety on a straight party vote.[31] Only section 19, requiring that "all votes for representatives in Congress shall hereafter be by written or printed ballot," survived.

Where do the 1870 and 1871 laws rank in our search for major developmental events? First, by requiring that ballots be used for all congressional elections, "any law of any State to the contrary notwithstanding," the 1871 act clearly brought about change—and change that proved durable. Previously, states could allow viva voce voting in federal elections. Oral voting had only recently been eliminated in West Virginia (1863), Missouri (1863), and Arkansas (1868). Oregon and Kentucky still voted viva voce for Congress as of 1871; Oregon moved to ballots immediately after the act's passage, in 1872, as did Kentucky for House elections. But Kentucky persisted in voting orally for every other election, and did not abandon the voice vote altogether until 1891.[32] At the very least, Oregon and Kentucky appear to have been compelled to alter their mode of choosing congressmen by federal legislation.

But the meaning of these laws in political development goes well beyond that particular change in the "manner" of voting. Almost two decades before state ballot reform began in earnest (and a century before the Voting Rights Act) the federal government tackled fraud, coercion, discrimination, and incompetence in American election administration. The 1870 law was part of that response, but the 1871 law was particularly important. It was national in scope, not just regional; it penetrated into practical elements of the electoral process, not just qualifications; it set up a supervisory regime, not just rules; and it aimed at partisan corruption in the North, not just racial discrimination in the South. It cost a lot of federal money, was controversial, and had visible impact. Though the law took some knocks, it survived repeated testing in the highest national courts. It included no automatic expiration date and was in effect for decades. (For comparison's sake, its tenure was about as long as the period we have seen since the Court ratified the 1982 amendments to the Voting Rights Act in the 1986 decision *Thornburg v. Gingles*.) And its implementation employed members of both the federal executive branch and the federal courts, taking specific authority away from states, localities, and parties. Indeed, the Enforcement Acts of 1870 and 1871 were important beyond the election-law field itself, as they were among the very first American efforts to use national law enforcement to protect the rights of citizens.[33]

The 1870 and 1871 statutes stand among the most significant developmental shifts in the history of American voting practices. Yet even the 1871 law followed the developmental pattern displayed in lesser acts of suffrage-practices transformation: although it moved American elections toward centralization and uniformity, it was also deeply limited. The statute's effects were spatially constrained: while drafted in a national way, most of it was applied only to cities.[34] It was also temporally limited, repealed almost entirely less than twenty-five years after its passage. And the single section of the 1871 law that survived, requiring the use of ballots in federal elections, effected only an incomplete transfer of meaningful power away from political parties, because parties remained able to manipulate ballot design to their hearts' content until state Australian-ballot laws intervened. And certainly the use of ballots subsequent to the law's passage did not mean voting was secret.

The ultimate reason why the 1871 law brought about only limited developmental change is probably that it never transcended its close connection to a single political party. Indeed, it may be that the law's enforcement gave national involvement in election administration a bad name—or at least an

utterly partisan one. That was clearly the case among Democrats who believed they were defending state authority against federal encroachment. As
Woodrow Wilson himself wrote in *Congressional Government* (published in
1885, when enforcement of the 1871 law was alive and well), "The federal
supervisor who oversees the balloting for congressmen represents the very
ugliest side of federal supremacy."[35]

What Justice Brewer Saw: *Giles* and Election Administration in American Constitutional Development

In his 2001 book on *Bush v. Gore*, federal judge and law professor Richard A.
Posner wrote that though the body of Supreme Court case law on elections is
large, "virtually none of it deals with election administration."[36] It is true that
prior to 2000, few if any cases had taken locally varying voting technology
itself as their central constitutional problem. But American constitutional
law has not ignored election administration or the role of local officials in
American suffrage. In fact, in the late nineteenth century, the federal courts
routinely decided cases that required them to look closely at local voting
practices. Cases from this period leave no doubt that the Court and the legal
community clearly understood the importance of local authority and local
variation. Moreover, Congress and the courts together developed a body of
theory, statutes, and doctrine supporting a broad federal ability to supervise
and constrain state and local administration of elections. The 1870 and 1871
enforcement laws were essential parts of this period, but they only begin to
tell the story of mixed election-supervision authority and constitutional development in the late nineteenth century. A fuller picture comes from a Supreme Court case decided in 1903 that helped bring an end to the era—*Giles
v. Harris*—and in particular from a short, straightforward dissent written in
that case by Justice David Josiah Brewer.

In *Giles*, the Supreme Court rejected a challenge to the Alabama constitution's voter-registration scheme, patently written to enable the disenfranchisement of blacks and administered accordingly by county boards. Writing
for the Court, Justice Oliver Wendell Holmes concluded that while racism
was indeed the reason why the Montgomery County board of registrars refused to register Jackson Giles to vote, "relief from a great political wrong"
like this must come from "the people of the State and the State itself," or from
"the legislative and political department of the government of the United
States."[37] Holmes noted the existence of the Fifteenth Amendment only in
summarizing Giles's claim at the outset of his opinion; he did not see any

need to mention it again. Justice Brewer dissented, focusing on the question of jurisdiction. Brewer did not say what relief, if any, he thought Jackson Giles should receive; he simply stated that the federal courts did have jurisdiction over such a case, and that the question should be sent back down for trial. Though not particularly long or impassioned, the opinion points to an abandoned path in American election law and offers us a chance to recover a lost legal narrative.

Giles brought an ignoble end to a generation in which the Court went back and forth on questions of federal power over elections, race, and the meaning of the Fifteenth Amendment. In order to place *Giles* in American political development, it helps to return to the quotation from the 1876 case *United States v. Reese* that begins this chapter, and to briefly review doctrinal and political developments in the thirty years between *Reese* and *Giles*. In *Reese*, the Court voided the conviction of a local official who refused to register a black man to vote in a municipal election in Louisville, and threw out two sections of the 1870 Enforcement Act because they failed to include language about voting exclusion on the basis of race. Interpreting narrowly both the Fifteenth Amendment and Congress's ability to enforce it, the Court scolded Congress for its poor draftsmanship and called the 1870 Enforcement Act "a most important change in the election laws," and "a radical change in the practice" of voting.[38] In *Reese* (and its companion, *Cruikshank*), the Court essentially tried to rein in those changes. Despite its bald statement that the Fifteenth Amendment "does not confer the right of suffrage upon any one," the *Reese* Court did at least acknowledge that the Fifteenth Amendment forbids the states "from giving preference" in voting rules on account of race. In other words, the national government could not use its new authority to protect the right to vote generally; it could protect only against discrimination based on race, color, or previous condition of servitude.

Congress reenacted the nullified sections of the act.[39] In terms of our developmental interest in federal power to govern voting practices, the interesting point is *how* Congress reenacted the law voided in *Reese*, and how the federal courts interpreted the new law. The original statute had rested its ban on voter intimidation on the Fifteenth Amendment. But the new section 5506 of the Revised Statutes was "a general law," enacted "by virtue of the power given to congress under the *fourth section of the first article* of the constitution," as a Virginia federal court put it in the 1883 case *United States v. Munford.*[40]

That reference, of course, is to the Elections Clause, which gave Congress the authority to "make or alter" rules affecting the "times, places, and manner" of elections for senators and representatives. *Munford* reads the clause as a broad grant of authority: "If congress can provide for the manner of election, it can certainly provide that it shall be in an honest manner; that there shall be no repression of voters and an honest count of the ballots."[41] Distinguishing *Reese*, the *Munford* court said that Congress had "general powers" concerning *federal* elections based on Article I; Congress could reach *state and local* elections only when employing its new Fifteenth Amendment authority to prevent and punish racial discrimination.[42] Despite that restriction, the slumbering Elections Clause now appeared to have come to life as a meaningful source of national authority.

Other lower federal-court decisions adopted this same broad view of Congress's Elections Clause power. *United States v. Goldman*, decided in a Louisiana federal court in 1878, concluded that the Elections Clause was "framed to secure the existence of the government itself." State law was still the ultimate source of a man's right to vote, but once he had the franchise, the *Goldman* court reasoned, Congress had "the power to protect him in that right."[43] Despite its cramped *Reese* decision, the Supreme Court would soon emphatically endorse this sweeping view of the Elections Clause as a source of congressional authority. In several cases decided in the 1880s, the Court upheld federal power to regulate election practices and punish those who obstructed voting—and rested that power firmly on the Elections Clause. In *Ex parte Siebold* (1880), *Ex parte Clark* (1880), and *Ex parte Yarbrough* (1884), the Supreme Court declared that under the Elections Clause, the federal government could legislate against interference in voting in federal elections for any reason—not just racially discriminatory motives.[44] In *Siebold*, the Court upheld the conviction of a Baltimore election judge and ruled that Congress could make it a *federal* crime for a state official to neglect his duties under *state* law in a federal election. In *Yarbrough*, the Court upheld the conviction of a Klansman for beating a black man to keep him from voting, and gave a much stronger interpretation of the Fifteenth Amendment than had the *Reese* Court. Not only did the Court point to the Elections Clause as the source of congressional authority over elections in these cases, but it offered a deep and principled theory for that conclusion. If Congress did not hold and execute this power, said the Court in *Siebold*, "it is no government."[45] In what is still a startlingly broad declaration, the Court said Congress could, if it saw fit, "assume the entire control and regulation of the election of Representatives," including "the appointment of the places for holding the polls, the times of voting, and the officers for holding the elections; . . . the regulation of the duties to be performed, the custody of the ballots, the mode of ascertaining the result, and every other matter relating to the subject."[46] Certainly, said the Court in *Yarbrough*, Congress could "make additional laws for the free, the pure, and the safe exercise of this right of voting," to ensure "that the votes by which its members of Congress and its President are elected shall be the free votes of the electors, and the officers thus chosen the free and uncorrupted choice of those who have the right to take part in that choice." Accurate, un-polluted elections, the *Yarbrough* Court declared, are "essential to the healthy organization of the government itself."[47] Strikingly, the unanimous *Yarbrough* decision held that the Fifteenth Amendment empowered Congress to reach and punish *private* action.

Ratification of the Constitution granted ultimate voting-supervision authority to Congress in federal elections. But until now, Congress had been "slow to exercise the powers expressly conferred upon it" by the Elections Clause, as the *Yarbrough* Court put it.[48] Congressional ability to "make or alter" voting rules hadn't figured much at all in American political life; the Elections Clause had lain all but dormant. Now, that latent authority seemed to be coming to full flower, with Congress and the courts essentially sharing the belief that it was right and proper for Congress to reach past state and local election-administration authority and tell states *and* individuals what to do (and not do) at election time. As Richard Valelly writes, this was a "centralizing and muscular reading" of the Elections Clause.[49]

It didn't last. By the 1890s, elite white opinion had turned against universal suffrage, and not just in terms of race. As we have seen, partisan change had led to the 1894 repeal of almost all congressional election-supervision statutes. The membership of the Court had changed almost entirely: Democrat Grover Cleveland had appointed three justices, including Chief Justice Fuller, and even the Court's new Republican appointees held a much more skeptical view of national power than had their predecessors. That showed in the Court's election-law decisions.

A typical case from the 1890s is *Mills v. Green*, in which the Court heard a challenge to the exclusionary rules South Carolina erected to keep blacks from voting in elections for its 1895 constitutional convention. In a decision one modern critic calls "disingenuous nonsense," the Court dismissed the challenge as moot—because the election in question had already been held.[50] Next, the Court in 1897 simply ignored the Fifteenth Amendment and refused to strike down an obviously racist state constitutional provision governing the franchise in *Williams v. Mississippi*. Mississippi's 1890 constitution enacted literacy tests, poll taxes, and other devices with the proud and explicit purpose of restoring white supremacy, a purpose the Mississippi Supreme Court had clearly identified a year earlier.[51] But while the U.S. Supreme Court quoted that state decision at length, it resolved the federal case with a statement as chilling as it is bland. "There is an allegation," said the Court, "of the purpose of the convention to disfranchise citizens of the colored race, but with this we have no concern, unless the purpose is executed by the constitution or laws or by those who administer them."[52] Of course, there was abundant evidence of discrimination by those who administered elections, but the *Williams* Court simply covered its eyes and let the state constitution stand. And in the 1903 case *James v. Bowman*, the Court would ignore *Yarbrough* and void a surviving federal statute as an impermissible restriction of private action.[53]

This brings us back to *Giles*, decided in the same year as *Bowman*. The Court majority concluded that Jackson Giles's problem was simply not one federal courts could help with: if state and local actors wanted to deprive blacks of the ballot, that might be a "great political wrong," but it wasn't one the Court could address. Justice Brewer, joined by Justice John Marshall Harlan, argued that the courts did have jurisdiction over such a case. To Justice Holmes's conclusion that no relief could be granted in such a voting-rights case, Brewer said bluntly, "That such relief will be given has been again and again affirmed in both National and state courts."[54] Brewer's opinion reviews those precedents, beginning with simple citations to *Siebold* and *Yarbrough*, as demonstrations of "the general jurisdiction of Federal courts over matters involved in the election of national officers."[55]

Brewer also pointed here to *In re Coy*. In that 1888 decision, the Court affirmed the propriety of a federal indictment against at least eleven men accused of interfering with an Indiana election—despite the fact that they had meant to interfere with a *state* election, and not the congressional contest occurring simultaneously. The Court was mindful of what it called "the difficulty and delicacy" of laws allowing federal courts to punish interference with a state contest: "The difficulty and delicacy of the position arises from the circumstance that Congress, instead of passing laws for the election of such members and delegates from the States and Territories under the supervision of its own officers and at times when no other elections are held, has remitted to the States the duty of providing for such elections."[56] The national government, said the *Coy* Court, had not chosen to require separate elections for congressmen, instead enacting statutes that essentially "adopted the laws of the State." While that made applying laws regarding the "casting, returning, and counting of votes somewhat complex," it also meant that ultimately congressional power to secure fair and honest elections "cannot be questioned."[57]

After noting *Siebold*, *Yarbrough*, and *Coy*, Justice Brewer focused the balance of his dissent on two more recent cases: *Wiley v. Sinkler* (1900) and *Swafford v. Templeton* (1902).[58] Both affirmed federal jurisdiction in cases involving the casting and counting of votes in congressional elections. *Wiley* arose after precinct managers in Charleston, South Carolina, refused to let a man vote; the Court insisted that the right to vote "is not derived merely" from state law, but "has its foundation in the Constitution of the United States."[59] *Swafford* emerged out of Rhea County, Tennessee, and repeatedly referred to the right to vote in congressional elections as a "Federal right."[60]

The heart of Justice Brewer's *Giles* dissent is a long passage taken from Justice Edward White's opinion for the Court in *Swafford*. White had in turn quoted from *Yarbrough*, insisting that the right to vote in congressional elections was "fundamentally based upon the Constitution of the United States."[61] Intriguingly, in supporting that conclusion Justice White would then use a phrase prominent in the racial jurisprudence of the period. White wrote that the lower federal court should not have dismissed Swafford's claim, because the right to vote in congressional elections "was one *in the very nature of things* arising under the Constitution and laws of the United States."[62] That language—"in the nature of things"—appeared more than once in leading cases dealing with federalism and race over the preceding decades, as Mark S. Weiner has emphasized.[63]

Race and federalism held no monopoly on the Court's use of this phrase.[64] And it is probably impossible to know just why Justice White had used these words in *Swafford*, and whether Justice Brewer gave any thought to reproducing them in *Giles*. But reading *Giles* and *Swafford* today, the statement that the right to vote was "in the nature of things" fundamentally based upon the federal Constitution reminds us how deeply the Court's election-administration decisions were connected to its struggles with federalism and race. And most important to us here, both opinions employed the phrase to support an *expansive* reading of congressional authority—and a very modern-sounding, nationalized conception of the right to vote. Famous passages from cases like *Reese* and *Minor v. Happersett*, in which the late-nineteenth-century Court stated in one way or another that the federal constitution does not confer any right to vote, seem to have eclipsed for us the powerful alternative legal narrative developed during this period in cases like *Siebold, Yarbrough, Wiley, Coy,* and *Swafford*.[65]

These latter cases also make it emphatically clear that many Supreme Court cases have indeed dealt with election administration. Here the Court demonstrates a clear-eyed understanding of the nitty-gritty details of American voting practices—"the casting, returning, and counting of votes," as the *Coy* Court put it. As I said earlier, this book is premised on the belief that local officials should be understood as part of the interpretive community that constructs constitutional meaning. And I have acknowledged that in order for this to be true, locally varying suffrage practices and the work of local officials have to have been *visible*. That is, we need to see evidence that other, more prominent shapers of constitutional understandings—particularly judges and legislators—knew full well how crucial local discretion was to the exercise of the right to vote. In Chapter 1, I argued that among other sources, the records of contested congressional elections, the proceedings of state constitutional conventions, and occasional congressional debates plainly indicate that the local dimension of American suffrage was indeed visible through the early nineteenth century. Set in local contexts and predominantly concerned with the conduct of county and city officials, the decisions leading up to *Giles* support the same conclusion.

Wiley recounts the alleged actions and inactions of election managers in "the first precinct in the sixth ward of the city and county of Charleston" and includes a detailed explanation of voter-registration procedures required by South Carolina law.[66] *In re Coy* wades repeatedly into the nuts and bolts of Indiana elections. Votes for congressmen, the Court explained, "are generally put into the same box with those cast for the various state and municipal officers" and are "printed upon ballots, composed of one piece of paper, containing a long list of names." A number of precinct election inspectors apparently mishandled "ballots, tally papers, poll lists, and certifications of the board of judges of election." By Indiana law, *Coy* notes, "it was the duty of these inspectors to take the certified lists of the voters, with the returns of the judges, and safely keep them until they delivered them to the county clerk or to the board of canvassers who were to examine and count the votes of all the precincts in the county."[67]

Swafford, meanwhile, focuses on whether the small population of Rhea County exempted it from Tennessee law regarding registration and ballot laws, such that the election judges were wrong to make the plaintiff "mark his ballot, and fold it in a particular way."[68] And *Mills v. Green*, the 1895 South Carolina case, nicely directs our attention to the contents of "the registration books in the defendant's hands."[69] For a generation, the Court made a habit of looking closely at such books and such hands. These cases are about federalism, jurisdiction, and the constitutional foundations of the right to vote—*and* about tally papers, registration books, folding ballots, and canvassing boards.

Expanding national supervision of elections had been a major Republican priority in the election of 1888, but an unrelenting Senate filibuster kept the strong Federal Elections Bill of 1890 from becoming law.[70] As the South became solidly Democratic, Congress repealed voter-intimidation and election-supervision statutes and abandoned the aggressive use of its power to review and void congressional elections. The Elections Clause would not disappear from Court doctrine—as I explain later, it would anchor primary-election cases such as *Newberry v. United States* (1921) and *United States v. Classic* (1941)—but Congress dramatically scaled back its use of the powers that the clause nominally bestowed.

As the new century began, the Republican coalition no longer ruled national politics. And the year after the Court handed down *Giles,* Congress announced what amounted to an important constriction of its own constitutionally granted power to directly supervise elections. Having done away with almost all of the election-supervision statutes sustained by the federal courts under the Elections Clause and the Fifteenth Amendment, the House now declared a major shift in its own understanding of its power under a third part of the Constitution: the Qualifications Clause. Recall that the Qualifications Clause empowers the House and Senate to judge the "Election and Qualifications" of their own members, and both bodies had employed that power hundreds of times to overturn what they considered faulty elections. Between 1880 and 1901, the House had twenty-six times seated Republican or Populist congressmen in southern seats after Qualifications contests.[71] Significantly, Congress reasoned in many of these proceedings that the Qualifications Clause combined with the Fifteenth Amendment allowed it to decide that *state* election laws were unconstitutional.[72]

But by the late 1890s, Congress had indicated that it would not look favorably on official elections contests challenging the new southern disenfranchising constitutions and statutes. The Court in 1903 turned away Jackson Giles, suggesting that he and his southern black comrades should seek help from the "legislative and political department" of the government. In 1904, that legislative department emphatically refused. Rejecting an election challenge out of South Carolina and completely reversing the principle that had guided it for a generation, the House Committee on Elections said that "a legislative body is not the ideal body to pass judicially upon the constitutionality of other bodies." Adding a punch line, Congress advised those deprived of the franchise to "bring suit in a proper court," such as the "Supreme Court of the United States."[73] There was nowhere left to turn.

The balance of authority between Congress, the states, political parties, and local governments shifted in the 1870s, as Congress and the courts together built a doctrine of expanded national power to oversee voting practices. National authority in this sphere seemed so clear that to its supporters it achieved the ultimate rhetorical pinnacle: it became common sense. It was "in the nature of things," as the Court said in *Swafford.* "These questions answer themselves," said the Court in *Yarbrough.* The only reason anyone could possibly doubt Congress's authority over elections, the Court declared, was that Congress had refrained from exercising its Elections Clause power "through long habit and long years of forbearance" and "in deference and respect to the states."[74]

While the statutes of the 1870s were in effect, local officials in many parts of the United States saw their independence and election-administration powers severely constrained. Not only could the federal executive prosecute local officials for failing to conform to national and state election laws, and not only would the federal courts support such prosecutions and shine the light of the highest courts in the land on local conduct, but federal marshals could take over the entire electoral process—and frequently did so, particularly in northern cities. But just as national institutions together built a doctrine and a practice of expanded national power to supervise voting practices, so together did they eventually abandon it. The Court adopted the understanding of federal judicial authority espoused by Justice Holmes rather than Justice Brewer. And Congress made sure that there were few statutes left to enforce, even had the Court been so inclined.

Woodrow Wilson won: the idea that federal supervision of elections was the "ugliest side of federal supremacy," as Wilson had written in 1885, became widely accepted. There were partisan objectives behind that change, surely, but there was also probably another reason. In the 1883 *Yarbrough* case, the Court noted that Congress had found it "necessary to make additional laws for the free, the pure, and the safe exercise of this right of voting."[75] And four years later, in *Coy*, the Court said that "crimes against the ballot have become so numerous and so serious that the attention of all legislative bodies have been turned with anxious solicitude to the means of preventing them, and the object of securing purity in elections and accuracy in the returns."[76] The Court was slightly ahead of the game to say that "all legislative bodies" were engaged in election reform, but only slightly. Between 1888 and 1896, Australian-ballot reform would sweep across the American states—bringing about a set of changes that would obviate the need for strong federal action to secure fair and free elections, at least in some eyes.[77]

"Responsible Agents of the State": The Australian Ballot and the Transformation of American Suffrage

In their study of viva voce voting in pre–Civil War Washington County, Oregon, Paul Bourke and Donald DeBats point out that less than half of American electoral history "has occurred in a legal environment that permitted voting to be defined and enforced as a private and permanently secret act."[78] Not until the period between 1888 and 1896 did states require votes to be secret, marked on ballots produced by the state or local government. Because Australia had been first to use the secret, state-produced ballot broadly, the reforms became known as the "Australian ballot," though some American opponents preferred the terms "penal-colony voting" and "kangaroo voting."[79]

Both in terms of what it changed and what it did not change, this reform was a crucial step in the story of the local dimension of American suffrage. The reform was clearly designed to limit the impact of local contexts on voter choice, particularly when partisanship, coercion, and cash were features of those contexts. In addition, it brought about deep changes in how the act of voting itself was conceived and marked a major expansion of the state role in election administration, with a corresponding diminution in the range of local discretionary and interpretive authority. However, state lawmakers stopped far short of eliminating local responsibility for running elections; indeed, they ultimately renewed and reinforced it.

We saw a similar phenomenon in the Jacksonian period, when state constitution-drafters engaged in close analysis of the right to vote's essence. Those conventions asserted the state's ability to set formal voting qualifications, but while lawmakers sometimes looked directly at local variation, they did not move toward homogenizing voting practices. Now, state legislators did so, promulgating new policies dealing with the precise mechanical details of suffrage. But rather than choosing to set up statewide election-administration bureaucracies, reformers directed their rules at county and municipal officials. As one advocate put it, "Ballots should be taken from the political organizations and put into the hands of the responsible agents of the State."[80] Legislators did just that: they took the ballots from the parties and effectively constructed a public, election-administration bureaucracy—in county, city, and town governments. The "responsible agents of the State" would be local officials.

The decades prior to the advent of the secret, state-produced ballot marked the high point of American parties' control of American suffrage practices, and to modern sensibilities, the results were not pretty. Men sometimes literally feared for their lives on the streets during elections, and bribery was a fact of life. "Knives were drawn and freely used, revolvers discharged with a perfect recklessness. . . . The police had they interfered would have stood a chance of being annihilated," reported one observer of a California election.[81] Political parties engaged in "systematic organization for the purchase of votes," and savvy voters routinely demanded to be paid for their support.[82] Where printed ballots were used, they were usually different sizes and colors according to the party, so it was a matter of simple observation either to bribe or to force someone to vote a certain way. New York's Tweed Ring specialized in registering and pressuring new Irish immigrants in droves just before elections, sometimes swelling the rolls by 30 percent in a matter of weeks.[83] Bribery, ballot-stuffing, registration fraud, intimidation, and simple disregard of election results were all common.[84] Parties demanded huge contributions from would-be candidates in order to finance both bribery and the above-board aspects of elections, such as printing and distributing ballots; this restricted the pool of those who could afford to compete.[85] And voters with poor reading skills were often duped by ballots bearing the insignia of one party but a list of names belonging to another.

The Australian ballot was fundamentally designed to cure these ills, protecting voters from the possibility of coercion and bribery (not to mention knives and revolvers) at the polls. By 1872, Britain had done away with oral voting in parliamentary elections and had adopted the set of methods pioneered in the Australian colonies in the 1850s: the government designed, printed, and distributed paper ballots, and stipulated secrecy in voting. Canada, Belgium, and Italy followed.[86] The idea caught on among American mugwumps in the 1880s but was not enacted into state law until Kentucky (in Louisville only) and Massachusetts (statewide) tried it in 1888. Localities were often the laboratories of change, as many states initially used the Australian ballot only in certain municipalities and parts of the state.[87] The reform spread with remarkable speed: by 1891, thirty-two of forty-five states had adopted Australian-ballot laws, and seven more did so by the end of 1896.[88]

"Safeguarding the suffrage and getting a true expression of the will of the voters" was the goal, wrote one southern advocate.[89] Kentucky's first-in-the-nation law was aimed at "protecting the ballot and securing a fair expression of the public opinion," wrote Abram Flexner.[90] Having just observed Louisville's 1888 elections, Flexner argued that secrecy enabled a man to vote "as he really prefers." The reforms, wrote another contemporary, were "introduced for the purpose of enabling the voter to express his opinion by the ballot without the interference of others."[91] In the voting booth, wrote William Glasson, "it is each citizen's business to decide according to the dictates of his own conscience how he shall vote."[92]

Those references to "conscience" and "interference" capture a constitutive transformation brought about by the secret ballot. As Australian Les Murray wrote in his 1996 poem "My Ancestress and the Secret Ballot," the voting booth became "a closet of prayer."[93] As Murray's apt phrase reflects, the reforms effected a new privatization of American suffrage by making voting a silent, solitary activity. As one contemporary supporter wrote, the secret ballot "makes every voter directly responsible to himself for his individual actions."[94] It was a new ideal image of the voter: the "solitary and independent citizen," rather than a participant in collective, communal political action.[95]

At the same time, voting also underwent a kind of centralization. Major parties were not displaced entirely, of course, and they would eventually find the new rules very much to their liking. But by removing the parties from their dominant mediating role and establishing public control over making ballots, the Australian ballot enabled the state to "enter into direct communication" with the voter.[96]

The new ballot laws also fundamentally altered the formal relationship between state government and local elections officials. Locally employed clerks, judges, and supervisors still performed most election-administration functions—indeed, more than before, since they had taken the place of partisan volunteers. But now, when paid local officials or party workers administered elections, they did so essentially as agents of state government, to a degree that represented a significant departure from prevailing U.S. election practices. To be sure, certain state laws, such as those regarding literacy tests and registration, had included specific instructions to local officials before this time. For example, in *Wiley v. Sinkler* the Court points to South Carolina's 1868 constitution, which set out the duties of election supervisors and described the use of registration books for state elections.[97] And *In re Coy*, the Court recounts that an Indiana statute of 1881 told township trustees to serve as inspectors in congressional elections and required that ballots be placed "in a strong and stout paper envelope or bag, which shall then be tightly closed and well sealed with wax."[98]

But the new laws went further, so much so that the change was one of kind rather than degree. They had to: the use of official ballots entailed rules for the production, distribution, and secure and accurate counting of those ballots, and the secrecy mandate required detailed physical and logistical instruction that had been unnecessary before. One cannot read the Ohio law of 1892, for example, without being struck by the depth and specificity with which state power now penetrated into local voting contexts. Precinct elections officers were told which state-written oath they were to swear; how to call in all election judges at least three days before the election and supply them with the "sealed packages of ballots, poll-books, tally sheets, and all other necessary papers"; what time to open the polls and how to arrange rails, tables, booths, and ballot boxes; how to interview voters and assist them; and which ballots to reject during counting.[99] North Dakota's 1891 law instructed county officials that "the form of ballots under the Australian Election Law [must] be uniform throughout the State, and to this end the department will recommend a form and supply county auditors with samples of same prior to the general election of 1892." The law has forty-one different sections, ranging from "Ballots, how printed" to "Election booths, how built" to "In case of spoiled ballot." Local officials were directed to "see that the tables, guard-rail, booths and ballot-boxes are properly placed."[100] In Massachusetts, the law defined state and city officials' obligations to inform and instruct voters of upcoming elections, required delivery of certain numbers of ballots at certain times, stipulated how to arrange "voting shelves or compartments," and even included a drawing that demonstrated how to lay out the room.[101] Vermont's thirty-nine-section 1890 statute similarly mandated a "guard rail" to keep people at least six feet from voting booths and required those booths to be at least three feet square, with a shelf at least one foot wide across one side.[102]

A colorful account of privacy rules comes in a small book called *Hill's Political History of the United States*, published in 1894. Hill offers the text of a typical law:

You will not be allowed to occupy a voting booth with another voter.... If you will declare upon oath that you cannot read the English language, or that by reason of physical disability you are unable to mark your ballot, upon request you will be assisted by two of the election officers, appointed for that purpose, of opposing political parties.... Intoxication will not be regarded as physical disability, and if you are intoxicated you will receive no assistance in marking your ballot.[103]

Reformers might have *hoped* voters would be praying inside those booths. But at least some knew they had to be ready for drunks too. "No election shall be held in a room in which spirituous or malt liquors are commonly sold," North Dakota's 1891 law sternly instructed election inspectors.[104]

Just as the federal Constitution's Elections Clause had constituted the first "unfunded mandate," the Australian-ballot laws formally passed most of the election-administration buck to localities. Some advocates did indicate that "the state" would pay. For example, New York's Governor David B. Hill argued that "the distribution of all ballots by the state would be an enormous expense to the state," while reform supporter Richard Henry Dana of Boston contended that "the self-respect in voting under the new system is alone worth all the extra expense to the state."[105] But these references to the state appear to have been mostly a way to contrast the new system with the party-funded regime that preceded it. The Massachusetts law of 1888 does imply that the state government carried the cost of ballots, declaring that "State Ballots will be printed by the Secretary of the Commonwealth, and city ballots by the city clerk."[106] But in an introduction to its 1891 law, North Dakota stated in no uncertain terms that "county auditors and commissioners are reminded of the fact that all election machinery is a county charge and must be provided at the county's expense."[107] Vermont's 1890 law stated that the cost of ballots would be "defrayed by the county," while for local elections, the city, village, or town in question would bear the financial burden.[108]

The cost went well beyond ballots. As Vermont's law made clear, booths, compartments, and the ballot boxes themselves were also to be "a public charge." An 1889 survey of voting practices concluded that while many states and territories insisted that ballot boxes have certain characteristics, it was up to towns, cites, counties, and school districts to pay for and furnish them. Many states set out the characteristics of those boxes in some detail: Colorado stipulated use of "a circular box of glass enclosed in a wooden frame, with a lid fastened with three unlike locks."[109] New Jersey's 1887 law also required all counties to use boxes of glass.[110]

In *The People's Welfare* (1996), William J. Novak describes prevailing ideas about good governance in eighteenth- and nineteenth-century America.[111] "In contrast to the modern ideal of the state as centralized bureaucracy," Novak writes, "the well-regulated society emphasized local control and autonomy."[112] While acknowledging the limits of such sharp lines, Novak marks the end of that older regime at 1877, at which point the modern ideal—the centralized liberal state—took over. The Australian-ballot reforms began a decade later, and in some respects they fit Novak's conception well. State lawmakers were eager to abolish the evil influences they associated with local variation and control, and to establish a kind of direct, unmediated connection with the voter. The result was that control of American voting practices shifted from a system run by political parties and localities to one directed by state governments. By privatizing and centralizing the act of voting and converting local officials into agents of state government, these reforms effected a significant change in the character of American suffrage.

But the limits to this centralizing change are clear. Measured in terms of partisanship, the Australian ballot did not dramatically alter American voting behavior, and in practice, it fell far short of the substantive, instrumental transformations reformers hoped for.[113] And of course, no statewide election-administration bureaucracies were created. (As in the Jacksonian period, there is again no evidence that lawmakers even considered such bureaucracies.) These reforms are quintessential illustrations of the developmental and institutional paradox of American voting. Asserting their own authority over minute details of suffrage mechanics, states simultaneously reinforced the locally managed system by directing county, city, and town governments to run elections and pay for them. We have seen before that when the national government acted to shape election rules and practices, it consistently exercised that authority in limited ways that left substantial power in local hands. The Australian-ballot reforms mimic this pattern, substituting state government for national, and they were a key step in the construction of our localized suffrage systems.

The Australian-ballot example also illustrates another theme of American electoral history: the flexibility and durability of the big political parties. Unlike virtually all other major changes in American election law, these reforms had been driven not by either major party but by good-government advocates, labor groups, and radical parties.[114] Not surprisingly, neither major party consistently supported the reforms, but the system became so popular that "even the party workers have to profess to like it, whether they do or not," as one reformer remarked.[115]

The big parties adapted. In a classic instance of election-law irony, what began as a nonpartisan effort to minimize the political parties' stranglehold on voting practices ended up placing them in an even stronger position. Parties taught voters about the need to write on the ballot and showed voters with poor literacy skills how to recognize the vignette or symbol of their party. In Minnesota, one Republican argued that rather than offering "profound dissertations on the tariff and the currency," the best way to secure votes was to instruct partisans in "the art and science of casting a ballot under the Australian system."[116] In Maryland, both major parties carried mock voting booths to rallies around the state so they could show voters how to use them.[117]

Beyond such benign responses, the parties quickly saw that since government now controlled the making of ballots, whoever controlled government could decide which parties made it onto the ballot. For small parties, it was a hard lesson in unintended consequences; before the new rules, as Lisa Jane Disch points out, "to act as a party was to qualify as one," but now "party fitness [became] a matter for the states to decide." State legislatures dominated by major parties made life hard for smaller parties through new ballot access and design policies, including new barriers to "fusion" voting, in which a minor party seeks to raise its profile and increase its chances of influencing the outcome of an election by endorsing a candidate already backed by a major party. [118] Beneath these practical powers, the new policies helped parties gain a firm foothold in American constitutional thought. Having begun the nineteenth century as essentially private associations with a very uncertain status in American law, the major parties ended it as quasi-public utilities, secure in their ability to shape election law and voter choice.[119]

On the eve of the twentieth century, Congress again legislated with regard to voting practices, doing so in a way that solidified its own authority while simultaneously empowering the states. As Roy Saltman shows, the 1880s and 1890s were a fascinating time for voting technology, with inventors all over the country developing and marketing new voting machines.[120] But the last standing piece of the 1870 election law required that all votes for Congress be "by written or printed ballot," and some worried that this stipulation might preclude the use of machines. Responding to a contested election in Rochester, New York, Congress resolved this question with new legislation passed on Valentine's Day, 1899. Congressional elections could now be conducted by written or printed ballot, or by "voting machine the use of which has been duly authorized by the State law."[121] The statute enabled voting-machine use to increase dramatically in the decades ahead. States would declare which kinds of machines could be used, and localities would choose, purchase, and run the machines. The twentieth century could hardly have begun with a finer example of the triply mixed nature of American election-administration authority.

3

"To Promote the Exercise of That Right": The Twentieth Century

There is probably no other phase of public administration in the United States which is so badly managed as the conduct of elections. Every investigation or election contest brings to light glaring irregularities, errors, misconduct on the part of precinct officers, disregard of election laws and instructions, slipshod practices, and downright frauds.
Joseph Harris (1929)

We never pay any attention to election laws.
Anonymous Georgia justice of the peace with fifty years' election-administration experience, quoted by V. O. Key (1949)

The Congress finds that (1) the right of citizens of the United States to vote is a fundamental right; (2) it is the duty of Federal, State, and local governments to promote the exercise of that right.
National Voter Registration Act (1993)

Nineteenth-century federal interventions in election law altered how and when Americans voted, erected supervisory regimes that endured for decades, changed the constitutional text itself (with the Reconstruction Amendments), and strengthened doctrines interpreting older text (particularly the Elections Clause) in a way that would provide crucial support for later statutes. State legislative and constitutional changes altered the formal boundaries of the franchise and required secrecy in voting. Yet unlike the developments of the twentieth century, these changes were relatively scattered, and many were reversed or abandoned after partisan or doctrinal shifts. By contrast, twentieth-century voting-rights laws have self-consciously built on each other, placing the national government in at least a loose supervisory role over most nuts-and-bolts elements of voting. National authority over the mechanics of suffrage has unmistakably expanded, as has the federal government's underlying conception of its own role in elections: "to promote the exercise of that right," as the National Voter Registration Act of 1993 says. Yet as that same statutory sentence makes clear, the national government still shares that responsibility with "State and local governments." So, while the twentieth century clearly tells a tale of continuing reform and accumulation of national authority over election administration, it is a story of uneven and gradual accretion, rather than one of clear, durable shifts in which both practical institutional power and underlying constitutional theory are transformed. Indeed, many specific aspects of the electoral process receiving most attention today—registration, record-keeping, facilitating participation by disabled voters, and the consistent imposition of formal voter-qualification rules, for example—have actually been subject to repeated federal legislation.

Voter Registration, the Elections Clause, and V. O. Key's America

If the twentieth century concluded with a generation of statutory centralizations of election-supervision authority, the major reform of its early decades tugged in the other direction. For even as state governments asserted their ability to structure the voting process itself by enacting Australian-ballot requirements, many states enacted voter-registration laws that had the opposite effect. As the National Commission on Federal Election Reform said in 2002, the adoption of mandatory voter registration in most states would bring about "*a new decentralization of power* to determine the eligibility of voters, devolving from state governments down to the local and county governments that managed this process and maintained the rolls."[1] Even where state government had acted to harmonize voting rules, voter qualification was as a practical matter almost entirely at the discretion of local officials.[2] Local decisions could take colorful forms: until at least the late nineteenth century, it was quite common for the legal test of a voter's residency to be "where he had his washing done."[3]

Few states outside New England required registration prior to the Civil War, and from 1860 to 1880, older northern states enacted requirements applying only to large cities. Federal courts ruled that such distinctions were constitutional, as there was no requirement of uniformity in registration laws.[4] Western and southern states followed between 1880 and 1900, and registration procedures came under new scrutiny in the early twentieth century.[5] Vulnerabilities to fraud had been addressed by in-person registration, limited-enrollment policies that enabled voters to register only a few days per year, a house-by-house canvass, annual purges of the rolls, and required identification at the polls.[6] By the 1920s, many advocates saw these systems as "expensive, cumbersome, and inconvenient," as well as overly exclusionary, and advocacy for reform was widespread.[7] As a study produced for the National Municipal League in 1927 concluded, registration rules were enacted "before any consideration was given to the idea that participation in elections should be made easy and convenient for the voter."[8] Some reformers, such as Progressive William U'Ren of Oregon, pushed for automatic universal registration by the state, observing that some European countries already employed such a system.[9]

U'Ren's proposal failed, but his comparative note raises an illuminating point. Even as the U.S. government was renewing the importance of state and local authorities in running national elections, peer nations were building *national* electoral bureaucracies. Australia, a former British colony with a strong federal system (like the United States), established the Australian Electoral Office as a branch of Home Affairs in 1902. The Commonwealth Franchise Act of the same year required the secret ballot and provided that both men and women (but not aboriginals) could vote. Today, Australia retains some electoral variations among its states and territories, but national authority over administrative matters now has a century-old pedigree.[10] In Canada, each province was responsible for running elections prior to 1920; in that year, the position of Chief Elections Officer was created, with the aim of diminishing partisan influence and standardizing election administration.[11] Naturally, Australia, Canada, and the United States each faced their own unique political and social circumstances. But the Australian and Canadian moves toward centralization show that there was no technological or grand historical reason why a former British colony with a federal system could not nationalize and standardize control of national elections in the early twentieth century; the United States simply chose not to. The reasons for this were diverse and complex, wrapped up in partisanship, political tradition, and the lack of bureaucratic capacity.[12] Having decided to erect a new portal to voter participation, state legislators decided that local officials could best manage it.

The National Municipal League report (published in 1927) and Joseph Harris's *Registration of Voters in the United States* (1929) return us to the question of visibility, demonstrating that local control and its problems were no secret in the early twentieth century. "There is at present," the league's report states, "very little control or supervision over registration exercised by state officers." Some governors and secretaries of state had "nominal" powers over registration and elections, but local and party officials generally ran the show; in sum, elections were "largely decentralized."[13] Harris was disgusted: "There is probably no other phase of public administration in the United States which is so badly managed as the conduct of elections. Every investigation or election contest brings to light glaring irregularities, errors, misconduct on the part of precinct officers, disregard of election laws and instructions, slipshod practices, and downright frauds."[14] The league suggested three reasons for local control's persistence: expertise born of experience; state governments' reluctance to take on what had become a significant expense; and necessity, because of high population mobility and the tendency for local elections to accompany state and national contests.[15]

Registering to vote did get easier in the early twentieth century, and state reforms curbed some local discretion. But despite this withering exposure, those obstacles to centralization remained, and local control of voter lists and registration practices endured. One result was that virtually all states lacked statewide voter rolls until the 2002 Help America Vote Act (HAVA) mandated their creation.

Of course, other major changes to election law took place in the early decades of the twentieth century. For starters, the national Constitution was amended to require direct election of U.S. senators and to extend the franchise to women. Certainly these amendments reinforced ultimate national authority over some fundamentals, but local responsibility for election administration remained almost total. And despite the Nineteenth Amendment, important voter-qualification rules remained under state control. The voting rights of Native Americans offer an important example. In 1924, Congress passed the Indian Citizenship Act, granting all Native Americans national citizenship. By implication at least, the Indian Citizenship Act should have entailed full state and local citizenship for Native Americans and firm possession of the right to vote. But many states continued to bar American Indians from voting; as many as seven still did not let native peoples vote in 1938.[16] States offered several reasons for such exclusion: that Native Americans were not true "residents" of the state; that they needed to terminate their tribal ties to become full citizens; that they did not pay enough in taxes; that like people in mental institutions, they were under "guardianship"; that they were not literate in English; and that allowing them to vote would simply give them too much political power. Utah did not fully enfranchise American Indians until 1957, when the state legislature did so in response to a legal challenge.[17]

For its part, the Supreme Court in these years stayed in the business of scrutinizing local electoral practices and gauging their compliance with federal law. But it did so only occasionally, and without much immediate effect.

For example, in the 1915 case *United States v. Mosley*, the Court upheld a federal fraud prosecution of two members of the Blaine County, Oklahoma, election board, ruling that it was "unquestionable" that "the right to have one's vote counted is as open to protection by Congress as the right to put a ballot in a box."[18] But within three years, the Court would step back from that position, reading the statute in question more narrowly in cases involving party primaries and a candidate's right to participate in a bribe-free election.[19]

Though there was precious little statutory action during this period, the Elections Clause did resurface as a source of congressional authority. In the 1932 case *Smiley v. Holm*, the Court declared that the clause gives Congress the "authority to provide a complete code for congressional elections" and "comprehensive" power over "the numerous requirements as to procedure and safeguards which experience shows are necessary in order to enforce the fundamental right involved."[20] (*Smiley* figured prominently in the 2001 term-limits case *Cook v. Gralike*.)[21] The landmark ruling of the period from the perspective of institutional development was *United States v. Classic*, decided in 1941. In *Classic*, the Court applied a federal anticonspiracy law to primary elections, upholding the new Civil Rights Division's prosecution of Louisiana elections commissioners for altering and falsely counting primary ballots.[22] The *Classic* Court said that congressional authority extended to any "primary election which involves a necessary step in the choice of candidates for election as representatives in Congress."[23]

Classic effected an important shift, dissolving the doctrine that had protected the white primary and paving the way for the Supreme Court to strike down that crucial exclusionary device just three years later in *Smith v. Allwright*. This was a real and consequential enlargement of both national judicial power and the federal executive's Civil Rights Division, and it led to a corresponding weakening of the parties (particularly the Democratic Party in the South). Moreover, it rested on a strong reading of the Elections Clause. According to a biographer, Justice Harlan Fiske Stone said that when *Classic* came to the Court, "I made a thorough study of the clauses dealing with federal elections and came to the conclusion that the purpose was to *give the Federal Government power over the whole electoral process*."[24]

As we have seen, neither the bench nor state and federal legislators ever held long to such a sweeping interpretation of the Elections Clause, and even today, many might squirm a bit at Justice Stone's all-encompassing language. At any rate, in 1941, the federal government was still decades away from enacting its most famous voting-rights measures, and when it did so, the Elections Clause would play second fiddle to the Fifteenth Amendment as a source of national power. And local governments at the time enjoyed virtually complete discretion over election administration, as a landmark book was about to demonstrate.

Despite repeated federal statutes, prosecutions, and court rulings, across American history periodic probing inquiries into American election practices, whether conducted by advocates, scholars, legislators, or judges, had revealed localities to be running elections almost totally unsupervised. Published in 1949, *Southern Politics in State and Nation*, V. O. Key's extraordinary combination of scholarship and muckraking, offered the latest such investigation. The spectacular quantity and quality of electoral corruption across the South is one of the book's central themes. As Key writes, "In these communities free and honest elections would be radical, or revolutionary, for an honest count would overthrow the established order."[25] *Southern Politics* shows emphatically that despite the Elections Clause, Court decisions, Australian-ballot statutes, registration rules, and congressional contested-election hearings, counties still had virtually complete independence in supervising the suffrage.

Sounding much like Joseph Harris two decades earlier, Key wrote, "The conduct of elections is the most neglected and primitive branch of our public administration, and the South is no exception to this general rule." Key ranked the states in their sheer quantity of election irregularities (Tennessee first, Arkansas second) but concluded that the real "habits of fraud and of rectitude" in election administration were to be found at the *county* level. "One county will year after year conduct its elections honestly and fairly and an adjoining county will with equal regularity operate irregularly," he wrote.[26]

Key found a remarkable lack of secrecy in southern voting. Recall that since 1871, federal law had required that "all votes for representatives in Congress shall hereafter be by written or printed ballot," and most southern states had adopted the Australian ballot *fifty years* before Key and his colleagues roamed the region. But in South Carolina, where the state constitution guaranteed secrecy, parties produced the tickets, and voters picked up the party ballot they wished to cast for a given office and dropped it in the appropriate box in full view of all present.[27] Other states were worse. Texas, Alabama, Georgia, and Arkansas all openly marked ballots in one way or another, usually by a numbering system or a requirement that voters sign their ballots. Nominally done to prevent fraud, this exposure had real consequences for voter behavior.[28]

State laws criminalized unauthorized inspection of ballot numbers or copies. But Key found everywhere a pervasive lack of confidence in the secrecy of votes, and in many areas, it "seem[ed] to be a matter of common knowledge" that officials checked up on how their neighbors voted.[29] Some states that did mandate secrecy, such as Louisiana and North Carolina, required any challenged voter to indicate their identity on the ballot—a policy guaranteed to facilitate intimidation. Others lacked polling booths altogether. In one revealing incident from 1946, it took what locals called a "GI revolt" against the local political machine in Crittenden County, Arkansas, to bring in booths so that voters could enjoy real secrecy—despite the fact that state law already required the use of booths. Covering the story, the *Arkansas Gazette* mused publicly whether any other counties had ever followed the state's law.[30]

The Early Expansion of National Power

Even as GIs were rebelling in Crittenden County, the institutions of U.S. national government were beginning to insert themselves more aggressively into election mechanics. *Smiley, Classic,* and *Smith v. Allwright* were not the only important cases of the 1940s from the perspective of voting practices. In 1949, a lower federal court anticipated later developments when it criticized an "understanding" test for giving a registrar too much discretion and "arbitrary power" in violation of the Equal Protection Clause.[31] In 1942, Congress hastily enacted legislation allowing absentee voting by soldiers to accommodate those serving in World War II. Indeed, because of the millions of voters who left home during the war to serve in the armed forces, work in factories or government offices, or accompany a spouse who did so, about one-quarter of voters were away from their polling place during the elections of that year. (The Civil War had sparked the first absentee voting rules; Vermont in 1896 had been the first state to let civilians vote absentee, but few states had done so prior to World War II.)[32] Only about twenty-eight thousand soldiers voted under the new 1942 national law, which pertained only to military personnel; in the next three years, the forty-eight states put more than one hundred different absentee-voting laws on the books, most of them temporary and partial.[33]

Of course, these were baby steps compared to what would follow. One could fill a library with the books and articles interpreting the voting-rights statutes and federal court rulings of the late twentieth century. The brief tour that follows tries to capture how each legislative action did and did not transform the mix of federal, state, and local power over voting practices, and particularly how each constrained local administrative authority. While each statutory change was widely seen at its enactment as transformative or even radical, in hindsight the limits of each soon became apparent.

The Civil Rights Act of 1957

The first national civil rights law passed since Reconstruction, the Civil Rights Act of 1957 created the Civil Rights Division within the U.S. Department of Justice as well as the Civil Rights Commission, which was established to investigate allegations of voting discrimination. The commission did so, holding hearings across the South.[34] The U.S. Attorney General won new authority to bring lawsuits challenging violations of the Fifteenth Amendment or join such lawsuits already in progress. The federal government was thus newly empowered to take action against any person engaged in discriminatory practices, including local registrars. Of course, such suits were not entirely new— the nation saw two full decades of such prosecutions while the 1870 and 1871 statutes were in effect—but the law was controversial. The Supreme Court upheld the statute in a 1960 case affirming the prosecution of deputy registrars in Terrell County, Georgia, for racial discrimination in voter registration.[35] But fierce southern Democratic opposition made the final bill and its enforcement relatively weak. The requirement of jury trials and the need for individual southern judges to uphold the act made successful prosecutions of white southerners difficult, and both of these features would lead future statutes to take a different path. Yet, although litigation proved cumbersome, expensive, and ultimately ineffective in redressing massive inequities in voting practices, the 1957 Act did help "set the stage" for the major voting-rights laws of the 1960s.[36]

The Civil Rights Acts of 1960 and 1964

The Civil Rights Act of 1960 tried to rectify one of the major flaws of the 1957 statute, and the new law constrained local discretion in powerful ways. In addition to mandating registration in any area found to be practicing discrimination, the 1960 statute did something not seen since the 1871 law: it established that federal courts could appoint referees to register voters after a judicial finding of racial discrimination in voting.[37] The 1960 act also included an intriguing item relating to election records, an excellent example of the penetration of federal power into the local sphere. Title III of the act stated that "every officer of election" must "retain and preserve" any and all documents, papers, and records relating to any national election for twenty-two months. It became a federal crime to destroy, conceal, or alter voting records, and if the federal attorney general asked for any "record or paper," local and state officials had to provide it.[38] The statute thus acknowledged the enduring importance of state and local officials in running elections, and simultaneously placed those officials formally under (at least hypothetical) federal supervision. Yet while the national government would now have a hand in registering voters, Congress stopped far short of displacing those state and local election administrators: despite the "referees," the law's enforcement mechanisms lacked teeth, and poll taxes and literacy tests remained in place. Nevertheless, "outrage" was expressed in Congress at the provision of federal referees, as Roy Wilkins of the National Association for the Advancement of Colored People and the Leadership Conference on Civil Rights would later comment in a 1962 subcommittee hearing on a subsequent, more aggressive bill. Pointing back to *Siebold* and *Yarbrough*, Wilkins argued that "Congress has the power to take over the . . . management of Federal elections machinery lock, stock, and barrel." In hindsight the 1960 measure looks quite tepid, but at the time it aroused such a "clamor" that "one would have thought the proposal was completely foreign to American democracy and had never been broached before."[39]

The Civil Rights Act of 1964 is most famous for its ban on discrimination in places of public accommodation. But its preamble pledged "to enforce the constitutional right to vote," and it marked a major expansion of national authority over the suffrage. Both building on and responding to the limitations of previous statutes, the law enabled the federal executive branch to insist on expedited hearings of voting-rights cases in a three-judge federal court. It implemented the "freezing doctrine," forged in previous litigation, preventing any discriminatory jurisdiction from quickly putting in place a new exclusionary practice. And it included the first prophylactic measure in any federal voting-rights statute: a rebuttable presumption that anyone who had completed sixth grade was literate.[40]

These were substantial and consequential changes. Jim Crow now faced a full federal assault, and the old Democratic coalition was under enormous strain. Yet the 1964 Act stopped well short of a full ban on literacy tests, which at that time still claimed the protection of Court doctrine and extensive practice, and is thus accurately described as only a "tentative, limited step" toward what the Voting Rights Act of 1965 would accomplish.[41] Moreover, the statute's literacy-test provisions illustrate well a developmental paradox we have seen before: even when Congress acted to expand its own control of voting practices, it sometimes reinforced local administrative authority. Given the presumption of literacy for graduates of sixth grade, literacy tests were banned—unless conducted in writing, with a copy of the completed test provided to the testee if requested. But that is not all. The act provided that "appropriate State or local authorities" could enter into agreements with the attorney general to preserve their literacy tests, "in accordance with the provisions of applicable State or local law." The act represented a new level of federal restriction and supervision of literacy tests. Yet its very language recognized the important continuing role of state and local authorities, and incorporated "local law" within a national voting-rights statute.

The Voting Rights Act of 1965

As we have seen, there have been many landmark events in the construction of our triply divided system of managing election administration. The Elections Clause, the Fifteenth Amendment to the Constitution, the 1871 elections statute, and state Australian-ballot laws can all lay claim to being among the most substantial alterations of existing power relations. Yet each has pertained to only part of the serial electoral process and left a great deal unfinished.

While Warren Court decisions like *Baker v. Carr* and *Reynolds v. Sims* would have their advocates, most students of election law would probably rank passage of the Voting Rights Act (VRA) of 1965 as the single greatest developmental shift in national power over elections—and in the effort to bring uniformity to American voting practices. The VRA considerably enlarged federal authority in contrast to that of states and localities, has been repeatedly affirmed in the federal courts, and has shaped minority voting and office-holding far more than its predecessors. Yet like its lesser forebears, the VRA was in important ways a deeply limited transfer of authority. The national government asserted the power to shape *some* aspects of the voting process, in *parts* of the country, as a *temporary* response to a grave problem. Without a doubt, the law did mark "a dramatic restructuring of the existing voting system, shifting authority away from state governments to the federal government," but it also unequivocally left de facto administrative responsibility with states and localities.[42]

The VRA did change a great deal. Indeed, some of its particulars, such as the suspension of all literacy tests, were "truly radical," because nondiscriminatory tests had for a generation been upheld by the Supreme Court, by statutes like the 1964 Civil Rights Act, and even by various civil rights commissions.[43] Never shy about the power of his office, President Lyndon Johnson told Martin Luther King Jr., "We may have to put [voter registration] in the post office. Let the postmaster [do it]. That's a federal employee that I control. . . . If he doesn't register everybody, I can put a new one in."[44] And urging Congress to pass the VRA, President Johnson spoke directly of local, procedural obstacles to voting: "The Negro citizen may go to register only to be told that the day is wrong, or the hour is late, or the official in charge is absent. And if he persists and if he manages to present himself to the registrar, he may be disqualified because he did not spell out his middle name or because he abbreviated a word on the application. And if he manages to fill out an application, he is given a test. The registrar is the sole judge of whether he passes this test."[45]

The VRA tackled such problems by moving from litigation to a direct-action strategy to protect African American voting rights.[46] The act succeeded in doubling African American voter registration in covered states in just a few years, mostly because of its suspension of literacy tests and its deployment of federal examiners to register voters. The act outlawed any "voting qualification or prerequisite to voting" that denied voting rights on account of race, including restrictions based on educational achievement or understanding and tests for "good moral character."[47]

Previous statutes had set national legislative and litigative power against both states and localities. But the VRA's "coverage" formula and "preclearance" requirement (an extension of the 1964 statute's "freezing" doctrine) went much further and applied to any state or locality where a given percentage of voters were not registered or had not voted in recent elections. Since the early years of the act, litigation has often targeted localities.[48] Advocates have instructed citizens on how to challenge voting procedures erected by counties, cities, and special election districts, like changing polling places or new voter-registration procedures.[49] It has made a difference: one recent study concludes that the act successfully "sensitizes local officials to the need to consider the impact on minorities of changes in electoral structures and rules."[50]

Despite all this, as a transformative developmental shift in the history of American voting mechanics, the VRA was constrained in a few essential ways. First, the act did not emerge fully formed from the void (or the head of Zeus, as played by Lyndon Johnson) in response to the Bloody Sunday charge at the Edmund Pettus Bridge in Selma in 1965. As Brian Landsberg has convincingly demonstrated (and as the preceding pages should make clear), the VRA emerged from a process of statutory enactment, litigation, new legislation, and more litigation.[51] Landsberg argues that each major provision of the VRA had a precursor in either legislation, litigation, or both, extending back through the 1964 and 1960 statutes to the 1871 measure.[52]

Second, like its 1871 predecessor, the VRA was limited temporally, spatially, and substantively. The law's temporal restrictions were straightforward: some of its provisions had to be renewed in five years, others in twenty-five (the literacy-test ban would eventually be made permanent). The need for these renewals lies in the very nature of the VRA, which was and remains formally "emergency" legislation—something meant to fix a problem rather than to establish permanent structures. The spatial limitations of the VRA are also fundamental to its nature, as some parts of the country are "covered," but most are not. Section 5 of the VRA applies preclearance requirements to much of nine states (excepting communities within those states that have successfully "bailed out") and parts of seven others, requiring these jurisdictions to seek Department of Justice approval before changing any voting procedure. Most but not all covered states are in the South; Alaska and Arizona also remain covered, as do parts of California, Michigan, New Hampshire, New York, and South Dakota.[53]

Subsequent legislation reveals the substantive limits of the original VRA. The 1970, 1975, and 1982 extensions and amendments dramatically increased its reach, limiting the degree to which the 1965 act can be understood as a defining stand-alone transformation. Bilingual-ballot requirements in many parts of the country, permanent suspension of literacy tests, the reduction of residency requirements to thirty days in presidential elections, and the requirement that "opportunity districts" be drawn for language and racial minorities—we owe these things and others not to legislation passed in 1965 but to statutory amendments added over the following years. (Numerous Supreme Court decisions have further pushed what Richard Valelly calls the "Extended Voting Rights Act" into areas previously managed by state and local governments, but statutory changes at the VRA's renewal points have been most important.)[54] Searing criticisms of the American voting regime published in the 1970s and 1980s, such as Penn Kimball's *The Disconnected* and Frances Fox Piven and Richard Cloward's *Why Americans Still Don't Vote*, would document structural inequities in American suffrage that survived the VRA.[55] And naturally, later legislation like the National Voter Registration Act (NVRA) of 1993 and Help America Vote Act (HAVA) of 2002 helped illustrate just how much state and local variation remained.

The VRA is fundamentally an antidiscrimination measure and is not aimed at protecting "the right to vote as such," as Richard Pildes has put it. The act's intrusions were "uniquely justified not to secure the right to vote itself, but to protect against racially discriminatory manipulation of the vote."[56] Remember, in nineteenth-century cases including *Siebold, Clark,* and *Yarbrough* and twentieth-century cases like *Classic,* the Court had rested a general congressional power to regulate voting practices in national elections (and punish local sins of omission and commission) on Article I's Elections Clause. But while some congressmen did argue that the VRA was enacted partly pursuant to Congress's Elections Clause authority, by far the stronger conception of the VRA has been that it is an antidiscrimination measure based on the Fifteenth Amendment.[57]

In sum, in addition to being "one of the most important and successful pieces of legislation of this century," the VRA is aptly called "a curious milestone."[58] Part of what makes the VRA remarkable is that it intrudes so deeply on federalism, setting different rules for different parts of the country and requiring some states and localities to get federal permission before doing things others may do just on their own say-so. As Nate Persily points out, no other national law works this way, and without question this was a major enlargement of federal authority.[59] Yet its very uniqueness draws us back to the VRA's temporal, spatial, and substantive constraints.

The VRA's curious history is still unfolding. Several of its mandates are now intensely controversial (including uneven preclearance coverage, multilingual ballot requirements, and the role of race in drawing congressional districts), so commentators anticipated a pitched battle over those parts of the statute requiring reauthorization in 2007. Yet while partisan conflict was occasionally fierce early in the process, Congress not only reauthorized the VRA earlier than necessary (in July 2006) but did so with a unanimous vote in the Senate. Partly for that reason, some critics have derided the 2006 renewal as purely symbolic rather than substantive.[60] But in fact, the 2006 VRA forcefully articulates the standards that will prevent covered jurisdictions from employing voting laws that "diminish" minority voters' "ability to elect their preferred candidates of choice"—explicitly overturning two recent Supreme Court decisions in the process.[61] Still, some opponents of the VRA hope the somewhat odd legislative history behind congressional renewal of the statute will facilitate a legal challenge.[62] Indeed, the renewed VRA has already been challenged in federal court—appropriately enough, in a case dealing with the humblest of election matters, a Texas utility district's attempt to move a polling place from a residence to a school. A federal district court sustained the VRA's preclearance requirement against that challenge in early summer of 2008, but that ruling is unlikely to end the tale.[63]

One history of the American civil rights movement says that in 1965, "Congress passed the Voting Rights Act, giving African Americans in the southern states the right to vote."[64] In some ways that is true. In raw voter-registration figures, in its killing-off of the literacy test, in the doctrinal developments it fostered, in the voting-rights bar it helped create, and in its constraining effects on local decisions in covered jurisdictions, the VRA is a colossus in American political and constitutional development. Yet it was not a zero-sum, plenary developmental moment, shifting the authority to regulate voting mechanics and qualifications fully and decisively from one level of government to another. Retrospectively, too much had gone before: constitutional enactments and amendments, statutes, and court decisions reaching back a century had previously "given the right to vote" to African Americans. Those grants had not proven durable, but they had laid crucial groundwork for the VRA and indeed shaped its content. Prospectively, many parts of the serial process constituting the right to vote fell outside the VRA's ambit. Voter registration, record keeping, writing and interpreting some qualification rules, selecting polling places, choosing and designing ballots, setting counting and recounting rules, and paying for it all remained, for the vast majority of Americans, in state and local hands.

Federal statutes and regulations have continued to define and constrain state and local suffrage authority since the 1965 passage of the VRA. In carrying the narrative from the VRA to the present, I describe here the most substantial of these laws, the NVRA (1993) and HAVA (2002), again trying to place them in historical context and focus on what each changed and did not change in terms of local administrative responsibility.

The National Voter Registration Act of 1993

Enacted pursuant to Congress's general Elections Clause authority, the NVRA represents a major developmental step in the history of U.S. election administration. The 1871 statute came first, the VRA wrought far greater change, and HAVA would push further in a few specific areas, as we'll see. But with the passage of the NVRA, the federal government stepped forcefully into several aspects of electoral mechanics, telling states and localities what to do in more areas—and in stronger terms—than ever before.

That aggressive assertion of national power was one reason President George H. W. Bush vetoed the measure when it reached his desk in 1992. He too wanted to see increased electoral participation, Bush said in his veto message, but this law "would impose unnecessary, burdensome, expensive, and constitutionally questionable Federal regulation in an area of traditional State authority." States should "retain the authority to tailor voter registration procedures to unique local circumstances" rather than be forced to implement "nationally standardized voter registration procedures."[65] But less than a year later, President Bill Clinton hearkened back to the VRA when he signed the NVRA into law in 1993, calling the measure "a sign of a new vibrancy in our democracy."[66] Clinton also referred to the statute by its more familiar tag, the "motor-voter" bill. The law's most famous provision required states to make registration available in driver's license agencies and in many other "state or local government offices," including social-service agencies, county clerks' offices, and "fishing and hunting license bureaus."[67] Indeed, the NVRA told states how and where to register voters, "right down to the layout of the registration form."[68] The statute also mandated by-mail registration, which could be carried out either with a federal form or with an optional state-designed form.

Congress enacted the law with four general purposes: to increase registration, enhance participation by eligible voters, protect the integrity of the electoral process, and ensure that accurate registration rolls were maintained.[69] The precise language that opens the statute is particularly valuable for our purposes here. Congress finds that "the right of citizens of the United States to vote is a fundamental right," and that "it is the duty of *Federal, State, and local governments to promote the exercise of that right*." Congress hoped to "make it possible for Federal, State, and local governments to implement" the statute, and to enhance voter participation. It is a nice example of Congress's penchant for reinforcing the local dimension of American suffrage, even while extending its own reach.[70]

In addition to voter registration, the NVRA put in place new federal rules governing several other areas of election administration. As we have seen, Congress had effectively placed local record-keepers under federal supervision with the 1960 Civil Rights Act (not to mention various prosecutions under other statutes going back a century), but the NVRA went much further. States now had to "conduct a program to maintain the integrity of the rolls," and any such program had to be "uniform."[71] The law included detailed rules regarding "purging" voters: no longer could a voter be struck from the rolls simply because she did not vote, and elections officials had to take clearly articulated steps in an effort to notify anyone that was to be removed from the voter roll.[72] Finally, the law required U.S. attorneys to notify state elections officials of felony convictions in federal court, so that those state officials could "determin[e] the effect that a conviction may have on an offender's qualification to vote."[73]

Several states actively resisted the new law's implementation. The Justice Department sued California, Illinois, and Pennsylvania to force them to comply with the NVRA, while other states, including New York and South Carolina, either openly rejected the law or implemented it only reluctantly, usually pointing to its cost.[74] Partisanship divided politicians on the NVRA, as had happened before with federal election-administration legislation (with post-Reconstruction laws) and is now happening again (with the implementation of federal laws and passage of new election-administration laws at the state level).[75] Virtually all governors resisting implementation were Republicans. But in two 1995 decisions, the Seventh and Ninth Circuits firmly upheld the NVRA against challenges by Illinois and California, respectively. Both decisions rested the law firmly on the Elections Clause.[76] Writing for the Seventh Circuit, Judge Richard Posner said that while Congress's power under the clause is not "infinitely ductile," over the course of two centuries Congress had "passed a large number of laws altering state regulations of federal elections on the authority of that provision."[77] Citing the nineteenth-century *Siebold* and *Yarbrough* cases and the 1932 *Smiley* case among others, Posner wrote that the Constitution had erected an "intricate balancing or offsetting of governmental powers," and that the NVRA did not upset it.[78]

On its face, the NVRA clearly asserts new federal authority over several aspects of election administration, and the states' resistance underscores that fact. Yet while voter-registration levels have increased under the law, overall voter turnout does not appear to have been significantly affected; the hopes and fears of the major parties have not been realized.[79] With the passage of time, reform-organization studies, governmental reports, and court decisions have revealed serious limits to the NVRA's centralizing and harmonizing effects—and to how much it shifted meaningful authority from one institution to another. As has happened before, uneven implementation and enforcement has called into question just how sharp a developmental turn the law's passage really constituted. A 2008 advocacy report argued that many states have "failed" to fully implement the law, and that the federal Department of Justice has "largely ignored violations of the law in recent years."[80] Some public-assistance agencies are not offering registration at all, and many states have not supplied registration data to the Election Assistance Commission (EAC), as required by the law.[81]

Indeed, the EAC's own 2007 report to Congress on the NVRA's implementation clearly indicates that for all its interventions, the NVRA left our triply mixed system of election-administration authority firmly in place. Summarizing the data contained in the report, the EAC notes that some state officials had filled out its questionnaires themselves, while others allowed local jurisdictions to complete the surveys. Moreover, the report "does not cover all local (i.e., county and township level) jurisdictions in each State." Some states included local-level data, but others did not, and "in a number of instances the States' data were incomplete." In sum, the EAC acknowledged, the report was based on data from "at most 2,978 jurisdictions (out of 3,524 total jurisdictions possible)."[82] Fourteen years after the NVRA's passage, states and localities still exercised ample discretion in registering voters and maintaining records, and even the federal government's ability to collect comprehensive data was limited by our hyperfederalized election-administration system.

The Help America Vote Act of 2002

The 2000 election probably would have led to new state and national laws even if *Bush v. Gore* hadn't happened. But the judiciary sometimes serves as a catalyst for legislative action.[83] Naturally, states and localities took note of the majority's willingness to subject ballot-counting standards to equal-protection scrutiny, despite the per curiam opinion's statement that it was not likely to do so again any time soon. But the opinion also offered a more direct nudge: "After the current counting, it is likely legislative bodies nationwide will examine ways to improve the mechanisms and machinery for voting."[84]

HAVA aimed to do just that. At the time of its passage in 2002, HAVA was often described as a transformative piece of legislation. Indeed, one scholar calls HAVA "the first piece of major national legislation structured to provide general protection for the act of voting itself."[85] That might be slightly overstated—the 1871 law and the NVRA could both make similar claims—but HAVA has effected considerable change. For the first time, the national government spent money directly on routine election administration. The statute banned certain types of voting technology; it created a new body, the EAC, to centralize and disseminate "best practices" information; and it required that states accept provisional ballots from certain voters. Federal law now required *states* to compile and maintain lists of eligible voters, and it mandated that states coordinate their new computerized voter rolls "with State agency records on felony status."[86] The federal government had regulated some of these areas before, but never so comprehensively. HAVA set states scrambling to create statewide voter rolls, induced states and localities to purchase new voting machines, and provided money to help make town halls and other public buildings used for voting more accessible to people with disabilities.

In a 2007 assessment, the indispensable *Electionline.org* found that HAVA had thus far led to the disbursement of more than $3 billion in federal funds to states for voting equipment and accessibility. The Department of Justice had sued four states for failing to comply with the law. And some states had innovated under the law's pressure, setting up large voting centers, allowing voting by mail, and designing electronic poll books to facilitate on-site registration, for example.[87] Academic studies show that administrative, legal, and statutory actions have all been necessary to implement the complex technical, logistical, and financial changes called for by HAVA. And while HAVA clearly empowers state government, states have relied on the expertise of local officials as they try to come into compliance with the law.[88] Though initial implementation was slow, a 2008 report by the Congressional Research Service showed that 90 percent of local elections officials surveyed believed every jurisdiction within their state was in compliance with HAVA's manifold requirements.[89]

Yet HAVA has not brought about the level of centralization and harmonization many expected. Setting up the EAC was not a priority for Congress: it took a full year just to confirm the first four members of the commission, and as of 2008, Congress still had not released almost a quarter of promised funds. States have taken years to implement the law.[90] Resistance has sometimes been overt, as when the National Association of Secretaries of State formally requested that Congress let the EAC die after the 2006 election.[91] Since 2005, HAVA has been described as "somewhere between a disappointment and a fiasco," "toothless," and "a weak piece of legislation."[92] Various examples of that weakness have become clear in just a few years. Because the EAC's commissioners are essentially chosen by congressional party leaders, the commission is very unlikely to exercise any meaningful independence.[93] The EAC is formally an advisory body, without enforcement authority, and even its surveying capacity is limited: as we saw with the NVRA study, the EAC receives incomplete data from states and localities, and lacks the tools to force more comprehensive reporting. Gaps are apparent even in the most mundane matters. HAVA made the EAC responsible for administering the National Mail Voter Registration Form in 2004, but some states still do not use that form. Wyoming state law *prevents* officials from accepting it, and New Hampshire's local clerks accept the national form only as an application for a *state* form.[94] As one analysis concludes, "None of the standards put forward under the Help America Vote Act will fundamentally alter the decentralized character of the administration of federal elections."[95]

The 2008 election brought sharp evidence of that point on two specific fronts. Prior to the election, conflict erupted over "matching" of data in voter-registration files. HAVA directs states to coordinate voter lists with other state databases, but the statute leaves it up to states to decide what to do if a driver's license or Social Security number on file does not exactly match that on a voter-registration application. Human error and inaccurate data naturally make such occurrences common, but many states have not yet developed any data-matching standards, "suggesting that matching and verification is left to localities," as one study concluded on the eve of the 2008 election.[96] Second, HAVA requires poll workers to provide provisional ballots for voters whose eligibility is uncertain, but it does not set clear rules regarding the counting of those ballots. That became abundantly clear in 2008. With vote counting in three extremely close Ohio congressional contests hanging in the balance, a federal judge ruled in late November 2008 that poll-worker errors in labeling ballots and other voting materials should not lead to the rejection of about one thousand challenged ballots.[97]

In an intriguing 2008 report on election reform, the Congressional Research Service found that local elections officials, whom it calls "LEOs," had very mixed views of HAVA. The law had brought about moderate improvements in the voting process, said the LEOs, but the federal government now had too much influence on their choice of voting systems. While most LEOs thought the law had made "moderate" improvements to voting, the percentage of respondents saying HAVA had made *no* improvement exceeded the percentage who thought it brought about *major* improvements.[98] Most responding LEOs supported HAVA's major provisions, but some won only very narrow majorities. Not surprisingly, provision of federal funds to states was most popular; centralizing voter registration files, allowing some form of voter-error correction, and facilitating participation by military and overseas voters also won strong support. But in 2006, less than half of LEOs surveyed (48 percent) thought the establishment of the EAC had been an advantageous aspect of the law, and only 51 percent said as much about provisional voting. Overall, local officials said that HAVA had made elections more expensive and more complicated to administer. And when asked whether HAVA had "made elections more fair" and "more reliable," sizable majorities either disagreed or were neutral.[99]

Scholars disagree about how to understand HAVA's place in constitutional development. Like the NVRA before it—but unlike the VRA—it is nationally uniform legislation clearly based on Congress's general Elections Clause power, rather than a targeted antidiscrimination measure based on the Fifteenth Amendment. Richard Pildes is among those who conclude that HAVA is a powerful new stroke, aimed at protecting "the right to vote as such" in a way the VRA simply did not.[100] Pildes, a critic of our decentralized suffrage systems, hopes this is a sign of more to come.[101] But Richard Saphire and Paul Moke emphasize practical effects rather than constitutional foundations and reach a very different conclusion. Pointing to the fact that HAVA "empowers states to make fundamental decisions about election technology reform, the purging of voter registration lists and identification requirements for first-time voters who register by mail," they argue that HAVA creates no new substantive rights and endorses "a highly deferential model of federalism." In their view, the law is thus so weak that it is "fundamentally at odds with the framework of voting reform that has evolved over the last four decades since the adoption of the Voting Rights Act."[102]

Saphire and Moke have a point, particularly in terms of HAVA's deferential posture toward state authority. But there are ways in which HAVA continues the developmental sequence we have seen unfolding, a pattern of layered, partial, repetitive federal legislation regarding election practices, bringing about a secular increase in central authority over election administration but accompanied by enduring state and local variation. As an illustration, consider one specific aspect of HAVA: its rule that the disabled receive the same level of access and ability to participate as all other voters.

This requirement has brought about real change in the past few years. Local officials have moved and closed polling places because of the accessibility mandate, and many have received federal money to make existing polling places accessible. The ability of the blind to vote now figures prominently in disputes over voting technology at all levels of government. But HAVA was not Congress's first legislation dealing with disabled voters. The 1982 amendments to the VRA stated that any voter who needed assistance "by reason of blindness, disability, or inability to read or write" could be helped by a person of their choosing, as long as that person was neither their employer nor an officer of their union.[103] Two years later, Congress passed the Voting Accessibility for the Elderly and Handicapped Act (VAEHA), which pledged "to promote the fundamental right to vote by improving access for handicapped and elderly individuals to registration facilities and polling places for federal elections." The statute required that within each state, "each political subdivision responsible for conducting elections shall assure that all polling places for Federal elections are accessible to handicapped and elderly voters." Exceptions were provided for, but only if the chief elections officer of a state determined that a given "political subdivision" was unable to provide an accessible polling place, and alternate means of voting were made available to affected individuals.[104] The VAEHA's enforcement mechanisms were weak.[105]

The third piece of legislation that dealt with disabled voters was the Americans with Disabilities Act (ADA) of 1990. Unlike the 1982 VRA amendments and the 1984 VAEHA, the ADA itself did not directly mention registration or voting. But in a kind of powerful revisionist history, the federal courts (joined by some prominent legal advocates) subsequently interpreted the ADA as reaching the franchise. In 1996, the Federal Election Commission joined with the National Association of Secretaries of State to try to develop accessibility guidelines that would "satisfy the requirements of the ADA"; about forty states adopted the guidelines.[106] In *Tennessee v. Lane*, the Supreme Court explained the discriminatory conditions that led Congress to enact the ADA: a history of "systematic deprivations of fundamental rights," offering as the first example the right to vote.[107] In 2007, retired Supreme Court Justice Sandra Day O'Connor pointed to *Lane* when she joined a federal appeals court's study of whether Missouri's law barring some mentally ill people from voting violated the ADA. "I thought it covered voting," she said in open court.[108] Deciding the case later that year, the Eighth Circuit panel agreed, but in a cautious way. The judges (including O'Connor) agreed that *Lane* had criticized state laws barring "idiots" from voting, but noted that it had done so "not in constitutional terms." Moreover, the court noted that another piece of federal legislation mattered here too: the NVRA of 1993, in which "Congress specifically preserved the States' authority to make mental capacity a voting eligibility requirement."[109]

Authority over treatment of disabled voters has unequivocally shifted: federal law now routinely compels state and local officials to take certain actions. If we could simply determine *when* this definitive assertion of federal authority came about, we would identify a somewhat narrow and discrete but nonetheless meaningful instance of political development in the election-administration context. Instead, history offers a sequence in which federal statutory law *and* legal doctrine become gradually more aggressive, while leaving interpretation and enforcement to other actors in the federal system. In part this is because like other aspects of election law, the challenges posed by disabled voters merge administrative questions with matters of formal eligibility. Enabling a blind person to vote is a technical challenge; providing wheelchair access to polling places is an architectural and financial one. But trying to define disability, in terms of both "elderly individuals" (of whom Congress spoke admiringly in the 1984 statute) and those diagnosed with mental illness (as in the Missouri case), is something else. It gets judges, lawmakers, and elections officials very quickly into matters of competence and formal eligibility—things ill-defined in many states' voting laws but nonetheless firmly under state and not federal control in the United States.

In sum, HAVA is a new chapter in a familiar American tale. The federal government increased its authority over the practice of suffrage—over the institutions that structure and constitute the American right to vote—but it was also constrained by federalism and partisanship. HAVA itself is not temporally limited, despite occasional state calls for the EAC to be abolished. Spatially, HAVA does apply to the entire country—except North Dakota, which is exempt because it has no voter registration. Substantively, HAVA clearly leaves state and local officials with day-to-day responsibility for most areas of election administration. And the ongoing debate over voting reform offers many illustrations of how, after more than a generation of federal intervention, state and local officials continue to believe that election mechanics are theirs to manage. A particularly stark example came in late 2007, when Congress considered legislation that would reverse the move toward touch-screen voting machines and insist on some form of paper ballot in national elections. Doug Lewis, executive director of the Election Center of the National Association of Election Officials, said that the proposal's timelines and the financial and logistical burdens it would impose were so severe that if the law were passed, he would recommend that state and local officials refuse to run future federal elections.[110]

A constitutional order is composed of both institutions and principles. And as Mark Tushnet writes, sometimes a statute can express the guiding principles of that order as effectively as any Supreme Court decision.[111] HAVA is such a statute. Substantive and important, it has altered the balance of authority between the national, state, and local governments, changed the way many Americans vote, and brought new attention to election administration. But HAVA stops far short of nationalizing any part of the voting system. It established a small federal agency with advisory powers, but in practice the agency is subject to partisan influence, and its enforcement rules are so mild that years later, it cannot even say for sure how close we are to full compliance. The federal role in many areas is greater than it was a decade ago, but responsibility for voter registration, ballot technology, voter purges, voter identification, and most election funding remains shared by national, state, and local officials.

Lawmakers in different eras, different parties, and different ideological settings have concluded that despite its flaws, local administration of national elections is fully compatible with American democracy. As I argue in the next chapter, one reason is that local variation in American suffrage practices fits comfortably within our understandings of popular sovereignty, and even today holds the potential to enhance the exercise of self-rule.

4

Mediated Popular Sovereignty: Local Suffrage Practices and American Self-Rule

> We confront anomalies within our beliefs, within our
> practices, and most important in the relationships between
> the two. And our goal is always to make the broader
> web of beliefs and practices as coherent as we can.
>> Don Herzog (1989)

> I'm on them to register when they come in
> for dog tags and dump stickers.
>> Barbara Swann, town clerk, Monterey, Massachusetts (2003)

> I don't think there was anything wrong with those
> machines. But if it gives the voters more confidence,
> then it's the change we're going to make.
>> Kathy Dent, election supervisor, Sarasota County,
>> Florida, explaining the county's move away from
>> touch-screen voting machines (2008)

Between the disc jockey's tables and the food tent, Gadsden County election supervisor Shirley Green Knight set up her new optical-scan voting machine at a Sawdust town party one late-spring evening in 2004. One of Florida's poorest counties and its only majority-black county, Gadsden had the highest rate of disqualified ballots in the presidential election of 2000. Knight, who took on the job of election supervisor in 2001, spent a good deal of time in 2004 showcasing the new voting technology at churches, carnivals, school classrooms, and other gatherings. Knight's message was, "Your vote will count this time, so please come out." The DJ took the microphone between songs to remind partygoers to register.[1]

Far to the north of Sawdust, the clerk of a predominantly white, prosperous town in the Massachusetts Berkshires told a similar tale. Asked by a skeptical visitor about the wisdom of having registration and elections run by officials in each tiny town—in Massachusetts, towns and cities rather than counties choose election machinery and supervise voting—Monterey town clerk Barbara Swann responded that she and her peers took great pride in high rates of registration and turnout. Like Shirley Green Knight, Swann actively encouraged political participation. "I'm on them to register when they come in for dog tags and dump stickers," she said.[2]

These stories capture both the peril and the promise of the distinctive, decentralized American way of voting. The reason Shirley Green Knight was making the rounds is that many Gadsden County voters felt they were effectively disenfranchised in 2000 by a badly designed ballot, too few polling places, and other factors, some of which were directly under county control. Such problems are not exclusively or necessarily linked to local authority. But a centralized, standardized system of election administration would be unlikely to permit such inconsistencies and inadequacies. Meanwhile, in addition to a robust civic culture of voter engagement, the Massachusetts town has enough money and a sufficiently small population to continue using hand-counted paper ballots—the method that results in the lowest percentage of "lost" votes, according to at least one estimate.[3] These contrasts suggest that local administration of elections has the potential to *compromise* American popular sovereignty.

But there is another side to the story, for both Knight and Swann are public officials who work hard to recruit people to register and vote, and who are eager to ensure that votes are easily cast and accurately counted. Each official feels intensely her duty and obligation to facilitate voting by her neighbors—that is, her constituents. This immediacy, close connection, and linkage of the political and social realms would be difficult to achieve under full federal or even state administration. These factors suggest that the local dimension of suffrage actually *enhances* the exercise of self-rule in the United States.

Casting a ballot remains the central activity of American civic membership and the most direct tool by which we exercise authority over the state, and how we do it has profound implications for popular sovereignty. In the years since *Bush v. Gore*, authors like Thad Hall and Michael Alvarez, Paul Gronke, John Mark Hansen, Spencer Overton, Roy Saltman, Steven Schier, and Dennis Thompson have touched on the theoretical connections between localized voting practices and self-rule. Important empirical questions remained almost entirely unexplored until quite recently: in 2006, scholars working with the CalTech/MIT Voting Technology Project observed that despite reams of research on trust in government, virtually nothing had been published on citizens' trust in the electoral process itself.[4] Today, a growing empirical literature is closely examining the connection between election administration and popular sovereignty, exploring how to "make voting work."[5]

The phrase "popular sovereignty" is often treated as a "God word," one observant scholar recently noted, as if its meaning were "immediately clear and descriptive of an unqualified good."[6] In fact, it has always been one of the central contested concepts in American political thought. But a defining attribute of American popular self-rule has not been fully understood, for very little of the massive literature in political science, history, and law exploring popular sovereignty engages with suffrage practices. And even the best analyses of the theoretical premises behind electoral structures, such as the work of Arend Lijphart and Richard Katz, pay very little attention to election administration.[7]

As we have seen, even as the national state expanded in sheer size, power, and wealth—and repeatedly regulated the voting process—voting supervision remained largely in local hands. As a historical matter, then, the American exercise of national electoral self-rule has always had a local texture, mediated by small institutions and varying practices. This chapter turns from the developmental and historical questions—what has *caused* localism—toward an inquiry into the *consequences* of localism in national suffrage. At its core is a normative question prompted by that history and implicit in a good deal of popular and academic literature today: do our distinctive, locally varying voting practices obstruct the exercise of popular sovereignty in the United States?

This is a complex question, and my answer is not Panglossian, for in different ways localism alternately diminishes and improves our ability to govern ourselves through elections. Meanwhile, empirical research is necessary for resolving important aspects of the question, and scholars are just now beginning to explore them directly. (I describe some of this research later in the chapter.) But I argue that on balance, and contrary to what seems to be the current conventional wisdom, the decentralized American way of voting enhances and facilitates our exercise of meaningful popular sovereignty. To draw on the frame set up by Don Herzog in the quotation that opens this chapter, in this area our beliefs and our practices are not so anomalous, and are in fact much more coherent than they may appear.

The first section of the chapter offers what I think is an improved description of the problem itself. A lot of contemporary debate over election administration treats the matter of popular sovereignty as if it were a simple binary question: this or that voting procedure is either good or bad for democratic self-rule. But electoral popular sovereignty has two important aspects, complementary but not identical, and it helps to separate them. The *instrumental* component of popular sovereignty focuses on outcomes: whether an election in fact accurately translates voter preferences. The *constitutive* side of popular sovereignty deals with beliefs: whether citizens sense that voting is meaningful, worthwhile, and fair. A particular localized practice may either enhance or diminish popular sovereignty, on one or both dimensions.

The second section of the chapter makes what might be called the "weak" argument for decentralized election administration. This claim argues that a certain amount of locally patterned variation in voter registration and in the casting and counting of ballots fits coherently within our federalized electoral structure. The reason for this is simple, if counterintuitive: uniformity is actually not a central value of American elections, even national elections. Our intense disputes over how to apply the principle of equality to suffrage— together with the de facto nationalization of important aspects of the right to vote in judicial rulings and statutes—have helped obscure this fact. Even if we achieved the "technical perfection" that political scientist Stephen Ansolabehere calls for in casting and counting votes, constitutionally mandated structures such as the composition of the Senate and the Electoral College, as well as extra-constitutional devices such as the primary system and the drawing of congressional districts by state legislatures, would still leave American voters expressing their will through mediating structures that weight everyone's votes quite differently.[8] These structural features serve as a useful reminder that geographic places have always been essential to the theory and practice of representation in the United States. In sum, the weaker claim is that decentralization and local variation may well "interfere" with a certain vision of uniform, direct, plebiscitary national self-rule—but that in fact, almost everything about our electoral structure does so too. All told, decentralized election administration fits comfortably within what is now commonly called the Madisonian conception of American popular sovereignty.

The third section articulates the case for localism. Not only are locally varying suffrage practices consistent with other nonuniform electoral structures, but they have important redeeming characteristics for American popular sovereignty, on both the instrumental and constitutive dimensions. Drawing on a range of theoretical and empirical sources, I describe how local administration can improve citizens' sense of efficacy and ownership in the democratic process, provide opportunities for experimentation and innovation, place obstacles in the way of some corrupting influences, and increase turnout. The local dimension of American voting becomes much more intelligible and defensible, and much less a scandalous accident of history, when incorporated into the family of ideas built around popular sovereignty and the state.

The answers to these questions are certainly not black-and-white, however, and so I close the chapter on a cautionary note. The layered, even fragmented system of rules governing our democratic rituals clearly has been partly created by the renowned American fear of centralization, and that fear may inhibit the American citizenry's ability to act together as a united people.

The Instrumental and Constitutive Components of Popular Sovereignty

Election administration "may at first blush seem dull," Steven Schier writes, but it helps determine the stability and accountability of our government—and can also "indirectly affect governmental deliberation by influencing who is elected to direct the government's course."[9] At the same time, elections are "institutions for generating social capital," in the words of one study, and trust in the voting process is essential to a democracy.[10] People who are confident that the electoral process works are more likely to think other political institutions work well too, and to feel attached to the political and social order. Elections, writes G. Bingham Powell, "should not only provide symbolic reassurance, but also genuinely serve as instruments of democracy."[11]

As Powell's words suggest, an election must do two things. In the 1992 write-in-vote case *Burdick v. Takushi*, the Supreme Court said that the first and most fundamental task of an election is to pick a winner.[12] This is the instrumental aspect of voting: the citizenry's ability to choose their leaders, acting both individually and collectively, and so "direct the government's course," as Schier puts it. But despite *Burdick*, a successful election must also give voters the sense that they've participated in a fair and effective process and "provide symbolic reassurance"—the constitutive element of voting. The local dimension of American suffrage shapes and defines both aspects of popular sovereignty in the United States. Separating these concepts helps add a measure of precision to a question that can be abstract and amorphous. These ideas are key to a simple framework I propose for examining the relationship between voting practices and popular sovereignty (Table 1).

The instrumental component of voting is essential. A democracy "require[s] functioning institutions that are designed to, and really do, secure a government responsive to public interest and opinion."[13] When a person is made more likely to register, to travel to the polls (or mail in a ballot), to vote his or her intentions on a clear and intelligible slate, and to have that vote accurately counted (and, if necessary, recounted), the instrumental side

Table 1.

Popular Sovereignty and Suffrage Practices: A Simple Framework

	Instrumental (Outcomes)	Constitutive (Experiential)
Enhance	Practices that increase registration or turnout, help record preferences more accurately, and improve likelihood of a vote's being accurately counted	Practices that increase voters' sense of efficacy and civic engagement, regardless of whether favored candidates win or lose; give voters a valid sense of ownership of the electoral process; add depth to civic ritual; and advance perceived legitimacy of the system
Diminish	Practices that make registration and voting more difficult or decrease accuracy of ballot tabulation, particularly in any systematic fashion	Practices that increase voters' feelings of powerlessness, distance voters from sense of ownership of the electoral process, feed voters'sense that the state is incompetent or corrupt, and weaken legitimacy

of popular sovereignty is enhanced. Conversely, when any step in the serial voting process is made more difficult—or obstructed, either purposefully or accidentally—popular sovereignty is diminished. The ultimate demonstration of any variable's effect on the instrumental side of popular sovereignty is a showing that the factor in question can affect election outcomes. Evidence that local variation helped decide the presidential race in Florida in 2000 is a major reason why election administration has captured the attention of behaviorally oriented political scientists, journalists, and legislators around the country.

But the constitutive, or experiential, element of popular sovereignty is no less important. People do not vote merely to direct policy; indeed, rational-choice theory says only a fool would think any large election enabled him to do so. We vote to participate, to join in a symbolic ritual, and to affirm and express our membership in the polity. Voting is "not exclusively a matter of exercising a choice but is also an activity which helps sustain the feeling that the system is legitimate."[14] Judge Learned Hand may have captured it best: "I know how illusory would be the belief that my vote determined anything; but nevertheless when I go to the polls I have a satisfaction in the sense that we are all engaged in a common venture."[15]

A concern with the effects of voting not on policy but on citizens themselves runs through the work of normative political theorists from John Stuart Mill to Carole Pateman.[16] Election practices that foster and sustain a sense of efficacy, fair play, and participation in that "common venture" enhance this constitutive aspect of popular sovereignty. But structures, rules, and actions that diminish voters' belief that an election is fair and uncorrupted—that their vote matters, or at the very least is as likely to matter as anyone else's—undermine popular sovereignty as surely as practices that skew outcomes.

I will discuss empirical work exploring these questions in the American context later, but let me note here one piece of research in comparative politics that illustrates the point particularly well. Examining eight emerging democracies in sub-Saharan Africa, Jørgen Elklit and Andrew Reynolds found that both the perceived independence of the electoral commission and the quality of election administration had real effects on voters' sense of efficacy and their belief in governmental legitimacy. Voters' electoral experiences, they concluded, "have a direct bearing on how the sense of political efficacy develops in individual citizens" and on the "development of democratic legitimacy."[17] Thus the directly instrumental component of elections is only part of what determines whether we respect them: regardless of whether one's preferred candidates win or lose, voting practices can enhance or diminish voters' belief in the legitimacy of their government.

Because it rests ultimately on perceptions, this constitutive side of popular sovereignty can be a slippery and troublesome thing. For example, in one of the quotations that opens this chapter, a county election supervisor says that although she believes the county's touch-screen machines worked well, the county was getting rid of them because "it gives the voters more confidence."[18] A more consequential illustration of this problem comes from the Supreme Court's short opinion in the 2006 case *Purcell v. Gonzales*. That ruling allowed Arizona to put its new voter-identification requirements in place for the 2006 election, pending a full trial on the question of whether the statute violated federal law and the U.S. Constitution.[19] *Purcell* is important here because of the Court's commentary on the dangers posed by voter fraud—the ostensible target of Arizona's ID requirement. Though the Court professed to take no opinion on the merits of new anti-fraud measures, it reasoned that voter fraud "drives honest citizens out of the democratic process and breeds distrust of our government." Moreover, the Court worried that voters "who fear their legitimate votes will be outweighed by fraudulent ones will feel disenfranchised."[20]

What jumps out is the Court's emphasis on the possibility that some voters might "feel" disenfranchised because they "fear" fraud—and the tribunal's apparent willingness to balance such subjective speculations against the interests of voters who might be *literally* disenfranchised by onerous voter-identification requirements.[21] The Court's "feel" and "fear" approach in *Purcell* has been roundly criticized, and I will have more to say about voter-identification laws in Chapter Five. I raise the case here because the Court's casual use of the phrase "feel disenfranchised" highlights the need for scholars, advocates, practitioners, and judges to clarify which aspect of popular sovereignty—the instrumental or constitutive—they believe is or would be enhanced or diminished by a given voting practice. The Court was not identifying people whose votes might actually be rejected, wrongly weighted, or inaccurately tallied—the instrumental and more traditional sense of "disenfranchised." Instead, the Court implicitly said that the constitutive dimension of popular sovereignty is so important that diminished *confidence* in our electoral processes can properly be called "disenfranchisement." That conclusion raises serious questions as a legal matter, particularly to the extent that it justifies making voting more difficult and more costly for many eligible voters. But the *Purcell* Court was right to acknowledge directly the importance of the constitutive aspect of popular sovereignty: "Confidence in the integrity of our electoral processes is essential to the functioning of our participatory democracy."[22]

Madisonian Popular Sovereignty: Integrity, Federalism, and Geography in American Self-Rule

The Court's reference to "integrity" in *Purcell* was no accident. Few terms have been more prominent in recent debates over election administration, and many contemporary accounts set localism in suffrage practices against our commitment to integrity and equality in elections. At least since about 1965, voting has been understood not as a privilege but as a right, and a right that we insist must be distributed evenly among political equals. Variations in voting practices, this logic says—cloggy punch-card machines in one county, high-accuracy optical-scan devices in another, and so on—violate those principles and impair our exercise of popular sovereignty.

Equality and integrity are essential goals. My concern is that we are reflexively defining these terms using an overly simple metric. "Integrity," for example, suggests cleanliness; that is what we worry about when we talk about voter-impersonation fraud, errors in vote tabulation, partisan distortions, and voter intimidation. But "integrity" also denotes "the quality or state of being complete or undivided."[23] And that kind of wholeness or unity, that lack of division, is simply not a primary value or characteristic of the American electoral process writ large. Notwithstanding our equipopulous legislative districts, emphasis on the Equal Protection Clause in voting-rights cases, and underlying belief that we have a majoritarian political system, American elections do not establish anything like meaningful mathematical equality among voters. Even if voting practices became dramatically more homogenized than they are today—say, with the adaptation of a single voting technology and a common ballot in presidential elections, or even the creation of a national voter roll—many profound differences in the weight of individual votes in national elections would endure. Though this point is somewhat counterintuitive, the examples are well-known features of our electoral system, and it is important to spend some time looking at them here.

Some are mandated by the Constitution itself. The U.S. Senate, as Robert Dahl and Sandy Levinson have recently pointed out, is almost certainly the world's worst-apportioned legislative body.[24] Levinson observes that about 5 million people live in the seven smallest states; they enjoy representation by fourteen senators. The seven largest states total a population of around 124 million; they too have fourteen senators.[25] A resident of New York (population approximately 19,306,000) who moves across Lake Champlain into my home state of Vermont (population approximately 624,000) is handed a much more powerful vote in U.S. Senate elections: the voter's new state has *one-thirtieth* the population, but the same number of senators.

The presidential Electoral College reproduces the inequities of the Senate, because no matter what their population, all states get two votes derived from their two senators. Meanwhile, the common practice of delivering Electoral College votes in winner-take-all fashion leaves voters in most states casting ballots likely to have no direct bearing on the overall outcome, since the winner of their state's contest is a foregone conclusion. By contrast, voters in the dozen or so "battleground states" not only get to cast meaningful votes but also enjoy campaigns devoted to their needs and interests.[26] Voters in these states exert far more influence over presidential selection than their peers. In addition, the Electoral College allows the ultimate affront to the instrumental component of majoritarian self-rule: victories by presidential candidates receiving less than a majority of votes nationwide, and even by those defeated in the popular vote.[27]

Even the House of Representatives does not feature quite the level of mathematical equality we might assume. In part because the size of the House has been fixed for over a century, there are serious population deviations between districts across states. Wyoming, with about 515,000 people, and Montana, with 944,000, currently each have one representative.[28] And of course the half-million citizens of Washington, D.C., remain "represented" in Congress only by a House "delegate" who cannot actually cast consequential votes. Though living within the contiguous United States, D.C. residents are like their U.S. citizen counterparts in Guam, the U.S. Virgin Islands, Puerto Rico, the Northern Marianas, and American Samoa in that they lack any meaningful national right to vote.[29]

Less formal than the Constitution but still extremely durable, various other rules and practices of the American political order also result in differently weighted votes. Several fall well outside the category of "election administration" and are very unlikely to change any time soon. Among the most important are variations caused by the vagaries of our two-party system. A full accounting of the ways in which the two-party system facilitates and obstructs self-rule in the United States is outside the purview of this book. But parties contribute powerfully to the nonuniform nature of the American electoral process, as illustrated by the relatively long primary process in the run-up to the 2008 presidential election. First, voters in the early-primary states generally effect a crucial narrowing of the presidential field, a fact that increasingly irks voters and politicians in other states. And because their votes are so influential, most residents of Iowa and New Hampshire have multiple opportunities to meet each of the candidates before the primary. As the 2008 Democratic primary wore on, however, it became clear that states voting *later* exerted even more influence. In addition, as the campaign moved across the country, Americans were treated to an almost-infinite array of electoral devices: a caucus here, a primary there, a hybrid in Texas; closed primaries in some states, open primaries in others; delegates allotted winner-take-all on the Republican side, proportionally on the Democratic side; and so on.

U.S. congressional elections also feature deep nonuniformities effectively created by the parties. In most states, the state legislature designs U.S. congressional districts. There are commonalities in the rules and norms regarding how those districts should be drawn: for example, "communities of interest" may be recognized, existing town and county boundaries should be maintained, and districts should be as contiguous and compact as possible. But in practice, political parties dominate district-construction in most states, and they tend to try to draw the lines in a way that will guarantee victory by a given party in a given district. That means the instrumental weight of a person's vote—how likely it is to determine the outcome—rests heavily on where that person lives. Voters in some states (Republicans in Massachusetts, for example, at least recently) have virtually no chance of supporting a winning representative for their favored party in the U.S. House, because the opposing party runs the statehouse and draws the districts. (A winner-take-all Electoral College process in the state also means that the votes of those Massachusetts Republicans will have no direct impact on the presidential election.) Meanwhile, citizens in states where nonpartisan commissions draw the lines are likely to vote in much closer elections, because such nonpartisan bodies tend to aim for competitive margins. Whether one thinks this system is good or bad, it clearly results in voters in different states (and different districts within states) exerting varying amounts of power in U.S. House elections. Another example of parties' contribution to variation in U.S. elections concerns eligibility for seventeen-year-olds in primary elections. In most of the United States, a person must be eighteen years old to vote in any election, but in nine states, the major parties and state law together allow seventeen-year-olds to vote in primaries, as long as their eighteenth birthday will arrive before the general election.[30]

This brings us to election timing. Perhaps nothing illustrates the absence of uniformity in American suffrage today more powerfully than the shift toward early and absentee voting since 1980. "Without great fanfare," John Fortier writes, "our nation is steadily moving away from voting on election day." Fortier estimates that in 1980, just one voter in twenty cast an absentee or early ballot;[31] in 2004, about one in five did so. These calculations require reporting and analysis of data from localities as well as states, but it appears that in 2008 about 30 percent of Americans voted before election day. "A revolution has taken place," says one advocate. "The concept of Election Day is history. Now it's just the final day to vote."[32] (Federal courts have held that early, absentee, and all-mail voting do not violate national statutes setting the Tuesday after the first Monday in November as "the day of election." As the Ninth Circuit put it in a 2001 ruling, election day marks the "consummation" of the voting process rather than its entirety.)[33] Early voting allows in-person balloting, under the supervision and with the assistance of elections officials, in an official polling place; absentee ballots are usually mailed in, though they are sometimes delivered in person. Both early and absentee voting are increasingly popular, and state rules vary dramatically: for the 2008 election, thirty-two states allowed no-excuse, pre–Election Day, in-person voting in one form or another, while fourteen states and the District of Columbia required an excuse and four states did not allow early or in-person absentee voting.[34] From the perspective of popular sovereignty and the practice of suffrage, there are good and bad things about early and absentee voting, and I will comment on them further later in this chapter. I raise the topic here simply to note the deep differences in Americans' electoral experiences created by our abandonment of electoral simultaneity.

This list certainly is not exhaustive. Also varying by state are restrictions on the voting rights of people with felony convictions; ballot-access thresholds for candidates; standards for counting write-in votes (if they are legal at all); and name-order rules for balloting.[35] Each can shape both the instrumental and constitutive aspects of popular sovereignty. And none faces the prospect of national homogenization any time soon.

In part, all this variation emerges from the longstanding American commitment to geographically based representation. In both theory and practice, representation in Anglo-American thought has always been "overtly territorial," and electoral structures in the United States are still built around places.[36] Rosemary Zagarri has argued that Americans turned away from geographic theories of representation in favor of demographic representation by the middle of the nineteenth century.[37] To be sure, Americans now agree that politicians should represent "people, not trees or acres," as the Court said in *Reynolds v. Sims*.[38] But reports of our abandonment of geography should not be overstated. Partisanship, interest, and race now coexist uneasily in American theories of representation, but geographical entities have never yielded their fundamental position: those other variables play a role in *how* congressional districts are drawn, for example, rather than replacing place-based districts with an alternative system. Indeed, Sandy Levinson points out that in the United States "*all* elected officials within the national government, including representatives, senators, and even the president, owe their elections to their appeal to specific localities."[39] Writing about the construction of political districts, James A. Gardner identifies "a normative commitment to localness" in American theories of representation and observes that "to represent voters by territory is to organize the electorate according to bonds of local community and interest."[40]

Tacitly and sometimes explicitly, we accept the tradeoffs federalism creates. Those local bonds—what Levinson calls "the dispersion of loyalties and identities attached to federalism"—can certainly have negative as well as positive effects on popular sovereignty.[41] As Gimpel and Schuknecht write in *Patchwork Nation*, "The decentralization of power inherent in federalism acts against unity, making the political system a barrier to homogeneity."[42] A loss of unity, a diminishment of the ability to act together toward our shared goals and against our common problems, is a serious price to pay. But in the American political tradition, the paradoxical idea that a divided people can actually govern itself more effectively than a united one is familiar.

It is a fair summary of the Madisonian theory of democratic popular sovereignty to say that as long as the "the people" can act, it's perfectly acceptable and even desirable that it not be easy for them to act *together*.[43] Americans understand sovereignty not as unitary and total but as "divided and distributed to several levels of government."[44] Thus checks, filters, and limits are key to Madisonian theory, and a Madisonian understanding of popular sovereignty differs from a Populistic one, as Robert Dahl demonstrated more than fifty years ago.[45] Upholding the National Voter Registration Act against California's challenge in 1995, the Ninth Circuit said approvingly that by setting up a federal system, "the Framers split the atom of sovereignty."[46] (Daniel T. Rodgers writes of post-Revolutionary democratic thought that the majority's power was to be "carefully broken up," "divided in two," "buffered," made "indirect," "federalized," and, finally, "dismembered."[47]) Despite considerable differences between our assumptions about popular sovereignty and suffrage and those of the founders, in many ways their ideas still hold sway, as shown by the many introductory texts in U.S. government that offer Madisonian theory to explain federalism, the separation of powers, interest groups, and the legislative process.

Richard Katz has said that having "multiple sites and times for elections" is consistent with Madisonian democracy.[48] Because the founders took locally varying voting rules for granted, documentary evidence is scant, but I would go a step further and say that a decentralized system of election administration is *part of* the Madisonian conception of popular sovereignty. In addition to a comment by Madison himself, the words of nationalists such as Alexander Hamilton and Joseph Story suggest that the early architects of the distinctive structure of American popular self-rule understood local control of suffrage practices to be part of that system. Speaking in the Constitutional Convention during an argument over the House of Representatives, Madison worried most about manipulation of election procedures by *state* governments. His greatest concern appears to have been self-interested manipulation of election results by variations in the "mode":

> The policy of referring the appointment of the House of Representatives to the people and not to the Legislatures of the States, supposes that the result will be somewhat influenced by the mode. . . . The Legislatures of the States ought not to have the uncontrouled right of regulating the times places & manner of holding elections. These were words of great latitude. It was impossible to foresee all the abuses that might be made of the discretionary power. Whether the electors should vote by ballot or viva voce, should assemble at this place or that place; should be divided into districts or all meet at one place . . . these & many other points would depend on the Legislatures and might materially affect the appointments."[49]

Here Madison states bluntly that the manner (voice or ballot), balloting location, and basic representational structure (districts or at-large representation) employed in elections can all influence results. Yet Madison does not draw from this premise the conclusion that practices should be standardized. His concern is to restrain potential "abuses" by state governments, and his tactical goal seems to have been to place in the national government "a controuling power" over elections, particularly "in the last resort," as Hamilton would later put it in *Federalist* 59.[50] Madison appears to assume that thoroughly decentralized electoral regimes are satisfactory: it is the manipulation of such systems that worries him, not their normal operation. Certainly, Madison did not argue that the national government should write a national electoral law—let alone actually administer elections. He simply wanted an insurance policy written into the Constitution.[51]

That's what Article I, section 4, essentially does. Advocating ratification and defending the Elections Clause in *Federalist* 59, archnationalist Alexander Hamilton explicitly endorsed decentralized election administration. The Constitution was correct, he wrote, to assign "the regulation of elections for the federal government in the first instance to the local administrations; which in ordinary cases, and when no improper views prevail, may be both more convenient and more satisfactory."[52] (By "local administrations," Hamilton was probably referring to state governments as well as smaller units.) Only in crisis, Hamilton argued, would it be necessary for the national government to step in and guarantee that state governments did not debase the national representative process.[53]

For his part, Joseph Story wrote in 1833 that the Elections Clause encountered little opposition in the Convention, and indeed not even much attention.[54] Story's interpretation tracks Hamilton's closely (though without citation), placing discretionary power over elections not with *either* the state legislatures or national government but primarily with the former and ultimately with the latter.[55] Story did not believe that Congress would be able to draft "an election law, which would be applicable . . . and convenient for all the states."[56] Finally, recall that some opponents of ratification had denounced the Elections Clause: they wanted *more* decentralization of authority, not less, as they viewed even the possibility of congressional intervention in election practices as a dangerous usurpation.[57]

The founders understood the fact of local variation in election procedures and administration, and made no attempt to subject voting processes to routine national control. This should come as no surprise, for in the American constitutional order, popular power is exercised through the filters and channels of a federal system that enables voters to direct policy only in mediated, indirect ways. Uniformity is not a central value of that system; as a result, voters' power varies considerably and will continue to do so even as voting practices are standardized. Representational structures are shaped by the Constitution, by partisanship, and, in some cases, by race. But a commitment to geographic places remains the essential premise of American electoral institutions. Of course, beyond election law, important public policies in the United States also vary considerably from one state to the next. These include matters of the greatest importance, such as health care policies, educational funding and standards, family law, and criminal law. An election-administration system characterized by local control and local variation fits coherently within this structure.

The Case for Localism

Readers critical of the electoral structures featured in the previous section have probably found it to be a pretty thin defense of localism today. The fact that *other* archaic electoral structures violate modern understandings of egalitarian majoritarian self-rule, they might argue, does not mean that *this* electoral structure is worthy.[58] Beyond its historical compatibility with geographically based understandings of representation and American theories of divided, mediated popular sovereignty, what is the case for decentralized election administration?

As Dennis Thompson writes, "spatial variation" in election procedures (ballot design, technology, and recount standards) may "frustrate electoral justice" if such variation systematically makes some voters more powerful than others. But Thompson also argues that local administration of national elections can have salutary effects, because it "is likely to give citizens more control over the electoral process, encourage political participation, increase partisan competitiveness, and enable districts to experiment with different procedures."[59] I share that conclusion, drawing on an array of historical and contemporary sources to identify four ways decentralized election administration can enhance, rather than diminish, the exercise of popular sovereignty. First, local administration offers voters a greater sense of engagement and ownership in the political process and can provide a more meaningful voting experience. Second, it fosters experimentation and innovation. Third, it places obstacles in the path of systemic corruption, whether accidental or purposeful. Finally, it has the strong potential to increase voter turnout.

"The Strength of Free Nations": The Constitutive
Power of Local Election Administration

By broadly distributing responsibility and bringing voters into contact with local government, decentralized election administration increases voters' ownership of the political process. Embedding voting in local settings can also enhance the communal, ritual, and symbolic elements of casting a ballot. Where Madison's tacit approval of local variation emphasized the instrumental aspect of popular sovereignty (that is, election results), the work of Alexis de Tocqueville feeds this more constitutive case for localism in American electoral self-rule.

Tocqueville understood administrative decentralization as "one of the glories of the American political system," writes Stephen Macedo. Decentralization, Tocqueville believed, was "a way of placing governmental decisions within the reach of ordinary people, 'so that the maximum number of people have some concern with public affairs.' "[60] Local government was the main object of Tocqueville's affection, and an admiring study of local authority begins his assessment of "the form of government established in America on the principle of the sovereignty of the people." As a political entity, he writes, the township "is so perfectly natural" that it "seems to come directly from the hand of God."[61] Municipal institutions "constitute the strength of free nations. Town meetings are to liberty what primary schools are to science; they bring it within the people's reach, they teach men how to use and how to enjoy it. A nation may establish a free government, but without municipal institutions it cannot have the spirit of liberty."[62] The township is where power, sovereignty, and "the people" define themselves, where citizens are trained in both the "practice" and the "spirit" of liberty and order, learning both rights and duties.[63] The participatory habits built into local government provide civic benefits well beyond the township itself, disseminating a "bracing vitality to civil society as a whole," as Robert Gannett summarized Tocqueville.[64]

Politics in the New World have come a long way since 1830. But important modern works as diverse as Robert Bellah and colleagues' *Habits of the Heart* (1986), Robert Putnam's *Bowling Alone* (2000), and Anthony Lukas's *Common Ground* (1985) demonstrate Tocqueville's influence. And Tocqueville's concern for active citizenship is certainly timely today, since modern citizens have fewer and fewer opportunities to experience collective public activity of any kind. As sociologist Gianfranco Poggi writes, voting now "constitutes practically the only regular expression . . . of active citizenship."[65] Matthew A. Crenson and Benjamin Ginsberg make this same point in *Downsizing Democracy*, describing a "general political demobilization [in] the past several decades," which has "reduced the government's reliance on the active and collective cooperation of the people."[66]

Local administration of our national elections has stood against that demobilization, contributing to the vitality of civil society in two ways. First, localism multiplies the number of citizens who actually do the work of running elections. One of the themes of *Downsizing Democracy* is the declining number of "citizen administrators," as policies designed to run government more efficiently and smoothly diminish the space in which citizenship operates.[67] Working at the polling place—either as a regular employee of a town, county, or city or as a special, one-time volunteer or for-pay elections worker—offers Americans an opportunity to exercise an important, responsible role in our central act of self-rule. This is one message of Michael Schudson's *The Good Citizen*, which opens with an account of his own volunteer work at a California polling place.[68] Schudson brought his kids along for part of the day; he considered the work to be part of their political education. Dozens of voters thanked him, and many were "proud of their neighbor for volunteering."[69] Currently, about two million Americans work at the polls in a typical federal election, many of them volunteering or working for relatively little money.[70] Of course, a national election-administration bureaucracy would certainly still require a great deal of help at election time. But as local authority increases, the work of these citizen administrators—the army of clerks, recorders, managers, and one-day workers—deepens in importance. As Spencer Overton puts it, "Americans who register others to vote, work at community polling places, or see their neighbors performing these and other tasks gain a deeper sense of self-government. By providing hands-on democracy training, local control facilitates engagement among citizens. Complete federalization of elections, cutting out local input, would only make citizens even more detached from government."[71] Practices that allow local governments to register voters, choose polling places and ballot types, and count votes do sacrifice uniformity and may even threaten equality. But they also recognize the individual responsibility and capacity for choice of democratic citizens.[72]

A second salutary effect comes from the experience of in-person voting in local institutions. Many contemporary commentators laud the neighborly character of American elections as their finest feature. On Election Day 2004, economist and *New York Times* columnist Paul Krugman—not normally given to sentimentality—wrote, "I always get a little choked up when I go to the local school to cast my vote. The humbleness of the surroundings only emphasizes the majesty of the process: this is democracy."[73] Journalist David M. Shribman lamented that since he is always working on election day, he misses "the best part of politics," which is the "shared, community experience" of going to "my neighborhood polling place."[74] Political scientist Paul Gronke calls "going to the polling place and casting a ballot" our "most essential act of public participation," and Dennis Thompson emphasizes the "public affirmation" involved in the process of "walking to the polling station and standing in line with one's neighbors."[75] Analyzing the costs and benefits of continued localism in the wake of the Help America Vote Act (HAVA), Brian Kim writes, "There is something solemn and meaningful about citizens going to their local precinct, waiting in line with others, and casting a ballot for President of the United States or the local school superintendent."[76]

These responses are not mere nostalgia. When a democratic citizen chooses her national representatives standing in a local institution such as a school, firehouse, church, or business, after conversing with her neighbors and the town or county officials who perhaps helped her register to vote, may have selected (and paid for) the voting technology she will use, and now instruct her on how to mark her ticket (which they will ultimately bear responsibility for counting), she exercises electoral popular sovereignty and also builds civic community in a meaningful way.

Like others, John Mark Hansen is eloquently ambivalent about the relationship between localism and American popular sovereignty. On the one hand, as participation is increasingly privatized—by absentee and all-mail balloting, for example—Hansen worries that "the fabric of mutual engagement that supports self-government begins to unravel." Hansen laments the erosion of "the experiential connection between voting and place," because a citizen comes to understand other people and democracy itself by shared participation in democracy's rituals. "A placeless politics undermines the sense of common democratic purpose," he argues. On the other hand, participation detached from place "is also liberated from the parochialism of place" and is not necessarily worse for democracy.[77]

Some fascinating and important academic work has begun to explore these questions empirically. For example, Michael Alvarez and his coauthors found that voters' confidence that their ballot would be accurately counted varied according to what technology they used, among other factors. Yet they emphasize that further research is needed to better understand the interaction between voters' electoral confidence (or lack thereof) and their broader sense of civic duty—as well as the likelihood that they will keep voting.[78] Lonna Rae Atkeson and Kyle Saunders, meanwhile, surveyed voters after the 2006 midterm election and found that "local context matters a great deal in structuring voter confidence."[79] And Thad Hall and his colleagues have found that several locally varying factors, such as method of voting and the quality of voters' interactions with poll workers, affect voters' perceptions of the fairness of the voting process.[80] Notably, two recent studies conclude that the perceived quality of election administration "has a significant and independent effect on voter behavior and affect," as Robert Stein and his coauthors stated in a 2008 article. That is, voters who rated their polling place and its staffers highly were more likely to feel good about the voting technology they used and the likelihood of their ballot being accurately counted—regardless of whether they had just voted on a touch-screen system or a paper ballot.[81]

Local administration of national elections can be an engine of citizenship and deepen our exercise of popular sovereignty. My conclusion is that the gains to citizenship formation and participatory efficacy resulting from localism are worth the risks, particularly as those risks are minimized by further investments in election administration. But some careful observers disagree. Decentralized election administration presents numerous "managerial complexities," as Alvarez and Hall have explained, particularly the "principal-agent problems" created by the need for temporary election workers.[82] Ultimately the answer lies in how effectively local staff do the work, how well volunteers are trained, how well the technology functions, and how voters' particular experiences color their judgments.

"Great Diversity of Provision": Innovation and Experimentation

Concluding a survey of American voting practices in 1889, anthropologist James H. Blodgett wrote that "great diversity of provision will continue in different parts of the United States upon the leading features of representation and the conduct of elections, as no uniform legislation is practicable. . . . The inevitable diversity will serve to keep on trial a great variety of plans that find local favor, and may help toward a better solution of the problems of representative government."[83] Contemporary elections have only strengthened the experimentation argument for decentralization. Because of their experience and their proximity to voters in other settings, local authorities are well positioned to help address some of the problems vexing American elections, by proposing and testing novel ways of inducing voters to register and turn out to vote, disseminating election information, training poll workers, keeping records and collaborating with other officials (in their own state and elsewhere) in the interest of avoiding fraud, and, of course, trying new voting technology. We have little consensus on best practices in these areas, and allowing localities to serve as small laboratories of electoral democracy makes a great deal of sense—not least because when voters get upset, local governments are likely to feel the brunt of their anger and to be more responsive than federal authorities.[84]

Variation can also help identify problems when specific practices or technologies fail. This was part of the story in Florida's 13th Congressional District in the 2006 election, when the electronic voting machines used in Sarasota County did not record any choice for congressional representative from about eighteen thousand voters—most likely because of obtuse ballot design rather than machine malfunction. Because *other* balloting technologies were used elsewhere in the district, elections officials had a baseline for comparison and could see how odd it was that so many Sarasota County voters did not vote for that office. (In February 2008, a U.S. House task force ended its investigation into the matter, concluding that the voters had probably accidentally or purposefully failed to vote for representative and the machines had not malfunctioned.)[85]

As a 2004 study concluded, "it would ill serve us to adopt one uniform [voting] system for the whole country," because diverse ways of voting "encourages experimentation with new technologies and thereby improvements over time."[86] This is not a hypothetical point. After the election of 2000, touch-screen voting devices were regarded as a superior technology, best able to provide clear choices to voters, low error rates, accessibility, and fast results. Through HAVA, the federal government helped pay for touch-screen voting machines as replacements for older technology in many areas of the country, and about 40 percent of Americans used such machines in 2006. But with catastrophic events like that in Florida's 13th District supporting doubts about touch-screen machines—particularly their lack of a "paper trail"—Congress now wants optical-scan card-stock ballots to be used and is working with states and localities (and advocates for the disabled) to move in that direction.[87]

The experimentation point comes with two caveats. The first is that in order for localities to provide the kinds of "natural experiments" that can help move American democracy forward, they must publish more data about their election practices. This trend toward openness is already well under way as policy makers and academics take greater interest in election administration and in some instances work closely with local officials to develop and study new practices, and it should continue.[88]

The second caveat is that here too there will be difficult tradeoffs. On the one hand, in-person precinct voting on a common election day could well be seen as best harnessing the citizenship-building, efficacy-enhancing power of localism. It also facilitates the turnout-boosting work of parties, interest groups, and civic-minded individuals. But given room to experiment, localities may well choose to move away from that shared physical ritual in the interest of pursuing other sovereignty-enhancing goals. Early voting, which expanded dramatically in the 2008 election season, is a case in point. States such as Florida allow local supervisors considerable discretion in setting up early-voting and satellite voting sites, and Florida's election supervisors have been so impressed with early voting's capacity to boost turnout and ease congestion at the polls that they proposed getting rid of election day altogether, scrapping precincts, and moving to a system of dramatically enlarged, or "super," voting sites.[89] These large voting places would also have the potential to allow for better-trained poll workers and better machinery—thereby serving both the instrumental and constitutive purposes of elections, particularly if more voters participated and were more satisfied.[90] To be sure, not all localities have had similar experiences. When Cascade County, Montana, considered consolidating polling places in 2006, the county clerk found that her constituents "want to keep their own neighborhood polling place."[91] But the trend toward convenience for individual voters, and away from election-day precinct voting, seems strong, particularly in some large states. Indeed, Florida and Texas now offer "curbside" satellite voting facilities, where you can vote without leaving your car: truly an image to chill the Tocquevillian heart.[92]

Early and absentee voting hold the potential to improve electoral popular sovereignty if they can increase turnout, give voters more time to consider their choices, and diminish election-day mishaps at overburdened precincts. But, in fact, the empirical evidence of greater turnout is still thin, and absentee voting is quite vulnerable to fraud.[93] Moreover, by abandoning the civic ritual of a shared election day, early, absentee, and all-mail voting can detract from voters' experiences of self-rule in real ways. Absentee voting is "voting alone," Paul Gronke observes, and it erodes our sense of community rather than building it.[94] Perhaps most serious, abandoning electoral simultaneity threatens popular sovereignty because it means that voters will not be making choices with the same information.[95] This is not an abstract concern. It is easy to imagine a dramatic event that could change many people's minds just days before an election—the uncovering of personal or political scandal, victory or defeat in a battlefield abroad, a terrorist attack at home, a stock market collapse. With millions of early and absentee votes already cast, an election in such circumstances could lead to a weak and ineffective government without majority support, or even to instability.

"Diffusion of Power": Local Administration
as an Obstacle to Systematic Bias

Writing fifty years ago in one of the first modern works of comparative electoral studies, W. J. M. Mackenzie praised the British system under which many "autonomous local authorities" controlled elections. The setup was in some ways "peculiar and archaic," he acknowledged, but at the same time its "diffusion of power among different authorities" offered a safeguard against corruption:

> Responsibility for managing British elections is scattered. . . . It is both a weakness and an advantage of such a system that very few people understand fully how it works: it is an undoubted advantage that any attempt at improper action by an official somewhere in the system would be challenged at once by some other official independent of him. . . . This is not a matter in which it is desirable to seek administrative tidiness at all costs.[96]

Mackenzie is a bit naive here, even on his own terms—officials of the same party, for example, might well not challenge each other. And as an Englishman, he appears to be rooting for the "home" model. But his basic insight about the redeeming effects of "untidy" administration remains valid.

During the debate over HAVA in 2002, Congressman Bob Ney said Congress wanted to preserve dispersed responsibility for election administration in order to make it "impossible for a single centrally controlled authority to dictate how elections will be run and thereby be able to control the outcome."[97] As we have seen, Madison had also worried about the possibility that whoever controlled "the mode" could also dictate "the result." More recently, Federal District Judge Donald M. Middlebrooks made the point well in one case from the 2000 election. Rejecting George W. Bush's challenge to Florida's various hand counts, Middlebrooks called "electoral procedures and tabulations" a "traditional state province." Discussing the use of different ballot types, the judge praised even greater decentralization: "Rather than a sign of weakness or constitutional injury, some solace can be taken in the fact that no one centralized body or person can control the tabulation of an entire statewide or national election. For the more county boards and individuals involved in the electoral regulation process, the less likely it becomes that corruption, bias, or error can influence the ultimate result of an election."[98]

Judge Middlebrooks's final line is important. Mackenzie, Ney, and Madison all focused on how local variation can help prevent purposeful, self-interested manipulation. Middlebrooks reminds us that diverse practices and a national election effectively composed of small units can also help prevent *accidental* systematic corruption, such as might be caused by a misleading ballot or defective voting machine, for example. A decentralized system places a natural limit on the damage done by such mistakes—and can also help identify them.

In a fascinating 2006 paper, a trio of researchers at Stanford University concluded that *where* people vote can influence *how* they vote. Studying Arizona's 2000 general election, they found that people voting in schools were more likely to support an increase in the state sales tax devoted to education than those casting ballots in other types of polling place.[99] A similar thing may have happened in 2004, when several Iowa churches opposed to a riverboat-gambling initiative won the right to erect satellite voting stations in their houses of worship. (Iowa law allows people who collect one hundred signatures to demand an early satellite voting station at a location of their choice, as long as it meets basic accessibility requirements.) The initiative lost.[100] We do not know whether those early church-cast ballots were decisive, but it is likely that those advocating the placement of voting facilities in churches believed the setting would not only facilitate voting by their allies but also help sway undecided voters against gambling. Outside Houston, Texas, the sponsors of a special community-college bond election in May 2006 tried to put *all* the polling stations on community college campuses, so that students and employees could vote easily. The U.S. Department of Justice caught wind of that idea, and the election was postponed.[101]

Though it can be a bit unsettling to think that polling locations influence votes, the finding is consistent with what we know about the shortcuts and particular types of rationality that help some voters make decisions. Most important, what the Stanford study and the Houston community-college bond election illustrate is the need for polling-place variation. Bring on the small precincts, with their delis, laundromats, armories, and libraries along with the familiar schools, firehouses, town halls and churches. The problem to avoid is systematic polling-place bias, and the best way to accomplish that goal is with diverse polling places.

Local Administration and Voter Turnout

One of the most intriguing research projects to explore local voting practices involved election-day "poll parties" during various elections in 2005 and 2006. These events were staged by a most unlikely group of party hosts— political scientists—along with community-action groups in a dozen precincts around the country. Even in low-salience elections, these festivals increased turnout appreciably, and at a lower cost than other methods, such as direct-mail campaigns or phone banks. As Elizabeth Addonizio and her coauthors observe, festivals can "provide social approbation for and from those who perform their civic duty," and so it stands to reason that they help increase turnout.[102]

In fact, we have a good deal of historical and contemporary evidence that experiencing social approbation and communal connections not only increases voters' satisfaction with the electoral process but also helps induce us to vote in the first place. This is one of the strongest arguments for in-person voting in local settings, and it can claim support from recent empirical work. For example, an intriguing recent study directed by Alan Gerber, Donald Green, and Christopher Larimer sent voters mailings encouraging them to vote, then later checked to see which recipients voted in a subsequent election. Some voters merely received statements about the virtues of voting, but others got letters including information derived from public records about whether they and their neighbors had voted in recent elections. Exploiting social norms and "making public acts more public," Gerber and his colleagues found that substantially higher turnout resulted from these social-pressure letters. In fact, this was the only group of letter-receivers whose turnout rates increased appreciably.[103] Economist Patricia Funk's study of the Swiss response to the advent of postal voting reached a similar conclusion. Like the United States, Switzerland has a federal system, and the Swiss cantons adopted postal voting at different times. That enabled Funk to study how voting by mail affected turnout. Though it makes voting far easier, she discovered that the availability of postal voting *reduced* turnout, and she found a simple explanation: the Swiss had voted in part because they wanted the social benefits of being *seen* voting.[104]

In a marvelous descriptive passage, Richard Bensel writes that turnout in U.S. elections has declined "as participation in the social ritual of voting becomes increasingly irrelevant to the social standing of individuals": "There is no longer anyone at the polls to watch citizens vote; the crowds are gone, leaving behind only very small numbers of gentle-spirited people to mark down names as voters quietly, almost surreptitiously, trickle in to the polls."[105] Contemporary behavioral scholarship, meanwhile, offers a good deal of evidence that our political participation responds to the expectations of those around us.[106] We are more likely to vote if we know that people we respect in our communities are voting, and particularly if we *see* them voting. And while scholarship on this point is still developing, multiple recent studies conclude that Americans are more likely to vote when polling places are close to their residence or workplace.[107]

A second way decentralized voting can increase turnout is if local officials literally recruit voters. If the local government officials with whom citizens have the most contact—when we pay taxes, deal with property records, apply for permits, attend public functions, and so on—actively strive to increase the number of eligible residents registered to vote, the result may be increased participation, with the added benefit of a greater connection between citizens and the officials who run their elections. I began this chapter with anecdotal evidence that this type of recruitment does occur at least occasionally, with Shirley Green Knight at the Sawdust town picnic and Barbara Swann urging Monterey residents to register when they come in for "dog tags and dump stickers." But further empirical study is needed. We do not know how frequently such activity happens or how much of a difference it makes. Moreover, we should harness the power of friendly competition, further publicizing registration and turnout rates by locality, as well as "best practices" taken by local officials to induce people to vote—and to make the act of voting more celebratory.

Conclusion

"At the heart of American politics," writes James Morone, "lies a dread and a yearning." The dread is of centralized public power, particularly in the national government. Acting in part from that fear, we have constructed governing institutions that are "weak and fragmented, designed to prevent action more easily than to produce it." Paradoxically, Americans simultaneously yearn for a more effective democracy, one in which the people can function as "a single, united, political entity."[108] In this analysis Morone follows Tocqueville, who argued that the reason American government lacked a strong centralized hierarchy was that Americans exuded "dread of the consolidation of power in the hands of the Union."[109] Explaining the absence of national administration, Tocqueville wrote that "in America centralization is by no means popular, and there is no surer means of courting the majority than by inveighing against the encroachments of the central power."

That dread has survived. One author calls Tocqueville's remark about courting the majority by attacking centralization "a passage one might find in a memo from a political consultant today."[110] Indeed, former senator Alan Cranston illustrated just this sentiment in 2004 when he opposed a national identification card, calling it "a primary tool of totalitarian governments to restrict the freedom of their citizens."[111] Such distrust is surely one reason the

United States lacks a nationwide voter roll, election-administration bureaucracy, and strong standards governing the electoral process.

I have argued that on balance, decentralization and local variation enhance rather than diminish the instrumental and constitutive aspects of American popular sovereignty. I want to temper that conclusion, however, by acknowledging that the survival of local control over American national elections may be a manifestation of Morone's paradox. *If* inconsistent, obscure registration procedures prevent citizens from participating; *if* problems with ballot design, counting machines, and poll-worker support keep would-be voters from having their voices heard; and, most seriously, *if* such problems systematically skew or obstruct the will of the electorate, then local control limits the exercise of popular sovereignty and compromises the American people's ability to act together and govern ourselves well.

Ronald Hayduk writes in *Gatekeepers to the Franchise* that "election administration is not a neutral, ministerial process but a system that is highly susceptible to politicization and manipulation."[112] Together with vigilance against partisanship in election administration, local variation can be part of a good defense against such manipulation. But a certain level of error and a certain amount of discretion in election administration are both unavoidable. Where institutions exercise that discretion with as much public support as possible, and where mistakes are on a relatively small scale and are clearly understood, the legitimacy of elections will be strengthened.[113] In addition to fitting comfortably within Madisonian theory and federal structures, decentralization's redeeming features provide ample reason to keep many surviving elements of local control in place. Locally varying suffrage practices can improve citizens' sense of democratic efficacy, foster experimentation and innovation, obstruct corruption and systematic error, and increase turnout. But each of these points contains important empirical dimensions deserving further study.

Richard Pildes has written that democracy is like the "Banquo's ghost" of American constitutionalism, floating insistently over numerous principal issues but only rarely appearing at center stage itself.[114] The same is true of voting practices, which until very recently were only fleetingly integrated into analyses of American popular sovereignty. I have tried here to use the concept of popular sovereignty to better understand election administration. In closing, I would note that the arrow points in the other direction as well. To a degree that the literature on democratic self-rule has not adequately grasped, thinking about *how* we vote teaches us a great deal about the mediated, locally textured nature of American popular sovereignty.

5

Exclusion, Equality, and the Local Dimension of American Suffrage

> No democratic value is more important than a
> state's obligation to treat its citizens equally.
>> Steven F. Huefner, Daniel Tokaji,
>> and Edward B. Foley (2007)

> Unavoidable inequalities in treatment, even if intended
> in the sense of being known to follow ineluctably from
> a deliberate policy, do not violate equal protection.
>> *Griffin v. Roupas* (2004)

> When you get these minutes, you almost have
> to be a lawyer to understand them.
>> Louisiana parish elections official, explaining the
>> need to interpret court minutes in order to determine
>> whether or not a person is disenfranchised (2005)

A "Brave New World"?

Whereas the lasting images of the 2000 presidential contest were Palm Beach County's butterfly ballot and the faces of beleaguered recount officers peering deep into the dimples of chad, the 2004 election gave us the voters of Ohio. Some city voters gave up after inadequate numbers of voting machines forced them to stand in line for hours, while their peers in nearby suburban precincts had access to plenty of machines.[1] Only because George W. Bush carried Ohio by a margin of more than one hundred thousand votes were we spared "electoral meltdown" in a second straight presidential election.[2] This phenomenon recurred in 2008, with some localities in at least half a dozen states experiencing hours-long lines at the polls—but Barack Obama's edge exceeded that all-important "margin of litigation."

Americans now understand that the right to vote is constituted by local administrative practices, and evidence of discrimination and exclusion seems to be everywhere: malfeasance, misfeasance, ignorance, or inadequate machinery disadvantaging the blind, the disabled, non-English speakers, first-time voters, and others at every step of the registration and voting process. Even before the 2000 election dispute had concluded, some saw that the goal was not equal protection for voters but "equal protection for *votes*"—that is, for ballots themselves.[3] In *Bush v. Gore*, the Supreme Court did rule that the mechanics of Florida's presidential election had to meet the standards of equal protection, but the Court strove mightily to limit the precedential power of that holding, warning that the judgment was "limited to the present circumstances, for the problem of equal protection in election processes generally presents many complexities."[4] "Rehabilitationist" interpreters of *Bush v. Gore* hoped the decision might lead to a new level of equality and harmonization in voting practices, and they got a boost in 2006 when the Sixth Circuit Court of Appeals relied on *Bush v. Gore* in ruling that the use of deficient and error-prone voting machines in some Ohio counties may have violated the Equal Protection Clause.[5] (Ohio replaced the machines, and the case was eventually dismissed as moot.) The appeals court observed that while some authors consider such cases "simply variations of old challenges," others "have suggested that these types of voting rights challenges are taking us into a brave new world."[6] But generally, *Bush v. Gore* has proved a weak precedent, failing to "usher in a new era of searching equal protection review of electoral practices" in the federal courts.[7] Contemporary challenges are more likely to emphasize the Voting Rights Act, the National Voter Registration Act, the Help America Vote Act (HAVA), or various state laws.

Americans have periodically engaged in closely focused scrutiny of election administration since the nation's founding. But together with statutory and doctrinal change, the growth of advocacy organizations, and new communications technologies, the difficulties that have dogged recent elections have placed the mechanics of suffrage at center stage as never before, and equality is often the focus. Recall Justice Robert Jackson's concern that "small and local authority may feel less sense of responsibility to the Constitution."[8] Jackson was talking about freedom of expression, but his words are an apt summary of prevailing assumptions about local authority and fairness in election administration as well. Many Americans seem to have concluded that locally varying suffrage practices are a toxin to be expelled, a flaw that impedes progress toward national equality and inclusion even where officials do not act in bad faith. While localism in voting procedures may have a romantic appeal, "it works against the strong idea of equality," as law professor Akhil

Amar put it.[9] Because of locally patterned variation in technology, funding, competence, partisanship, and other variables, write Stephen Ansolabehere and Charles Stewart, "Americans' votes are not all counted the same."[10] Our locally administered suffrage, Lisa Disch concludes, "leaves the value of the vote to be determined by whatever tax dollars a given county can afford to invest in it."[11] Richard Niemi and Paul Herrnson write that varying ballot forms make voting difficult, particularly for "first-time voters, those not fluent in English, the elderly, the visually impaired, and those who simply have moved from one state (or even locality) to another."[12] Ronald Hayduk calls this phenomenon "administrative disenfranchisement of eligible voters."[13] City and county officials are doing excellent work in many areas, acknowledges a comprehensive analysis of election administration practices among the Great Lakes states, but "statewide equality should generally trump local autonomy."[14]

Even discrete election-administration questions press into essential concerns of American democracy. As Ansolabehere and Stewart write, the issue of differing voting machinery "goes to one of the core conflicts in the American polity—the conflict between the broad principles of political equality as it has been asserted by the national government and the practice of federalism and decentralized administration of government."[15] We have seen that from the start, the law and practice of suffrage in the United States have developed within this conflicted framework. And in examining the consequences of decentralized election administration for American popular sovereignty, I have argued that American self-rule derives an important part of its deeply mediated nature from our suffrage practices. In this chapter, I demonstrate that local election administration has always been an integral part of the American struggle with exclusion and inequality.

In some cases, local authority has clearly facilitated injustice, and the expansion of national power through congressional statutes and Supreme Court rulings has advanced the cause of equality and inclusion. But the relationship between local administration of elections and exclusion in American suffrage has been and remains complex, multidimensional, and multidirectional. Indeed, local variation and local administrative authority have also helped broaden the American franchise. I develop this argument in three parts, the first two historical and the third exploring contemporary questions.

The Post-Reconstruction White Backlash
and Jim Crow Voting Practices

At some points in U.S. history, local election administration has clearly ex-
acerbated exclusion and inequality. Indeed, for many Americans, the face of
localism in voting remains that of southern officials who implemented pro-
foundly racist policies in the long period between Reconstruction and the
Voting Rights Act. The literacy test in the post-Reconstruction South presents an archetypal use of local control for invidious exclusionary purposes.
As one early critic dryly put it, the "great difficulty" that a genuine, uniform
literacy test would have presented was "that it would also operate on more
than a million illiterate whites."[16] The solution was to rely on local officials
to allow whites, but not blacks, to pass the test. "I do not expect an impartial
administration of this clause," said a delegate to Virginia's 1902 state convention.[17] Sixty years later, the Supreme Court would say of Louisiana's "understanding" test that it "[left] the voting fate of a citizen to the passing whim or
impulse of an individual registrar."[18]

Copied from policies that the Know-Nothings used to disenfranchise immigrants in Massachusetts and Connecticut a generation earlier, literacy or
"understanding" tests were only part of a larger package of measures designed
to "eliminate the darkey as a political factor," as Carter Glass told fellow Virginians.[19] According to Rogers M. Smith, Southern lawmakers "frequently admitted, indeed boasted, that such measures as complex registration rules, literacy and property tests, poll taxes, white primaries, and grandfather clauses
were designed to produce an electorate confined to a white race that declared
itself supreme."[20] Commenting on the discriminatory use of registration rules
in 1929, Joseph Harris observed that "it is a matter of common knowledge
that the registration systems of the Southern states are designed to disfranchise the Negro. . . . The applicant for registration must prove his qualifications to vote 'to the satisfaction of the registration officer'—a provision which
vests such wide discretion in the registration officers that it permits them to
refuse arbitrarily to register Negro applicants."[21]

Southern white elites focused on voting practices and informal barriers,
constructing an intricate "maze," dependent on local administration, through
which any blacks bold enough to try to vote would have to pass.[22] As Morgan
Kousser writes, the southern states rarely employed any means that constituted an "absolute, unequivocal provision which [banned] a discrete category
of persons from the ballot box." Instead, laws focused on increasing the economic and social costs of voting and on implementing policies that "allowed
administrators to discriminate between voters with roughly the same legal

qualifications."[23] Opponents of black suffrage stood ready and willing to supplement such policies with extralegal violence.

Naturally, all this took place in the shadow of the Fifteenth Amendment, a guarantee that quickly proved hollow. The problem facing blacks for the next century would be "that local law and custom consigned them to a place outside the social boundaries defining membership in the local community."[24] One prewar Ohio law spelled out with unusual frankness how racial suffrage restrictions were made real. Ohio's statute required elections officers to contest the eligibility of anyone with a "visible admixture of African blood"; the challenged voter had to provide witnesses and answer questions, and could be barred from the polls at the discretion of the poll worker. This practice survived for a quarter century before state courts struck it down.[25]

For almost a century, both Congress and the federal courts either tacitly or openly approved of these exclusionary practices. The turn-of-the-century Supreme Court was deeply unwilling to involve itself closely in electoral practices, to sustain Congress's power to punish those who discriminated against would-be black voters, or to reject elite ideas regarding race and suffrage. Recall *United States v. Reese* (1876), in which the Court reviewed a federal indictment of a local official in Lexington, Kentucky, who denied a black man's attempts to register. Refusing to sustain the indictment, the Court advanced narrow interpretations of both the Fifteenth Amendment's substantive protections and congressional powers to enforce the amendment's provisions.[26] In 1898, the Court in *Williams v. Mississippi* upheld that state's literacy test, ruling that it did not violate the Fifteenth Amendment because it was not on its face racially discriminatory.[27] And in the 1903 case *Giles v. Harris*, the Court refused to help a black man who had been denied by his local voter-registration board in a blatant act of discrimination.[28]

For the next sixty years, localized exclusion would prove recalcitrant, stubbornly resistant to change. V. O. Key found that neither federal nor state laws had much bearing on what county officials across the South did when they ran elections in the 1940s, and the voluminous scholarship on the Voting Rights Act and its predecessors shows that it took decades of concerted action by Congress, the federal executive branch, civil-rights activists, and the voting-rights bar to dislodge many exclusionary practices. As Brian Landsberg demonstrates particularly clearly, local registrars resisted change even after their discriminatory actions were revealed by federal investigations: "The real civil disobedience came from the state and local officials."[29]

"To Elevate and Purify the Suffrage":
Progressive-Era Reforms

In the case of southern disenfranchisement of African Americans, we find ample support for the conventional understanding of the relationship between local administration of elections and voter disenfranchisement. Moving north and west, and examining state laws passed during the Progressive era, we encounter a more complex picture. A number of states passed registration laws and other requirements that were intended to be locally administered and, at a minimum, to make voting marginally more difficult—laws that had clear exclusionary effects, particularly on immigrants and members of lower socioeconomic classes. But in contrast with southern Jim Crow suffrage practices, discriminatory Progressive-era suffrage laws cannot be laid entirely at the feet of localism. With national elites turning against universal suffrage around the turn of the century, such voting laws would likely have been enacted no matter what level of government controlled elections at the time.

Today, there sometimes seems to be a kind of "Progressive bias" explaining why some Americans harbor a prejudice in favor of national standardization. Consider, for example, a recent commentary arguing that "the biggest threat to the integrity of our elections" is that "no one seems to be steering the ship. There is no central brain or team that has a handle on all aspects of the process."[30] This desire for a "central brain" is part of the "political piety" we have inherited from Progressive thinkers like Herbert Croly, who argued that democracy required "increasing nationalization of the American people in ideas, in institutions, and in spirit."[31] Other Progressives, such as Louis D. Brandeis and Woodrow Wilson, disagreed, particularly on economic matters, but in terms of voting, Croly's preference seems to have won out.[32] This is doubly ironic, for the suffrage legacy of the Progressives is one of neither nationalization nor greater inclusion.

Bucking a classic American preference for dispersed power, many Progressives sought centralization in various policy areas. But turn-of-the-century reforms, particularly new requirements that voters register, did not nationalize administrative authority—in fact, the opposite happened. Recall the 2002 report of the National Commission on Federal Election Reform, which concluded that compulsory registration effected "a new decentralization of power to determine the eligibility of voters, devolving from state governments down to the local and county governments that managed this process and maintained the rolls."[33] Meanwhile, Progressives' opposition to corruption and their belief that enlightened policies were those harmonized at the national or state level did not at all lead to a preference for more people to be involved in elections, notwithstanding the 1920 passage of the Nineteenth Amendment. Instead, Progressives and other "professional students of political science" "rallied to the idea of . . . educational tests and higher registration laws to elevate and purify the suffrage."[34] Such requirements spread well beyond the post-Reconstruction South, and "by the 1920s a dozen states . . . adopted literacy tests, all but three states tightened their provisions governing registration, and about half of America's counties required personal registration before voting."[35] Indeed, if we consider compulsory literacy and personal-registration rules to be the Progressives' key contribution to American voting, theirs is a legacy of locally enforced, exclusionary practices.

It is important to remember that the other major reform of this period with exclusionary effects—the secret, publicly produced Australian ballot— was essentially a centralizing change. The secret ballot often functioned as a de facto literacy test, though not always, since many ballots did include party symbols to help voters who could not read well. And some states allowed voters to use "pasters," essentially labels listing a party slate which a voter would affix to his ballot. However, in the same period, many states also implemented a new formal barrier, to be administered at the polls: de jure literacy tests, typically requiring voters to read and explain an excerpt from the state constitution or another official document. Twenty-one states put in place some form of literacy or understanding test between 1870 and 1924.[36]

Registration rules are particularly important for us here. Of the Progressive period's major reforms, only personal registration remains both on the books and controversial: literacy tests, poll taxes, and white primaries are gone, and secrecy is now democratic dogma. And although registration processes are subject to federal laws and states must now centralize registration lists, counties and municipalities remain deeply involved in registering voters, maintaining the rolls, and removing voters from the lists if necessary.

Prior to about 1880, most registration laws had mandated the creation of voter lists by town and county officials, but under new personal-registration rules, "it became the duty of individual voters to secure their own eligibility."[37] This was a national movement, employing local registration officials as its key agent. Particularly in the North, rural-dominated state legislatures sometimes imposed cumbersome registration requirements only on cities in order to suppress immigrant voting.[38] As late as 1927, eleven states in the Midwest, Plains, and West still had on the books registration laws applying only to urban areas. The most common justification for excusing rural areas from registration was that so many of the voters "are personally acquainted with one another," as the 1927 report by the National Municipal League put it. But as that same report acknowledged, "some of the worst cases of voting frauds appear occasionally in rural sections."[39] That it took decades for officials to reach this realization suggests that more than common sense and the desire to save money went into the decision to apply the procedure only to cities.

To be sure, late-nineteenth-century party politics were corrupt by any-one's definition. But Progressives also believed that big-city parties, with their working-class, immigrant members, were themselves "a corruption of the democracy envisioned by the founders."[40] Turn-of-the-century personal-registration procedures carried strong class biases, particularly since municipal offices were only open during business hours, and wage workers could ill afford to miss time on the clock. Meanwhile, Progressives were motivated not only by philosophy but also by partisanship. Urban immigrants and their "machines" did not fit the ideal of the well-informed, independent voter—and they were also likely to vote against Progressives.[41]

In the South, of course, black voters were targeted for exclusion; in the North, it was often laborers and new immigrants whom "the new registration boards hoped to bar from urban elections."[42] Another study concludes that registration rules "were enacted . . . in order to decrease voting, especially fraudulent voting, but also voting by transients, illiterates, blacks, immigrants, and poor whites."[43] Language like "hoped to bar" and "in order to" remains controversial, however. Were registration reforms primarily motivated by a genuine desire to fight fraud or a less-noble interest in shrinking democracy? Settling on a scientific metaphor, Alexander Keyssar writes that "widespread convictions" about the fallen state of American politics "were spawned by germs of fact, cultured in a medium of class and ethnic (or racial) prejudice and apprehension."[44]

If the purposes of personal-registration rules remain contested, their results seem clearer. The laws' impact varied with the ability of parties to register their members, but, according to Keyssar, "it can be said with certainty that registration laws reduced fraudulent voting and that they kept large numbers (probably millions) of eligible voters from the polls." One third or more of a national drop in turnout during this period was probably attributable to registration rules.[45] Reform "obstructed the actual ability of many people to vote," conclude Frances Fox Piven and Richard Cloward in *Why Americans Still Don't Vote*.[46] And some officials *celebrated* decreases in the size of the franchise, as when the Pittsburgh registration commission noted privately in 1907 that "the figures speak for themselves as to the good results obtained under the operation of the Personal Registration Act." The "good results" that the commission spoke of was the more than 50 percent decrease in the number of men registered to vote.[47]

Between about 1880 and 1925, state constitution writers and statute drafters in the South and North alike used local institutions to restrict the franchise. Along with the secret ballot and literacy tests, personal-registration rules made it difficult or even impossible for many American men who had previously been able to vote to do so. Elections had always been locally administered (with the brief exception of military Reconstruction in some places), and local men were the obvious choice to implement the new discriminatory rules.[48] Thus, local control clearly provided intellectual and historically grounded cover for deeply undemocratic exclusion. Without question, this is a mark against the local dimension of American suffrage, and localism's central role in this quintessentially exclusionary period should serve as a caution to Americans today.

At the same time, however, localized administration alone must not shoulder all of the blame. While the hyperfederalized American electoral system enabled and facilitated these important procedural contractions, neither that system nor its local administrators themselves caused it. Some responsibility falls on the judicial branch, for its cramped reading of the Reconstruction Amendments, and on Congress, for its relative inaction. State legislators and political parties obviously hold a share of the blame as well. But the fundamental culprit was a powerful national movement against universal suffrage. "Among élite thinkers, a retreat from the previous consensus in favor of manhood suffrage was among the most remarkable developments of the late nineteenth century," writes Eric Foner.[49] By the turn of the century, Morgan Kousser observes, the United States saw "a recrudescence of antidemocratic theorizing on the question of who was entitled to vote."[50] Michael Schudson concludes that "the concept of universal suffrage had lost hegemony."[51]

This antidemocratic "recrudescence" challenges the conventional Whiggish narrative of ever-increasing inclusion in American suffrage. Relatively few people had their right to vote legally, formally, and completely removed during this period. But a great many, in the North and South, saw a dramatic increase in the cost and difficulty of exercising that right. National and state-level actors hostile to political inclusion for racial, class-based, anti-immigrant, and partisan reasons consciously used localism for exclusionary and discriminatory purposes; no doubt many county clerks acted zealously in enforcing these restrictive codes. But the crucial variable was the powerful, carefully theorized, national movement away from universal suffrage. Local officials acted to restrict the franchise in ways that were discriminatory and unfair, along class, ethnic, and racial lines. But in doing so, they were not challenging the wishes of state or national elites. They were implementing a national ideology.

"Anything with the Appearance of a Man":
The Inclusive Tradition in American Suffrage

Across American history, local elections officials have participated in partisan fraud, racist exclusions, systematic discrimination against the poor and new immigrants, and money-grubbing corruption. A good deal of that behavior has been consistent with discriminatory elite ideas about voting among subordinate groups. That much is well understood. But there is another side to the story.

Local administration of U.S. elections has sometimes been a vector of inclusion in American voting, a pathway along which the franchise expanded. This tradition is as old as the country itself: despite property, citizenship, and residency requirements, Thomas Hutchinson wrote, "anything with the appearance of a man" was able to vote in Boston around 1772.[52] I show here that in at least three different ways, our hyperfederalized suffrage system has helped expand the polity. First, the history of the property test offers clear evidence that local practices were more inclusive than the law; that fact contributed directly to the restriction's demise. Second, local elections themselves seem to have played an important role in securing broader voting rights for women. In both of these examples, state and local experimentation helped to hasten the repeal of exclusionary rules. A third case illustrates a different phenomenon. Left to their own devices, states and localities throughout nineteenth-century America often allowed noncitizens who announced their intention to remain in the United States to vote in national elections.

Inclusionary suffrage practices are older than the country itself. Referring to recent elections in North Carolina, a speaker in Parliament in 1706 complained that "all sorts of people, even servants, Negroes, Aliens, Jews and Common sailors were admitted to vote."[53] English law stated unequivocally that aliens were not to vote, but differences between categories of subjects blurred in the New World, particularly at the polls.[54] Until 1647, the only requirement for political participation in a typical Massachusetts town had been church membership. A new law made men under twenty-four ineligible; subsequent acts imposed the first property test (1658) and raised the size of the minimum taxable estate required for a vote in town meetings (1670). But these laws usually grandfathered in all current voters and do not appear to have dropped actual participation much.[55] It became customary in most colonies, if not all, "to allow all adult males, when known to the community and to any degree respected or liked, to vote."[56]

Local officials were not always angels of inclusion and equality: decisions as to who was permitted to vote could be blatantly unfair, particularly when partisan passions were raised.[57] Thomas Paine agreed with Thomas Hutchinson's judgment that "anything with the appearance of a man" could vote in Boston before the Revolution, noting that as long as a man owned a few household utensils and a chest of tools, he would generally be willing to swear that he met the property qualification. And John Adams wrote in 1776 that Massachusetts officials had never been "rigid" in enforcing suffrage requirements.[58]

Independence did not change much. Analyzing a fierce dispute over whether to include a property test in the 1780 Massachusetts constitution, Chilton Williamson found that such a requirement might not have had any practical impact: "A strong possibility exists that the constitution did not change a situation in which adult male taxpayers were voting in both town and colony elections with the support of opinion at large."[59] New Jersey's 1776 constitution established a property test, but the standard soon came in for criticism when it became clear that the rule was not keeping many men from voting. The constitution permitted those "worth fifty pounds proclamation money" to vote, and apparently any number of men were willing to swear that they were in fact "worth" that amount. As one challenged voter said puckishly, he "valued himself a great deal more than that." Clearly, decisions as to the qualifications of voters were being made at the local level; one critic said that in his own county he knew of two hundred laborers who voted despite not paying taxes.[60] In South Carolina, numerous unqualified citizens were allowed to vote, "rather from want of information of the Constitution and Existing Law of the State, than from audacity, or intentionally violating the same," as one author put it in 1796.[61] Into the nineteenth century, officials in eastern Virginia worked to break "the pre-Revolutionary habit of ignoring the suffrage laws."[62]

This behavior became general. To be sure, ideological change was key to the gradual abolition of property tests in the early nineteenth century, particularly the growing sense that "it was no longer possible to equate the accumulation of property with wisdom and prudence," as John Dinan puts it.[63] But an equally important reason for the property's demise was the fact that local officials were not enforcing the tests. Pennsylvania abolished the freehold qualification in 1788 partly because it was so spottily enforced.[64] In New York, proponents of expanded suffrage in 1820 argued that to extend the franchise "would leave us just where we are now; since every man who can be trusted with a deed, is made a freeholder long enough to vote in elections." Meanwhile, evidence showed that in some towns "all adult male residents on tax lists were being permitted to vote."[65] At the Massachusetts constitutional convention of 1820–1821, debate clearly indicated that uneven local enforcement of the property test erred on the side of inclusion. The property test was "in this town, for a long time, a dead letter," one delegate noted.[66] Age and residence qualifications, another observed, "were commonly allowed upon the assertion of the voter himself."[67] (In nineteenth-century urban voting, age and residency requirements were generally "moot issues" simply because there were few records kept, and people had no consistent forms of identification.[68]) Even before the new constitution abolished the property test in favor of a taxpayer qualification, Massachusetts politics displayed "not a theory but a condition bordering on universal suffrage."[69] Inclusionary local practices acted as a kind of solvent, working hand in hand with changing ideological views to undercut the property qualification.

Of course, nineteenth-century "universal suffrage" only went so far: the female half of the adult population would be excluded in some states for another century. For some, the way Americans voted complemented more philosophical reasons for keeping women away from the polls: they were "no place for a woman."[70] As Richard Henry Lee argued, women ought not "press into those tumultuous assemblages of men where the business of choosing representatives is conducted."[71] Thomas Jefferson took the idea of women "pressing into" those assemblages further with this startling statement: "Were our state a pure democracy there would still be excluded from our deliberations women, who, to prevent deprivation of morals and ambiguity of issues, should not mix promiscuously in gatherings of men."[72] The polling places and halls of government Jefferson had in mind must have been tumultuous indeed.

The New Jersey constitution of 1776 referred to voters only as "inhabitants," rather than "men." Some local officials allowed women owning sufficient property to vote—but only widows and spinsters, since by law married women owned nothing. But other sources say that particularly after 1790, New Jersey women began voting in good numbers, and married women did so alongside single women. More surprising still, "negresses" apparently voted in several elections in New Jersey around the turn of the century.[73] All this apparently led to conflict between rural areas and towns, since the country people thought it was easier for partisans to drum up the female vote in the cities.[74]

The ideologies of the fight for women's suffrage have been well analyzed.[75] But women voted in some elections long before 1920, and in fact women's participation in local elections probably helped them win suffrage nationally. The Kentucky Assembly granted property-owning women the vote in school board elections in 1838, and in Kansas, women could vote in school board elections as early as 1865. Minnesota and Michigan allowed women such partial suffrage in 1875, and by 1890, thirteen other territories and states had done so.[76] In the late nineteenth century, state courts allowed legislatures to deviate from constitutional suffrage limitations in special elections, and state and local governments in many states allowed women to vote.[77] A significant number of counties, cities, and towns adopted partial suffrage, permitting women to vote in "municipal elections, on liquor licensing matters, or for local school boards and on issues affecting education." All told, prior to the enactment of the Nineteenth Amendment, twenty-six states allowed women to vote in school elections, thirteen allowed them to vote in presidential elections, and two allowed them to vote in primary elections. Women had full suffrage in fifteen states.[78] This development was uniquely American, "made possible by the complex architecture of voting laws."[79]

Partial-suffrage policies did not necessarily reflect deeply egalitarian ideas about gender: it was primarily women's property that won them such representation, not their status as citizens.[80] "Our speakers liked to enumerate these scraps of suffrage as signs of progress," recalled one suffragette later, but they were in fact sometimes a potential liability, since men could point to low female turnout in a school election as a sign that women did not actually want the vote.[81] The immediate effects of local voting rights were not always positive: a Kansas full-suffrage referendum failed in 1894 when women were unable to organize a nonpartisan campaign—because they were already engaged as partisans in municipal politics.[82] And scholarship is divided over the progressive impact of partial suffrage. Qualitative studies of three western states concluded that partial suffrage did help women achieve full voting rights: "As the public witnessed women voting in minor elections locally . . . with competence and good results, views towards women's political participation liberalized and acceptance of suffrage rights grew."[83] But a recent empirical analysis concludes that states granting women municipal voting rights were not more likely than others to subsequently enact full suffrage.[84]

Winning partial suffrage was a key strategic goal of some reformers, however, who were convinced it was a positive step. In the late nineteenth century, the "steady trickle of states and towns" granting school and municipal suffrage (and sometimes the broader franchise) "kept suffragists' hopes alive," and twentieth-century reformers such as Carrie Chapman Catt urged the strategic pursuit of municipal suffrage.[85] Local voting rights brought political leverage by increasing the costs to politicians and parties of opposing expanded suffrage. Local electoral participation also undercut antiegalitarian arguments against women's suffrage, which had insisted that women were entirely unfit for all political activity. Moreover, women's experience of voting in local elections, together with their expanding participation in various social-reform interest groups, must have helped support movements toward broadening state and national suffrage laws early in the twentieth century.

In a few areas, voting women had shuttered the saloons, but generally partial suffrage had not led to major challenges to the economic or social order. In a study of Portland, Oregon, published in 1919 called "How Women Vote" (and still discussed by social-science methodologists today), William Ogburn and Inez Goltra concluded that women appeared to be voting in a slightly conservative fashion, particularly on economic issues.[86] Big-city machines largely stopped opposing women's suffrage "after observing and reasoning that enfranchised women had not shown a habit of voting together to oppose existing political organizations."[87] Leading suffrage organizations such as the Women's Christian Temperance Union and the National American Woman Suffrage Association stressed that female voters had not wrecked the schools, liquor stores, or political parties, emphasizing "the absence of turmoil in partial suffrage jurisdictions" in their appeals for full voting rights, and noting that by 1902 twenty-six states "had adopted some kind of school suffrage without revolution."[88]

The case of noncitizens represents a third, though weaker, example of the inclusive potential of state and local variation. Here, our hyperfederalized franchise enabled states and localities to include an "outsider" group in the formal polity for a time, though eventually noncitizens would lose the right to vote. As we have seen, initially property ownership, not citizenship status, determined eligibility to vote among men in the United States; only slowly did noncitizens lose voting rights.[89] Most states permitted aliens to vote deep into the nineteenth century, particularly in the West—at least twenty-two did so in 1875. As a federal court summarized what it called Minnesota's "wise policy" in 1876, the state "invited an industrious and useful population from abroad to occupy her vacant territory, and, as an inducement, has said, 'You need not wait until you are naturalized and become citizens to exercise the elective franchise. . . .' "[90] Courts consistently denied that state laws letting noncitizens vote usurped federal power.[91] States began to withdraw voting rights from aliens in the latter half of the century, but it was not until 1926 that no states permitted aliens to vote.[92] The survival of alien voting in many states for a full century demonstrates at least a tacit confidence in the ability of local officials to control the suffrage.

As federal courts wrestled with citizenship puzzles prior to the Civil War, voting practices took on a fascinating, circular connection to citizenship law. Courts struggled to decide how a person could show their *animo manendi*— their "intent to remain." Residence alone was not enough. It appears that *exercising* the rights of citizenship—particularly the right to vote—was one way of effectively *securing* one's citizenship, by evincing that intent to remain. As Supreme Court Justice John McLean wrote, "Citizenship may depend upon the intention of the individual," and that intention was best revealed by actions: "An exercise of the right of suffrage is conclusive on the subject; but acquiring a right of suffrage, accompanied by acts which show a permanent location, unexplained, may be sufficient."[93] What may be most intriguing about aliens voting is that they had not been recognized as full citizens— formally defined as members of the American polity—by the national state. The U.S. Supreme Court has famously described citizenship as the "right to have rights."[94] But the history of alien voting in the United States shows that some Americans had the "right to vote" before they had the "right to have rights." They exercised one of the central political powers of members of the republic—by passing through suffrage portals controlled by local officials.

Voting rights for noncitizens remain a live topic today, with localities leading the way: noncitizens may vote in local elections in several municipalities, and many others have seriously considered extending the franchise to resident noncitizens.[95] But in the current anti-immigrant political climate, it is hard to imagine any such statewide legislative or constitutional change, particularly with state and national governments moving toward requiring voters to present proof of citizenship.

Localism and Contemporary Suffrage Practices

Bush v. Gore touched the issue of varying voting practices, but it stopped far short of resolving it, and many contemporary problems—such as those concerning registration and "purging" procedures, voting technology, polling-place location and accessibility, and voter "caging"—unite questions of equality and election administration. Behavioral election-administration literature has flowered in the past several years, examining various aspects of what one study of provisional ballots calls "the frictional interplay" of jurisdictions, precincts, and polling places.[96] This research demonstrates the complexity of the relationship between a diverse, locally run electoral system and equality. For example, Stephen Knack and Martha Kropf have found "remarkably little support for the view that resource constraints cause poorer counties with large minority populations to retain antiquated or inferior voting equipment."[97] Judge Richard Posner is among those who have argued that electoral democracy would be better served by *more* localism, at least when it comes to tallying votes: Posner has urged that ballots be "counted at the precinct level to enable as many spoiled ballots as possible to be revoted."[98] Several studies have concluded that precincts containing more African Americans and poor voters have more voided ballots—but while neither technology, education, language proficiency, voter experience, nor deliberate nonvoting seems to fully explain that discrepancy, technology seems to be the leading culprit.[99] Similarly, Michael Tomz and Robert Van Houweling examined precinct-level data from two states and found that while African Americans do appear to cast more voided ballots than whites, changing voting technology goes "a long way toward minimizing the racial difference in voided ballots."[100]

This section of the chapter explores the relationship between local suffrage authority and equality by examining two controversial policies: laws requiring voters to present identification at the polls, and laws barring people with criminal convictions from voting. The first is mostly procedural, the latter formal and fundamental. ID laws are of relatively recent vintage, while criminal disenfranchisement rules often date to the nineteenth century. Yet in the blended-authority American electoral "ecosystem," laws enacted by federal and state legislatures are ultimately made real by the work of local officials. The evidence is somewhat preliminary, but we can reach two tentative conclusions. First, local administration appears to aggravate the restrictive tendencies of each of these policies, contributing to the exclusion of eligible voters from the polls. Second, however, as proof of the administrative difficulties involved becomes clear, the fact of local variation may provide crucial support for principled arguments questioning the wisdom of such policies, particularly criminal disenfranchisement laws. That has occurred before in American suffrage history, and it may happen again.

Until a few years ago, most states instructed polling-place workers either to take voters' word regarding their identity or to make voters sign a form, match a signature, or present some form of ID not necessarily including a photo, such as a utility bill. Such laws have been giving way to tougher, more centralized requirements; in particular, voters are now often required to provide a photo ID. In 2002, Congress wrote into HAVA a requirement that a narrow category of voters provide some form of ID at the polls. The Commission on Federal Election Reform (also known as the Carter-Baker Commission) then supported photo-ID requirements in a widely publicized 2005 report. More than a dozen states have taken these cues and put in place new requirements; the most restrictive such laws require government-issued photo ID, though voters everywhere are able to cast some sort of provisional ballot if they lack ID.[101] Indiana was one of seven states requiring government-issued photo ID, and the Supreme Court upheld that statute in its divided 2008 decision in *Crawford et al. v. Marion County Election Board et al.*[102] *Crawford* is widely expected to encourage enactment of more such laws.[103]

The spread of photo-ID laws has been a somewhat curious development. While certainly there is concern about election integrity across the country (and across the legislative aisles), requiring voters to present ID at the polls prevents only a narrow type of problem—voter-impersonation fraud—that is by all accounts very rare in the United States. A growing body of literature shows that requiring voters to present photo ID will prevent an extremely small amount of fraud, if any, while imposing a burden on the millions of current and potential voters who do not have drivers' licenses, particularly low-income and elderly people. Much has been made of the fact that Indiana was unable to show that it had ever prosecuted a person for the type of voter-impersonation fraud its new requirement aimed to prevent. As critics have pointed out (and as is discussed in Chapter 4), such policies essentially restrict the exercise of a fundamental constitutional right because the public *fears* that fraud is occurring—regardless of whether such fear is well-founded or such ID requirements improve public esteem for electoral institutions. (In fact, Stephen Ansolabehere and Nathaniel Persily demonstrate in a 2008 article that neither of the two fundamental premises behind such laws is accurate. First, those who suspect that fraud is widespread are not, in fact, less likely to vote; second, those who have been asked to show ID at the polls are no less likely to perceive fraud in the electoral system.)[104] Despite broad public support for ID requirements, in practice this controversy is deeply partisan, as Republican-dominated legislatures have passed every recent such law.[105]

Naturally, responsibility for implementation of these new state and federal laws lies in the hands of the local officials and volunteers who run the polls. There is now a growing body of evidence, however preliminary and anecdotal, that implementation of these laws varies considerably at the local level, and that mistakes by polling-place staff may exacerbate their exclusionary effects. The most eye-catching example involved a dozen Roman Catholic nuns who were turned away from an Indiana polling place—by a fellow sister, no less, and in the very shadow of the University of Notre Dame, a Catholic university—in the state's May 2008 primary election. Other anecdotes from Indiana concerned a newlywed whose driver's license now featured a different name than that in her voter-registration file, and a student who offered her University of Notre Dame ID but was turned away. Apparently none of these would-be voters were offered the option of casting a provisional ballot and supplying an ID later.[106] This type of poll-worker error appears to be common. In Florida's 2004 primary election, poll workers in more than one county turned away would-be voters by telling them they needed to have photo ID—never informing them that the law allowed them the option of signing an affidavit swearing to their identities. The same thing happened in a previous election in South Dakota, where Native Americans without ID were turned away without being told about the affidavit option.[107] And in local elections held in November 2007 after Michigan enacted a photo-ID requirement, the NAACP (National Association for the Advancement of Colored People) alleged widespread poll-worker confusion and error, including the rejection of forms of ID that should have been acceptable and failure to notify voters of the opportunity to sign a sworn affidavit.[108]

As of the 2006 election, only Indiana and Florida required that voters present photo ID. Yet a study of that election found that nationwide, *half* of survey respondents said they had to present photo ID to vote. One scholar wrote that the study showed a "stunning lack of uniformity" in the use of such requirements, noting that results varied within states as well as across regions. African Americans and Hispanics reported being asked for ID somewhat more often than whites, even controlling for differences in region, age, party, and income.[109] A study of 2004 voting in Cuyahoga County, Ohio, found that while 31 percent of blacks were asked for ID, just 18 percent of others were, and a 2006 lawsuit alleged numerous inconsistencies in how Ohio's ID law was applied.[110] One culprit in all of this variation appears to be HAVA: the law requires only a very small subset of people—first-time voters registering by mail after January 1, 2003—to provide ID, but that distinction seems poorly understood by poll workers. In a major study of voting in nine states and the District of Columbia in 2006, the Asian American Legal Defense and Education Fund found that Asian Americans were often required to provide ID, sometimes while neighboring voters were not—despite the fact that the vast majority of those Asian American voters had registered years earlier and voted many times before.[111]

The number of people actually prevented from voting because they lack government-issued photo ID is likely to be relatively small, and we do not know whether, or how much, requiring photo ID depresses turnout.[112] At the least, it is probably safe to assume that such requirements will make some number of people who currently do not vote still less likely to join the American civic ritual. Indeed, some prominent observers, such as *New York Times* editorialist Adam Cohen, have concluded that new ID laws have in fact been enacted "not to verify voters' identities, but to stop certain groups from voting." Cohen refers to these laws as merely the latest installments in our "hidden history of disenfranchisement."[113]

Acting apparently out of confusion wrought by complex and varying new laws rather than animus, local elections staff seem to be exacerbating the exclusionary tendencies of new ID laws. Yet these are ultimately *centralizing* reforms: the source of this new burden on Americans has been not local authority but Congress (with the 2002 HAVA ID requirement) and the many state governments that have enacted these recent rules. Moreover, to some degree, the apparent confusion of some local officials probably reflects deeper inconsistencies in voter-identification laws. For example, absentee ballots are obviously far more vulnerable to fraud than those cast in person, yet while the number of people using such ballots has skyrocketed, few states have made serious efforts to combat absentee-ballot fraud.

Ongoing state experiments with voter ID—and growing evidence of the administrative difficulties these laws entail—may eventually help stem their disenfranchising effects in a couple of ways. First, other states may shy away once they see the difficulty of enforcing ID laws fairly. Indeed, when Missouri's legislature killed a photo-ID bill in May 2008, opponents pointed to the Indiana experience as a big reason why. "Once the nun thing was out there," as a lobbyist for the American Association of Retired Persons put it, the public became more sympathetic toward those who might be affected by the new laws, and the bill was stopped.[114] Second, if locally varying implementation of ID laws helps catalyze governmental and reform-group outreach, more infrequent voters and nonvoters could be brought into the process.[115]

Criminal Disenfranchisement: The American Crazy-Quilt

Little discussed outside a small group of litigators, scholars, and advocates just a decade ago, criminal disenfranchisement laws (or felony disenfranchisement, since felony conviction is the most common trigger of disqualification from voting) are now under virtually constant scrutiny. Recent years have seen several books, scores of law-review articles, litigation focusing on state and federal voting-rights laws, and statutory change in more than a dozen states across the country. Much has been written about the philosophical, historical, punitive, partisan, and racial aspects of this policy.[116] Yet as scholars, advocates, and lawmakers are increasingly realizing, this most fundamental type of suffrage law—one that manifests society's ideas about crime and the right to vote—has a crucial local dimension, since enforcement rests with the county, city, and town officials who register voters and oversee election-day voting.[117] In fact, until the advent of statewide voter rolls under HAVA in 2002, local officials in most states had to carry out these policies almost unassisted, working without statewide voter databases or a centralized notification process. As we have seen, local autonomy and authority have long been essential to many other aspects of American voting and election administration, such as registration, voting technology, and ballot-counting standards. But disenfranchisement is uniquely important and deserves our attention here because it concerns the formal, fundamental eligibility to vote.

In 1996, the U.S. Department of Justice described American laws barring people convicted of crime from voting as "a national crazy-quilt of disqualifications and restoration procedures."[118] The department had state law in mind. But in fact, the pieces of that metaphorical crazy-quilt are not just states, but the counties, cities, towns, and parishes within them. HAVA mandates that states coordinate their new computerized voter rolls "with State agency records on felony status."[119] This means that enforcement of criminal-disenfranchisement policy is changing in virtually every state, with state elections and corrections officials now sharing and centralizing eligibility information. Yet even with HAVA implementation well under way, in many parts of the United States the practice of voter disqualification and restoration varies by locality and rests ultimately on the competence and knowledge of local officials.

There are two main reasons why the voting rights of people convicted of crime depend so closely on the work of local elections officials. First, some states' disenfranchisement laws are intrinsically complex. Many states fail to draw sharp lines between eligible and ineligible people, lack clear procedures for suspending voters from the rolls, and have confusing rights-restoration procedures.[120] All this leaves a good deal of work (and practical voter-eligibility decisions) in the hands of local registrars. Second, most disenfranchised people are not in prison: nationwide, about three-quarters of the disenfranchised are on probation or parole, or have completed their sentences entirely (about one-third of the disenfranchised).[121] Therefore, even as disqualification procedures become centralized (with the implementation of statewide databases), restoration policy remains complicated and often locally administered. Many states multiply the complexity with a documentary requirement for restoration, leaving elections officials partly dependent on members of other state bureaucracies, including corrections, the judiciary, and sometimes the state police. As the *New York Times* editorialized in 2006, "The process for restoring voting rights for people who have been convicted of crimes can be so Byzantine that officials don't know who is eligible."[122] After a series of interviews with state and local officials in Washington State—and with many people who were accused of voting illegally in the state's extremely close 2004 gubernatorial election—the *Seattle Times* observed that the system designed to restore voting rights to those eligible while preventing illegal votes is "so bewildering that almost nobody negotiates it well." One official told the newspaper, "You need a degree in government to figure it out."[123] This problem is not unique to Washington.

Only recently have scholars and reform advocates begun to attend to the crucial local dimension of disenfranchisement, despite some prominent hints as to its importance. In *Richardson v. Ramirez* (1974), the U.S. Supreme Court quoted a California report showing that "a person convicted of almost any given felony would find that he is eligible to vote in some California counties and ineligible to vote in others."[124] A decade later, in *Hunter v. Underwood* (1985), the Court observed that Alabama boards of registrars often had to sift through case law to decide for themselves whether an infraction revealed disenfranchisable "moral turpitude."[125] While conscientious, hardworking, and well-intentioned, local officials often lack the information and resources even to understand disqualification and restoration law, let alone to implement those laws fully and fairly. Local staff err in administering criminal disenfranchisement law, and they often err in an exclusionary direction, helping foster confusion among the public and the ex-inmate population about who is and is not eligible to vote. A *Wall Street Journal* headline in 2008 referred to the "haze" surrounding the process of getting one's right to vote restored, and historian Morgan Kousser calls the obscurities and difficulties of some state restoration procedures "the bureaucracy of disfranchisement."[126] Surveys and studies conducted in at least seven states by advocacy groups and journalists since the election of 2000 have all revealed significant gaps in local officials' ability to implement state disenfranchisement and restoration policies, usually making it harder for former offenders to vote and sometimes clearly breaking state laws.[127] These problems are particularly acute in states that bar people who have been convicted of crime but who are not incarcerated from voting.

These conclusions found ample confirmation in a series of more than one hundred interviews conducted by the author with county elections officials in ten states, selected for the diversity of their disenfranchisement policies as well as their political culture. The interviews were supplemented by telephone interviews and surveys completed by dozens of state elections offices.[128] Even years after the Florida debacle of 2000 brought disenfranchisement to national prominence and prompted the enactment of HAVA, local registrars in states across the country differed in their knowledge of basic eligibility law; in how they were notified of criminal convictions; what process they used to suspend, cancel, or purge voters from the rolls; whether particular documents were required to restore a voter to eligibility; and whether they have any information at all about the criminal background of new arrivals to the state. "With 159 counties, I'm sure there's not as much uniformity as I'd like to believe," said one Georgia county official, when asked if all counties followed the same disqualification and restoration procedures.[129] That proved to be the case in states across the country.

Interviews began with a straightforward question about which people convicted of crime were ineligible to vote under state law, usually followed by a query about whether the county official would register an individual who stated that he or she was on probation or parole. On these initial questions, more than one third of local officials either described their state's fundamental eligibility law incorrectly or stated that they did not know a central aspect of that law. (That does not include the many who later erred in describing specific disqualification or restoration procedures.) Half of those who either did not know state law or described it incorrectly erred in an exclusionary direction—incorrectly stating, for example, that probationers may not vote when in fact only incarcerated people are excluded, or wrongly declaring that only an official pardon restores eligibility when in fact a routine corrections procedure will do. Just five erred in an inclusionary direction, wrongly saying that some people legally barred from voting may participate.[130]

This official confusion and uneven enforcement is partly traceable to deep ambiguities within disenfranchisement law itself. In an utterly atheoretical decision that shed no light on disenfranchisement's purpose or efficacy, the U.S. Supreme Court ruled in 1974 that an obscure passage in section 2 of the Fourteenth Amendment allows states to disenfranchise anyone convicted of crime.[131] State laws vary widely. In two states, Maine and Vermont, felons retain the right to vote even while incarcerated, and about one-fifth of the states disqualify only those currently serving time in prison. In most states, people in prison, as well as those sentenced to probation and those on parole following release from prison, cannot vote—but everyone who has completed their sentence may vote. And in nine states, at least some people are disqualified from voting even after all aspects of their sentences have been discharged—some for waiting periods of a few years, others indefinitely.[132]

Yet these formal lines only begin to describe the complexity of U.S. law. First, despite the commonly used term *felony disenfranchisement*, at least five states disqualify people convicted of misdemeanors and confined in jail, and that is almost certainly the de facto policy in other jurisdictions as well.[133] Meanwhile, several states employ a less clear cutoff point than felony conviction. For example, Georgia disqualifies people convicted of crimes involving "moral turpitude." Of ten county officials interviewed, only one knew that "moral turpitude" is today treated as effectively synonymous with "felony." (Some officials suggested the interviewer contact the courts or the state law library.) A 1993 Georgia case, *Jarrard v. Clayton County Board of Registrars*, suggested that the decision as to whether an offense revealed enough "turpitude" to warrant the loss of voting rights in Georgia (in this case, repeated violation of drunk driving laws) was sometimes formally made at the county level.[134] A 2007 Maryland statute made felony conviction, rather than commission of an "infamous crime," the threshold for disqualification. (The same statute did away with post-sentence disenfranchisement in Maryland, culminating a decade-long reform process.) Previously, the state attorney general reviewed criminal codes and determined which offenses were "infamous." The 2006 list included some misdemeanors, such as "misrepresentation of tobacco leaf weight," "unlawful operation of vending machines," and "racing horse under false name."[135] Before state law changed in 2008, Oregon's disenfranchisement laws challenged the assumption that one is disenfranchised for committing a felony, for being convicted of a felony, or even for being incarcerated for a felony. Oregon disenfranchised only those felons under Department of Corrections (DOC) supervision. Some of those convicted of a felony in Oregon and sentenced to less than a year's custody serve time in the county jails. Because these felons did not "enter DOC custody," explained an official at the Oregon secretary of state's office in a memo, they did not "lose their voting privileges."

One Louisiana parish official explained a "stickler" in the disenfranchisement law then in effect. Parish officials would receive records from various courts, and the local registrars would then purge people from the rolls. But Louisiana's constitution suspends the voting rights only of a person who "is under an order of imprisonment for conviction of a felony."[136] As the parish official explained, "We get the court minutes, and you have to read through them carefully. Sometimes, someone may be convicted of a felony, but the judge says 'imposition of sentence suspended.' You would think he'd be disqualified, but he's not—when you get these minutes, you almost have to be a lawyer to understand them." In June 2008, Louisiana Governor Bobby Jindal signed into law two bills changing disenfranchisement in Louisiana. One required correctional officials to notify elections staff of *every* conviction, with the purpose of removing from the rolls even those whose sentences may have been suspended. Another required correctional officials to notify those completing their sentences of how to register and be reinstated to the voter rolls.[137]

Similar uncertainties dog states with more extensive disqualifications. Tennessee law features several different policies, covering different time periods extending back to 1973.[138] During one interval, someone convicted of a felony in Tennessee suffered no disenfranchisement at all, while a few years later, the same conviction could bring lifetime disqualification. Thus, the process for restoring voting rights varies depending on the year of conviction, sometimes requiring the signature of a court clerk or probation officer. Local staffers described this variation differently, and some were clearly much more practiced in navigating it than others: one registrar had gone so far as to scan an important restoration document into her own computer so that she could help applicants fill it out.[139] Tennessee streamlined restoration procedures for most former felons by statute in 2006, but the state still permananently disqualifies those convicted of murder, rape, treason, or voter fraud. Both Alabama and Mississippi, meanwhile, contain simultaneously the nation's most restrictive and most inclusionary disenfranchisement laws. Alabama disenfranchises some offenders indefinitely, but a 2003 statute enables most offenders to seek restoration as soon as their sentence is over, and some can vote even while they are incarcerated. Not surprisingly, the state has had serious problems administering the policy in recent years.[140] In 2006, a judge briefly suspended all disenfranchisement in the state, ruling that the line determining which offenses revealed "moral turpitude" was too unclear. The law was reinstated on appeal, and the attorney general issued new official opinions. It was decided that drug offenders and those convicted of drunken driving, among other offenses, could vote even while in prison, but for other crimes, determination would remain case by case.[141] In 2008, the secretary of state explained that county elections officials routinely call asking whether those convicted of crimes not on the state's rough list can vote. "They're definitely allowed to vote, and that is the advice we give," said a legal advisor.[142] Remarkably, Alabama state law explicitly empowers registrars to act as "judicial officers" when deciding who may register to vote, stating that they "shall act judicially in all matters pertaining to the registration of applicants." Those denied by a county registrar may appeal in an Alabama probate court.[143]

Mississippi is renowned for the harshness of its postincarceration disenfranchisement law, but its policies actually contain a similar contrast. Mississippi's constitution specifically lists the offenses that bring about disenfranchisement, and people disenfranchised for committing those offenses may regain the right to vote after their sentence is completed only if their state legislator authors a bill specifically re-enfranchising that individual, and that bill is approved by both houses of the legislature and signed into law by the governor. Only about a dozen such bills pass each year.[144]

Drug infractions do *not* bring about disenfranchisement, however, and in 2008, the secretary of state estimated that less than a quarter of the state's inmates were actually prohibited from voting.[145] But the state constitution's neat list of ten infractions belies the confusion that prevails over which offenses bring about disenfranchisement. The attorney general is engaged in an ongoing process of deciding which offenses are disenfranchisable, responding to questions from state and local elections officials as well as court rulings. For example, the Mississippi Constitution disenfranchises those guilty of "theft," but there is no crime called "theft" in Mississippi, so in 1998 the Fifth Circuit Court of Appeals had to decide whether armed robbery is equivalent to theft—and therefore a disqualifying offense.[146] More recently, local and state elections officials queried the attorney general about whether the offenses of sexual battery, statutory rape, and carjacking are sufficiently similar to crimes listed in the Constitution that they should be disenfranchised. (He ruled that they were.) The state's online voter-registration form now lists two dozen disqualifying crimes, but new questions constantly arise.[147] As one county circuit clerk explained in 2008, his office gets absentee-ballot requests from inmates, and before responding, he must ascertain whether the offense of which the person was convicted is on the constitution's list of disqualifying crimes.[148]

One important problem would survive even full HAVA implementation: the question of whether people with criminal convictions gain or lose the right to vote by moving their domicile across state lines. We have no national data estimating how many formerly incarcerated people move into a new state each year, but the U.S. Census estimates that about twenty-two million Americans moved across state lines between 1995 and 2000.[149] About 7 percent of Americans have a felony conviction. If they were proportionally represented among interstate migrants, more than a million moved across state lines during that period, and many states likely received tens of thousands of them.

No state investigates the criminal backgrounds of new residents nationwide, though a few interviewees offered stories of occasional notifications from other states. And while some county registrars showed familiarity with neighboring states' disqualification rules in interviews, others openly acknowledged that they did not know other states' laws. In Delaware, some offenders must wait five years to be restored to the rolls, and others are disqualified indefinitely. When asked about a hypothetical person moving into Delaware who had finished a felony sentence but had been allowed to vote in their previous state while on probation, one Delaware official said, "You mean there are states that don't have waiting periods after the sentence before you can vote?" Asked a similar question, a Maryland staffer said, "I think disqualification for 'Infamous Crimes' is federal law, actually." (There is no federal law.) When asked whether a more robust statewide database would help, one county registrar in a waiting-period state said, "That might be helpful, but we'd need a file for the whole United States." One Louisiana parish registrar summed up the consensus about new arrivals: "There's no way for us to know, until there's a national database. And waiting for that is not something I'm going to lose any sleep over."

In every state, local officials were divided over whether it would be legal to register new residents who acknowledged old convictions. In interviews, some officials believed that the voting law from the state of conviction dominated, while others applied the laws of the new state of residence. It is important to emphasize that definitive answers to questions regarding new arrivals are often simply not available, either to the new arrivals themselves or the local officials receiving their registration forms, because U.S. law manifests deep uncertainty as to whether disenfranchisement is a sanction that remains attached to a person moving into a new state. In most states, neither statutes, constitutional text, voter-registration forms, nor judicial rulings offer a clear answer. This presents particularly serious problems for the dozen or so states that disqualify some people after their sentence is over, either during a waiting period or indefinitely, and for those states that require former offenders to present documentary proof of restoration. The Clark County, Nevada, elections chief explained in 2007 that his staff gets a lot of "shouting and yelling" from former felons who have moved to that state and are told they cannot vote without the right documentation proving their eligibility—even if they've been voting for years elsewhere.[150] (In Nevada, first-time non-violent offenders are automatically restored, but others must appeal and provide proof of restoration and eligibility at the polls.) One Tennessee registrar volunteered that "we have quite a few of those [newcomers] happen," and that "they get quite distressed" when they read the eligibility law. Another said, "They've got a panel of lawyers up [in Nashville] to answer those questions." Another, unprovoked, responded, "I wish all these laws would be changed, tell the truth, but that's Tennessee law right now. In other states, it's automatic. Everybody says, 'I was in Texas, and I didn't have to do any of this.' "

Even in states where disenfranchisement is limited to incarceration only, staffers face a potential problem: what to do if a newcomer explains that his former state had disenfranchised him indefinitely. While it might seem intuitive that the new state's suffrage law should prevail, few if any states have spelled this out in controlling legal texts, and many local officials interviewed were not sure what to do in such a situation. "I'd hate to have to answer that," said one Indiana staffer, before asking the county attorney, who happened to be in the office, whether someone disqualified after the sentence elsewhere could register in Indiana, which is an incarceration-only state. (The answer was yes.) "It's so bizarre how the states are so different—it's kind of scary," said another local Indiana official.

Every press account and advocacy study of disenfranchisement uncovers abundant evidence that many offenders who are eligible to vote do not even try to register. Elections officials' ignorance of the law contributes to this problem, though ultimately responsibility for knowing the law and complying with restoration procedures rests with the citizen. At the same time, we also know that public and official ignorance leads to mistaken voting by those who are ineligible. Hundreds of nonincarcerated Americans appear to have registered and voted illegally in state and national elections in recent years in some states.[151] Such behavior is no surprise, given both the complexities of such policies and the significant numbers of elections officials who do not know important parts of disqualification and restoration law.[152] Local administration of state disenfranchisement and restoration laws contributes to the exclusion of voters who are legally eligible *and* the inclusion of some who are not legally eligible. This is not just a voting-rights problem but a rule of law problem as well.

One possible root cause of the uneven implementation of American criminal disenfranchisement law is the possibility that these restrictions no longer serve a clear purpose or objective. To put it another way, one reason why Americans administer criminal disenfranchisement laws poorly is that we do not really know what these laws are *for*. Like other "collateral sanctions," disenfranchisement results from, but is not formally part of, a criminal sentence. American law is deeply ambivalent as to the purposes of such sanctions, which are partly punitive (meant to affect the offender and deter crime by others) and partly regulatory (meant to allocate society's resources to the most deserving, for example).[153] American colonial disenfranchisement was explicitly punitive, limited to certain crimes and publicly imposed by a sentencing judge.[154] Today, however, even some of our wisest legal minds, such as Judge Richard A. Posner, can fall into surprisingly sloppy logic when they write about disenfranchisement's purposes.[155] Perhaps it is because modern U.S. disenfranchisement law does not pursue any specific, practical goal that it has fallen through an enormous bureaucratic crack, as it were. The penalty is not formally imposed by the courts or the criminal-justice system, and neither the federal government nor individual states have ever given elections officials the data that would enable them to fully enforce complicated disqualification and restoration rules.

Disenfranchisement does emerge from two core ideas still attractive to many Americans. First, those who violate society's rules should forfeit, at least temporarily, the ability to "make" those rules indirectly through voting; second, voters should conform to some minimum level of civic virtue.[156] More prosaically, the survival of these policies likely rests on the high political sa-lience of criminal-justice issues today, and particularly on the "negative politi-cal leverage" felons possess.[157] But complex and ambiguous laws, data inade-quate to enforce those laws, and varying implementation undercut theoretical rationales for the policy. Certainly, would-be voters are ultimately responsible for knowing the law and assuring their own eligibility. But the governmental officials responsible for administering such laws should know what they are. And at a deeper level, it is also surely true that the law regarding who is for-mally, fundamentally qualified to vote should be clear and principled. When significant numbers of the people who actually run our elections do not know important aspects of disenfranchisement law, it is hard to conclude that the restriction is necessary to protect the social contract and the "purity" of the ballot box.

At least twice in American history—with the property test and the poll tax—uneven enforcement of a voting restriction has served as an important reason for its eventual abolition. As Americans continue to re-examine our voting-rights laws and practices, varying implementation of disenfranchise-ment law should provide leverage at least for movement toward incarceration-only disenfranchisement, the policy that is by far the easiest to administer in a fair and consistent way, if not outright abolition. Because they often involve complex restoration procedures—and because they fly in the face of the obvi-ous assumption that a person seen fit to discharge on parole or probation is not a threat to society—postincarceration rules appear to be the hardest for officials and voters to understand and administer, and the most prone to both overly exclusionary and overly inclusionary errors. Inevitably, states that bar nonincarcerated people from voting are going to disenfranchise people who are legally eligible and fail to disqualify some who are not.[158] The question is how many.

My purpose here has not been to engage with the core question of whether criminal disenfranchisement violates modern American understand-ings of the right to vote. Instead, I want to take seriously the *administrative* perspective: how the texts of the law are made socially real. From that vantage point (and assuming that some kind of disenfranchisement policy will remain in place in most states), policies disenfranchising only the incarcerated appear superior. Anyone who can walk up to the counter would be eligible, and the only problematic absentee-ballot requests would come from addresses in the prisons—a relatively small number of addresses for local officials to know. There would be no need to determine which illegal behavior is "infamous"; purges, conviction reporting, and complicated restoration procedures would be unnecessary; and there would be no worries about the eligibility of new arrivals to the state. States could easily make sure all public officials know the law and know how to implement it effectively and fairly.

Conclusion

In 1965, William Riker wrote that the "ballot box and all that goes with it" are "the essential democratic institution," and that the "first care of the democratic conscience ... ought to be the widest possible extension of the suffrage."[159] Americans now understand better than ever that the suffrage must be defined to include not just formal qualifications but also practices—what the *Bush v. Gore* Court called "the manner of its exercise." And while systemic inequality in election administration is not the same as de jure exclusion, they are certainly members of the same family. As Dennis Thompson says, a lack of democratic respect can show itself "not only in the laws that deny some individuals the right to vote, but also in the practices that discourage the exercise of that right."[160]

Despite its role in historic exclusionary episodes and its present-day negative effects, local administration of elections has sometimes aided that "extension of the suffrage" Riker spoke of, and the connection between local election administration and the enduring American struggle over exclusion and inequality is multidimensional and, indeed, multidirectional. Most simply, in the early days of American suffrage, local assemblies and officials allowed men who did not meet formal colonial standards to vote—but likely excluded others, based on whether those men had proved themselves to be virtuous and religiously orthodox. Nineteenth-century county and city officials continued this tradition, flouting state law on property, registration, residency, and other factors in the direction of inclusion when it suited them, often for partisan reasons. In the South, a different phenomenon occurred, as state lawmakers purposefully left substantial discretion with the local officials, with the explicit expectation that those officials would systematically keep blacks from the polls. An analogous development took place in the North, where personal-registration rules kept new immigrants and others from the polls. Registration rules increased municipalities' control of the portals of the franchise in some ways but decreased them unevenly in others—such as when state lawmakers applied new rules only to cities as a way of diminishing their political power. Local administration played a key role in the collapse of the property test, since local officials often violated such tests by allowing men without sufficient property to vote. In some states, two generations of women participated in local elections prior to women achieving national voting rights. The case of aliens was still another phenomenon, as many state lawmakers left formal control of new immigrants' voting rights in the hands of local officials into the twentieth century.

Still, the devil is in the details when it comes to contemporary questions. Variation in registration practices, ballot design, polling-place selection, and election funding can help create fragmented, complex voting structures that have systematic discriminatory effects—even if universal suffrage is on the books and in the courts, and most officials implementing those practices have no desire to discriminate. Yet we cannot assume that local variation is everywhere a threat to equality: differences have not always been discriminatory and are not so today. The challenge for reformers and lawmakers is to continue to pressure all three levels of American government to make the process of registering and voting more equitable and accurate, while preserving the historically grounded, democracy enhancing aspects of local administration.

Conclusion

Human affairs are always in a state of muddle; muddled
politics are not the worst sort of politics; and muddles
often have a curious stability of their own.
W. J. M. Mackenzie (1958)

Some sort of order, rather than chaos, is to
accompany the democratic process.
Storer v. Brown (1974)

In the United States, voting has always been a local practice. To say this is
not to deny the considerable importance of national and state constitutions
and statutes in shaping American suffrage. But we have erred by focusing too
much on the formal, symbolic, and constitutional aspects of "the right to
vote" and on the aggregate sense of "voter behavior." As powerful as these approaches are, they are incomplete if they do not understand suffrage as a *practice*. Across both time and space, American voting has displayed a remarkably
rich texture, a diversity of practices that invites and demands greater understanding. The American democratic process has long evinced "some sort of
order," as the Supreme Court said in *Storer v. Brown*—an order characterized
by considerable local variation.

Voting Practices and American Political Development

We began with a few central developmental questions presented by the en-
durance of local variation in U.S. national elections. How has our system of
mixed and shared election-administration authority come about? Can we
identify specific cut-points in this history, moments where zero-sum transfers
of authority from one level of government to another occur? And if not, what

does this story of democratic rights and institutional structures tell us about the nature of political development?

As I have tried to show, the arrangement by which local, state, and national governments share responsibility and legal authority over various parts of the electoral process is a product of federal and state action and engagement, not inaction and neglect. We have seen repeated federal statutory and judicial interventions into election administration; lawmakers have often declared loud and clear that they hold sway in such affairs, directing and chastising local officials for their work (or lack thereof) in setting and interpreting qualification rules, registering voters, maintaining records, securing privacy, and so on. Particularly in the twentieth century, we see a clear secular trend in which local and state discretion narrows as federal supervisory authority extends. But Congress has always left substantial power (and a significant financial burden) in state and local hands, and each new action reveals how much variation remains. And despite the common modern sense that localism is some kind of secret, the record shows that lawmakers, judges, and reformers through the centuries have clearly understood the existence of county-level variation in American voting practices.

One result is that we cannot identify sharp turning points in the development of laws supervising the suffrage. Often halting, sometimes cumulative, these events strongly resist an attempt to locate sharp developmental shifts, moments at which authority recognizably moves from one institution to another in a discrete, total, lasting way. The history of U.S. suffrage practices presents a continued layering of national, state, and local authority, with an unsteady secular trend toward increasing national control. This is political development in a kind of "sedimentary"[1] style, not a sequence of discrete, durable authority shifts. Whether you think the contemporary American election-administration order is an "ecosystem" or a "matrix," making sense of its development requires coming to terms with a lasting system of shared, overlapping authority.

The alternatives are deeply unsatisfactory. When did a durable, enforceable authority over election mechanics shift from states and localities to the national government? At one extreme, we might regard the definitive developmental moment as the ratification of the Elections Clause. But Congress has only occasionally employed that authority, and a great many political actors have always read the clause more narrowly. At the other extreme, we might say the national government has never yet taken on primary authority over election administration, because each passing week seems to reveal some important new phenomenon untouched or only partly regulated by the Help

America Vote Act (HAVA) or its predecessors. But that leaves us unable to make sense of a great many statutes and judicial opinions appearing to say something quite different.

In between, there is the possibility of disaggregating the right to vote into its many constituent pieces. But when we understand the right to vote as a practice, the list of those pieces becomes daunting. Begin with the simple matter of formal qualifications: which level of government decides who is allowed to vote in federal elections? The federal constitution addresses several qualifications (race, age, gender, poll tax), and a federal statute (the Voting Rights Act [VRA]) bans literacy tests. But several important qualifications remain formally up to states (citizenship, criminal status, mental capacity, voting age in party primaries), under the greater or lesser restraint of federal judicial rulings.

In terms of more practical, "mechanical" aspects of the suffrage, repeated state and federal action have left most questions under a blend of national, state, and local authority. Voter registration, for example, began as an entirely state-directed matter in the nineteenth century; it has been conducted in some parts of the country by federal officials acting under statutory and judicial authority periodically since 1871, and particularly since 1960. It is now regulated by federal statutes, including the National Voter Registration Act (NVRA) and HAVA, and partly administered by all three levels of government. Election timing, similarly, has been subject to federal legislation since statutes mandated simultaneity in 1845 (presidential elections) and 1872 (congressional elections), but states now exercise considerable discretion over early and absentee voting, with some delegating that authority to localities. Voting technology is a third triply mixed area: HAVA eliminated certain kinds of voting machines, but states and localities decide from among the kinds allowed which machines (if any) to use and pay for them (now with some federal assistance). The choice of voting locations is almost entirely up to localities and states, but federal laws have repeatedly mandated accessibility. And there are a number of other aspects of the practice of voting—whether identification is required at the polls, rules regarding election observers, poll worker training and pay, ballot design, and the order in which names appear on the ballot, among others—which, in most of the country (excepting jurisdictions "covered" by the VRA), are controlled by states and localities. Teasing out precisely how much authority states and localities have had over each area would be a daunting task indeed.

As Stephen Skowronek observed a generation ago, institutional politics in the United States are "distinguished by incoherence and fragmentation in governmental operations."[2] But when coherence is measured in terms of an order's ability to stand the passage of time, even fragmented political systems can cohere. The central developmental lesson of the history of American election-administration law is that systems of shared, even conflicting power can themselves be durable. To paraphrase W. J. M. Mackenzie, this "muddle" has had a stability of its own. In the history of American election-administration rules, multiple political orders have not engaged in a fight to the death.[3]

Election Reform Today

Recall Henry Glassie's definition of history as a map of the past, drawn to be useful to the present traveler. Today, our election-administration debates often turn on the question of how much the federal government can and should do to control electoral mechanics. For example, in May 2008 the *New York Times* editorialized in favor of new federal legislation to "set minimum voting rights standards" nationwide. Voter registration, ballot format, voter challenges, identification laws, and the number of machines per voter should all be federally regulated, the *Times* opined in a piece titled "Voting Rights Are Too Important to Leave to the States."[4] Meanwhile, the long 2008 primary season helped spark congressional proposals linking reforms in practices like early and Internet voting with formal constitutional change, such as abolition of the Electoral College.[5] But the historical record suggests that continuing adjustments *within* the American system of overlapping and shared authority are far more likely than such major restructurings of it. Developmental patterns etched so deeply do constrain policy choices, and Congress seems more likely to facilitate state and local change, nudging and moving incrementally further in those areas in which it has already legislated, than to directly require further uniformity.

Yet as that observant twenty-six-year-old Frenchman said back in 1835, Americans "accept tradition only as a means of information, and existing facts only as a lesson to be used in doing otherwise and doing better."[6] There is nothing in the history of American voting that suggests inevitability; indeed, the history recounted here is very much a record of change, certainly not a rebuke to the legions of present-day reformers pushing Americans to "do otherwise and do better" in how we vote. Alert to the importance of unnecessarily burdensome and inegalitarian practices, nongovernmental groups across the political spectrum have pushed hard in recent years to bring down the barriers to participation our localized suffrage system sometimes erects. At the same time, many reformers have also come to see that nationalization and standardization is no panacea, as illustrated by the recent spate of state and national laws placing new burdens on voters.

What blend of local, state, and national authority over suffrage practices will best "promote the exercise of that right," as the 1993 NVRA put it? My view is that because of the benefits localism can bring in terms of experimentation, dispersed responsibility, voters' sense of efficacy, and responsiveness, we should preserve a measure of local autonomy in election practices. But to paraphrase Richard Bensel's assessment of the political culture accompanying mid-nineteenth-century elections, we should celebrate electoral localism today only with qualifications.[7] We are still learning which policies work best, and we should continue to allow our diverse election-administration systems to help answer those questions—how and where to register voters, assure that voter rolls are accurate, locate polling places, choose technologies that record votes most accurately, and design policies and procedures that improve voters' affective experiences of our national civic ritual. But localism can also contribute to real and damaging systematic discrimination, and we therefore need more oversight. Thus, diverse local practices should exist within a more comprehensive system that provides greater financial support for elections in exchange for mandatory reporting of registration and voting data.[8] One promising proposal along these lines calls for a published "Democracy Index" of voting practices, based on the assumption that public exposure of inadequate voting procedures will both demonstrate where reform is needed and provide pressure to facilitate such change.[9] Citizens, advocacy groups, academics, journalists, the voting-rights bar, and lawmakers should remain on the lookout for shoddy and partisan election administration, and judicial- and executive-branch enforcement of state and federal voting-rights laws must remain robust.

Our electoral vigilance must extend to state and federal policies as well, for statutory and regulatory harmonization of voting rules does not always serve equality and suffrage expansion. HAVA improved American elections in several ways, such as by allocating funds, publicizing best practices, and mandating accessibility. But by imposing a photo-identification requirement for some voters, the act injected unnecessary confusion into the electoral process and placed additional burdens on some voters (and elections staff). Or consider the question of voter registration for veterans living in federally run facilities. Until recently, the managers of nursing homes, rehabilitation centers, and homeless shelters run by the federal government could decide individually whether to permit voter-registration drives among veterans living on their premises. Obviously, that policy permitted inconsistency. But in

May 2008, the U.S. Department of Veterans Affairs set a clear national policy: it banned such voter-registration drives altogether, reasoning that federal employees should not be involved in the potentially partisan activity of deciding which outside groups could register veterans in public facilities. Republican and Democratic officials alike objected to the new policy, calling it an unnecessary obstacle to political participation by veterans, and the V.A. reversed its position in September 2008.[10]

Historically, local administration of elections has sometimes acted as a kind of solvent for burdensome and exclusionary voting rules, exposing those rules to new scrutiny and helping Americans to conclude that those policies lack firm theoretical foundations. Such a sequence was part of how both property and literacy tests were abolished; a somewhat analogous process occurred with women's suffrage. Though this has occurred only occasionally (and in hindsight, painfully slowly), it is a key part of the American struggle for suffrage equality. And while the national political climate does not now appear conducive to major progressive change, reformers may be able to make a virtue out of necessity. The current Congress may be unlikely to abolish either postincarceration disenfranchisement or burdensome photo-ID requirements. But seeing the administrative difficulties such policies present may help nudge Americans toward reconsidering whether these rules serve any important purpose. Reform groups surely will continue to push for changes at the state level and to help local officials better enforce these rules in a way that enables all eligible voters to participate.

In short, Americans should continue to insist on the importance of full participation, equal respect, transparency, and integrity in voting practices, while embracing the virtues of a locally run system—even where it does not provide uniform experiences for voters. Such an approach to the past and present of American election administration calls for a kind of ironic appreciation of the right to vote, an attitude already on display in some of the best recent analyses of voting rights and electoral structures. Bridging political science, history, law, and economics, election-law irony at its best retains a deep commitment to voting rights, believes in elections as expressive and instrumental elements of the political order, and holds in high esteem reformers who question and challenge the status quo. Yet this work also requires us to re-examine our assumptions about elections: how much voters know (and why that matters); what we think elections actually do; how we measure electoral success; and what phrases like "one person, one vote" and "the right to vote" actually mean. Election-law irony rejects absolutes, insists on the importance of contingency and context, and appreciates the role institutions play in making individual rights real.[11]

Of course, such an approach is not entirely new. W. J. M. Mackenzie sang the praises of electoral "muddles" in 1958. And Edmund Burke preceded Mackenzie by a couple of centuries, pioneering election-law irony with a meaner edge. Mocking those who criticized virtual representation and other aspects of England's voting system, Burke wrote that they judged the health of the political body not by its aptitude "but by their ideas of what ought to be the true balance between the several secretions."[12]

Naturally, contemporary practitioners of election-law irony are nicer to their debating partners than was Burke, less convinced of the rectitude of their positions, and far more open to the desirability of reform. Most important, present-day students of voting rights understand just how wrongheaded Burke's metaphor is. Electoral practices are not the epiphenomenal "secretions" of a political system; rather, they help form and define that system and manifest our fundamental political values.

Yet even those of us who believe that mundane electoral practices are fascinating and essential constitutive democratic behaviors must keep election mechanics in perspective. Modern mass elections have always been very blunt instruments with which to measure the public's will, if only because a great many voters cast ballots based on deeply partial information, raw partisan cues, or gut-level "throw the bums out" reasoning. To be sure, we need to count every one of those votes, and count them right. But in the face of mediating structures such as a polarized two-party system, plurality winner-take-all elections, and the Electoral College, even a procedurally immaculate election would not by itself move the United States significantly closer to the democratic ideal.

Adam Berinsky makes this point forcefully, arguing that "instead of making it incrementally easier for citizens to participate in politics, we should make people *want* to participate."[13] Todd Donovan takes a similar tack (and makes the irony explicit) in a recent article titled "A Goal for Reform: Make Elections Worth Stealing." Donovan acknowledges the importance of election administration but argues that the deeper reason so many Americans are disaffected about our elections lies not in procedural problems but in the broadly held public view that our electoral choices lack real meaning: too many elections are not truly competitive, and governments are insufficiently responsive to electoral results. A gerrymandered district, for example, will do far more to depress turnout than voting-technology problems. As Donovan writes, "Perfect scoring is meaningless if only one team takes the field."[14]

(Donovan's "scoring" certainly beats Burke's "secretions" as a metaphor for election administration.) And one comparative study of turnout rates concludes that when it comes to predicting increased rates of voting, the *salience* of an election—its perceived importance and impact on policy—dwarfs the effects of more procedural variables like compulsory, Sunday, and postal voting rules.[15] We can and should do more to make American voting easier, more accurate, and, yes, more celebratory, and local government can help us toward those goals. But it is just as important that we simultaneously remember the importance of making Americans want to vote in the first place.

Notes

Introduction

Epigraph: Bush v. Gore, 531 U.S. 98 (2000); Sally Engle Merry, *Colonizing Hawai'i: The Cultural Power of Law* (2000), 218.

1. Opinion *per curiam, Bush v. Gore*, 531 U.S. 98 (2000). The opinion begins with votes, disputes, and recounts in Leon, Miami-Dade, and Palm Beach counties, and manual vote tabulation in other counties.

2. Office for Democratic Institutions and Human Rights (OSCE/ODIHR), Limited Election Observation Mission, "Statement of Preliminary Findings and Conclusions, Nov. 5, 2008," 3. As the OSCE wrote in its report on the 2006 elections, "Federal oversight of election administration is primarily limited to specifying minimum standards." OSCE/ODIHR, "United States of America Mid-Term Congressional Elections, 7 November 2006," *OSCE/ODIHR Election Assessment Mission Report*, Mar. 9, 2007, 4.

3. See "Vote: The Machinery of Democracy," Smithsonian National Museum of American History, *www.americanhistory.si.edu/vote/index.html*. See also "America's Voting Patchwork," *www.americanhistory.si.edu/vote/patchwork.html*; this online exhibit describes and illustrates the "patchwork" of American voting practices.

4. Sheryl Gay Stolberg and James Dao, "Congress Ratifies Bush Victory after a Rare Challenge," *New York Times*, Jan. 7, 2005, A1. While Ohio received the most attention, at least a dozen states encountered serious human or machine errors in counting votes in the 2004 election. Brian C. Mooney, "Voting Errors Tallied Nationwide," *Boston Globe*, Dec. 1, 2004. See also Paul S. Herrnson, "Improving Election Technology and Administration: Toward a Larger Federal Role in Elections?" 13 *Stanford Law and Policy Review* 147, 150–51 (2002). Still, one million fewer votes were "lost" in 2004 than in 2000, due to improvements in ballot technology and design. Charles Stewart III, "Residual Vote in the 2004 Election," 5 *Election Law Journal* 158 (2006).

5. On the margin of litigation, see Richard L. Hasen, "Beyond the Margin of Litigation: Reforming U.S. Election Administration to Avoid Electoral Meltdown,"

62 *Washington and Lee Law Review* 937 (2005). On the problems affecting voters, see R. Michael Alvarez and Thad E. Hall, *Electronic Elections: The Perils and Promises of Digital Democracy* (2008), 26, 128; Ian Urbina and Christopher Drew, "Experts Concerned as Ballot Problems Persist," *New York Times*, Nov. 26, 2006.

6.   Mark Crispin Miller and Hans A. von Spakovsky, "Will This Election Be Stolen?" *Wall Street Journal*, Nov. 1, 2008, W1.

7.   See, for example, Tova Wang, "Voting in 2008: Lessons Learned," Common Cause, Nov. 10, 2008, *commoncause.org*; Rick Hasen et al., "Fixing Election Administration," Election Law Blog, Nov. 5–Nov. 17, 2008, *electionlawblog.org*.

8.   Though no such statement appears in *Cooper v. Aaron*, 358 U.S. 1 (1958), it is fair to say that the case did assert such a sweeping view of judicial supremacy.

9.   *Burdick v. Takushi*, 504 U.S. 428, 433 (1992), quoting *Anderson v. Celebrezze*, 460 U.S. 780, 788 (1983). The use of the phrase "electoral mechanics" in this context comes from Christopher S. Elmendorf, "Structuring Judicial Review of Electoral Mechanics, Part I: Explanations and Opportunities," 156 *Pennsylvania Law Review* 313 (2007).

10.   John A. Rohr, *Civil Servants and Their Constitutions* (2002), 141. Rohr writes, "The examples of how civil servants play their roles as constitutional actors are quite disparate ... but they all reinforce the point that civil servants 'run the Constitution,' i.e., they reduce its grand principles to practice by their actions both routine and extraordinary."

11.   It is surprisingly difficult to specify exactly which level of government bears legal and practical authority for varying aspects of election management. For particularly good analysis and summary, see "Working Together? State and Local Election Coordination," *Electionline.org*, Sept. 2002; "Election Reform: What's Changed, What Hasn't, and Why, 2000–2006," *Electionline.org*, Feb. 2006; U.S. Government Accountability Office (GAO), "All Levels of Government Are Needed to Address Electronic Voting System Challenges," Statement of Randolph C. Hite before the Subcommittee on Financial Services and General Government, Committee on Appropriations, House of Representatives, Mar. 7, 2007; Sharon Priest, "The Secretaries Speak: Sixteen Points to Improve American Elections," 1 *Election Law Journal* 71 (2002).

12.   Jimmy Carter et al., *To Assure Pride and Confidence in the Electoral Process: Report of the National Commission on Federal Election Reform* (2002), 27. Later tallies have produced smaller but still considerable figures. Spencer Overton, for example, writes that "local authorities within 4,600 different election districts control American democracy." Spencer Overton, *Stealing Democracy: The New Politics of Voter Suppression* (2006), 56.

13.   George Grayson, "Registering and Identifying Voters: What the United States Can Learn from Mexico," 3 *Election Law Journal* 513, 518 (2004); Jamin Raskin, "Suffrage Suffers in the Land of Rights," *Los Angeles Times*, Mar. 15, 2004.

14.   Forum on Election Reform, The Constitution Project, *Recommendations for*

Congressional Action (2001), 1. In 2002, *Electionline.org* calculated that nineteen states provided no funding for elections, and twenty-two funded only part of the costs of administering state elections. *Electionline.org* and the Constitution Project, "Working Together? State and Local Election Coordination," Sept. 2002, 3.

15. CalTech/MIT Voting Technology Project, "Voting: What Is, What Could Be" (2001), 48.

16. "In accordance with the decentralized nature of U.S. government, the majority of states have yet to introduce legislation to regulate observation. In some jurisdictions election administrators have used their discretionary powers to grant full access for observers, while in others access is limited or restricted." OSCE/ODIHR, "United States of America Mid-Term Congressional Elections, 7 November 2006," 28. Based on a full-access recommendation by the National Association of Secretaries of State in 2005 and the "strong support" of the federal Election Assistance Commission, OSCE observers "were granted access to all levels of the election administration in most cases, including polling stations on election day."

17. Allison Hayward, "Election Day at the Bar," 58 *Case Western Law Review* 59 (2007). For analysis of the beneficial aspects of having so many people (including lawyers) now closely observing U.S. elections, see "Case Study, Election Observation Dispatches from the Polls," *Electionline.org*, May 2008.

18. Bengt Säve-Söderbergh, Institute for Democracy and Electoral Assistance, "Broader Lessons of the U.S. Election Drama," *www.idea.int/press/op_ed_08.htm*.

19. Peter Schworm, "Activist Challenges the Use of Churches as Polling Places," *Boston Globe*, Mar. 31, 2003, B1; Matt Sedensky, "Man Sues over Church as Polling Place," Associated Press, Dec. 6, 2006. In the town of Weston, Massachusetts, all polling places were in churches. Voting in houses of worship, Schworm notes, is "a cornerstone of New England democracy."

20. CalTech/MIT Voting Technology Project, "Voting: What Is, What Could Be," 19. After California's 2003 gubernatorial recall election, the *New York Times* featured photos of California polling places, including a mortuary and a deli. *New York Times*, Oct. 8, 2003, 1.

21. Pam Belluck, "States Face Decisions on Who Is Mentally Fit to Vote," *New York Times*, June 19, 2007.

22. Shankar Vedantam, "Dementia and the Voter," *Washington Post*, Sept. 14, 2004, A1. For summary and analysis of state laws, see Kay Schriner et al., "Democratic Dilemmas: Notes on the ADA and Voting Rights of People with Cognitive and Emotional Impairments," 21 *Berkeley Journal of Employment and Labor Law* 437 (2007). One federal court has held that a state constitutional provision barring people under guardianship for mental illness from voting violates the Fourteenth Amendment and the Americans with Disabilities Act. *Doe v. Rowe*, 156 F. Supp. 2d 35 (E.D. Me. 2001). The Bazelon Center for Mental Health Law

offers a concise summary of federal law related to voting by people with mental disabilities, and litigates on voting rights as well as other issues. Bazelon Center for Mental Health Law, "Voting," *www.bazelon.org/issues/voting/index.htm*.

23.   Cheryl Wittenaur, "Lawyers Debate Alleged Ban on Voting Rights for Mentally Ill," Associated Press, Feb. 12, 2007.

24.   Becky Johnson, "Proposed Election Law Change Follows Swain Nursing Home Irregularities," *Smoky Mountain News*, May 23, 2007. Intriguingly, an 1875 treatise on American election law urged that while a person who has been adjudged non compos mentis ought not vote, a man "whose faculties are merely greatly enfeebled by old age, is not to be rejected." George W. McCrary, *A Treatise on the American Law of Elections* (1875), 41. "If the voter knew enough to understand the nature of his act, if he understood what he was doing, that is probably sufficient," wrote McCrary. Ibid., 42. This standard—essentially, that volition and the capacity to choose should be the standards for judging competency—is the one now proposed by those legal and neurological scholars who have studied the issue most closely.

25.   Jennifer Hochschild, "Introduction and Comments," 1 *Perspectives on Politics* 247 (2003). For some defenses of localized suffrage institutions, see Richard Briffault, "Home Rule and Local Political Innovation," 22 *Journal of Law and Politics* 1 (2006); Richard C. Schragger, "Reclaiming the Canvassing Board: Bush v. Gore and the Political Currency of Local Government," 50 *Buffalo L. Rev.* 393 (2002).

26.   See "How America Doesn't Vote," *New York Times* (editorial), Feb. 15, 2004. The editors wrote, "The lists of eligible voters kept by localities are the gateway to democracy, and they are also a national scandal." Just before the 2004 elections, the *Times* editorialized that "unfortunately, our election system leaves ballot design to the whims of local officials, who often make bad choices." "The Return of the 'Butterfly Ballot,' " *New York Times* (editorial), Oct. 29, 2004.

27.   Jack N. Rakove, "Introduction: Dangling Questions," in *The Unfinished Election of 2000* (2001), xv–xvi.

28.   "Interlude: Toner on Election Administration," *The Hotline: National Journal's Daily Briefing on Politics*, Nov. 30, 2006, *hotlineblog.nationaljournal.com/archives/2006/11/interlude_toner.html*; Heather Gerken, "How Does Your State Rank on 'The Democracy Index'?" *Legal Times*, Jan. 1, 2007.

29.   See Richard Morin and Claudia Deane, "Public Backs Uniform U.S. Voting Rules: Poll Finds Wide Support for Guidelines on Ballots, Closing Times, Recounts," *Washington Post*, Dec. 18, 2000; NBC News/Wall Street Journal Poll, Study #6050 (2004), p. 11, question 8, *online.wsj.com/public/resources/documents/poll20041217.pdf*.

30.   *West Virginia State Board of Education et al. v. Barnette et al.*, 319 U.S. 624, 637 (1943).

31.   Daniel Hays Lowenstein and Richard L. Hasen, *Election Law*, 2d ed. (2001), 65. A few prescient observers identified the division of "responsibility for defining

the nature and scope of suffrage between Congress and the states" as a consti-tutional problem before 2000. Jeffrey Rosen, "Divided Suffrage," in William N. Eskridge and Sanford Levinson, eds., *Constitutional Stupidities, Constitutional Tragedies* (1998), 81. Calling for "delegat[ion] of power over suffrage and redis-tricting to an administrative body that is less vulnerable to partisan interests" than state government, Rosen argued that "it makes little sense to tolerate a patchwork of inconsistent and parochial state restrictions." Rosen, *Divided Suf-frage*, 82, 83. For an earlier critique, see Dudley O. McGovney, *The American Suffrage Medley: The Need for a Uniform National Suffrage* (1949).

32. Richard A. Posner, *Breaking the Deadlock: The 2000 Election, the Constitution, and the Courts* (2001), 204.

33. Abner Greene, *Understanding the 2000 Election: A Guide to the Legal Battles That Decided the Presidency* (2001), 180.

34. For an excellent summary, see Brian Kim, "Help America Vote Act," 40 *Harvard Journal on Legislation* 579 (2003).

35. Robert Pear, "Congress Passes Bill to Clean Up Election System," *New York Times*, Oct. 17, 2002, A1; Robert Pear, "Bush Signs Legislation Intended to End Voting Disputes," *New York Times*, Oct. 30, 2002, A22.

36. "The Voice of Voting Reform," National Affairs Daily, *Rolling Stone*, June 6, 2006, *www.rollingstone.com/nationalaffairs*; Erica Werner, "Chairman of Voting Reform Panel Resigns," Associated Press, Apr. 22, 2005; Dan Seligson, "NASS to EAC: Three Years Is Enough," *Electionline.org Weekly Briefing*, Feb. 10, 2005.

37. Kelly McCormick, "Millender-McDonald urges election reform," *The Hill*, Feb. 16, 2007.

38. Bob Mahlburg and John Maines, "State Officials Defend List of Felon Voters," *Orlando Sentinel*, July 3, 2004; Marc Caputo, "Questions over Felon 'Purge List' Threaten Florida Governor," *Miami Herald*, July 4, 2004; Dara Kam, "County Elections Chiefs Worry about State Control of Voter List," *Palm Beach Post*, July 5, 2006.

39. David Postman, "Counties Opposing GOP Call to Reopen Vote Counts," *Se-attle Times*, Dec. 29, 2004. The canvassing boards that refused to recount ballots included some Republican-dominated panels.

40. Gregory Roberts, "Voter Database Should Fix Problems But New State System Won't Solve All Registration Flaws," *Seattle Post-Intelligencer*, Dec. 29, 2005.

41. C. J. Karamargin, "Ignore Voter Registration Ruling, State Official Says," *Arizona Daily Star*, Mar. 14, 2006.

42. Angela Couloumbis and Thomas Fitzgerald, "Pa. Law Sharply Restricts Poll Sites," *Philadelphia Enquirer*, May 13, 2006.

43. *United States v. Carnahan*, U.S.D.C. Western Mo., May 23, 2006, 16; David A. Lieb, "Judge: Missouri Not Responsible for Local Voter Roll Errors," Associated Press, May 23, 2006.

44. *United States v. Missouri*, Case No. 05-4391-CV-C-NKL, Apr. 13, 2007, 25.

45. As Liebschutz and Palazzolo write, "The rise of election reform as a major policy

issue has been accompanied by a rebirth of interest among political scientists in the administration and formation of election law." Sarah F. Liebschutz and Daniel J. Palazzolo, "HAVA and the States," 35 *Publius* 497 (2005).

46. Doug Chapin, "Director's Note," *Electionline.org Weekly*, May 12, 2005.

47. Spencer Overton, *Stealing Democracy*, 14. Another recent standout on voting rights and election administration is Ann N. Crigler, Marion R. Just, and Edward J. McCaffery, eds., *Rethinking the Vote: The Politics and Prospects of American Election Reform* (2004).

48. Steven F. Huefner, Daniel Tokaji, and Edward B. Foley, *From Registration to Recounts: The Election Ecosystems of Five Midwestern States* (2007), v.

49. Pessimistic accounts include Richard L. Hasen, "The Untimely Death of *Bush v. Gore*," 60 *Stanford Law Review* 1 (2007); and Doug Chapin, "Director's Note: Of Willy Loman and 'Whoopee,' " *Electionline.org*, Apr. 12, 2007. More optimistic is Gerken, "How Does Your State Rank on 'The Democracy Index'?"

50. The phrase comes from Dennis F. Thompson, "The Role of Theorists and Citizens in Just Elections: A Response to Professors Cain, Garrett, and Sabl," 4 *Election Law Journal* 153, 162 (2005). I should clarify what I mean in calling my conception of the right to vote as a local practice a "theory." In behavioral political science, a theory is an empirically testable, falsifiable hypothesis. In the course of this book I offer a good deal of empirical evidence for a variety of claims, but saying that the American right to vote is a locally constituted practice is a theoretical claim of a different kind. Developments in areas as diverse as campaign finance, ballot access, and the regulation of campaign speech—plus election administration—have made scholars today acutely aware of the inadequacy of "formal" definitions of the right to vote and increasingly interested in new ways to capture different aspects of a complex legal and political activity.

51. Stuart Scheingold, *The Politics of Rights: Lawyers, Public Policy, and Political Change* (1974). In her polemic against the two-party system, Lisa Jane Disch revived the term "catchphrase," borrowed from party historian Ronald Formisano. Disch, *The Tyranny of the Two-Party System* (2002), 59–61.

52. Sally Engle Merry, *Colonizing Hawai'i: The Cultural Power of Law* (2000), 218. For a leading theoretical analysis of practice from the anthropological perspective, see Pierre Bourdieu, *Outline of a Theory of Practice*, trans. Richard Nice (1977).

53. John Brigham, *The Constitution of Interests* (1996), x. Brigham defines a "practice" as "a structure of understandings that transforms a social phenomenon . . . into a highly organized part of political culture." Ibid., 95.

54. Michael McCann, *Rights at Work: Pay Equity Reform and the Politics of Legal Mobilization* (1994), 297. McCann continues, "The fact that legal conventions have no transcendant foundation should not obscure their constitutive authority as public knowledge in a lived history of social engagement."

55. For discussion of the "interpretive community" in American constitutionalism, see Carol Nackenoff, "Constitutionalizing Terms of Inclusion: Friends of the

Indian and Citizenship for Native Americans, 1880s–1930s," in Ronald Kahn and Ken I. Kersch, eds., *The Supreme Court and American Political Development* (2006). Nackenoff's use of "interpretive community" seems to include in that community those whose work is not necessarily concerned with *conscious* analysis of the document. A study that appears to define the "interpretive community" more narrowly is Ronald Kahn's chapter in the same volume, "Social Constructions, Supreme Court Reversals, and American Political Development: *Lochner, Plessy, Bowers,* But Not *Roe.*"

56. Karen Orren and Stephen Skowronek, *The Search for American Political Development* (2004), 133.

57. Daniel Wirls, "Regionalism, Rotten Boroughs, Race, and Realignment: The Seventeenth Amendment and the Politics of Representation," 13 *Studies in American Political Development* 1 (1999).

58. Richard F. Bensel, "The American Ballot Box: Law, Identity, and the Polling Place in the Mid-Nineteenth Century," 17 *Studies in American Political Development* 1, 5n10 (2003).

59. Brigham, *The Constitution of Interests*, x.

60. Bruce E. Cain, "Election Law as Its Own Field of Study," 32 *Loyola Law Review* 1095 (1999); Dennis F. Thompson, *Just Elections: Creating a Fair Electoral Process in the United States* (2002), 199n2. See also Angus Campbell, Philip E. Converse, Warren E. Miller, and Donald E. Stokes, *The American Voter* (1960); Warren E. Miller and J. Merrill Shanks, *The New American Voter* (1996). With far more modesty than warranted, Miller and Shanks describe their long and complex compendium of the antecedent and proximate causes of voting as offering merely "the skeleton of a complex causal structure" (ix).

61. Jonathan N. Wand et al., "The Butterfly Did It: The Aberrant Vote for Buchanan in Palm Beach County, Florida," 95 *American Political Science Review* 793 (2001).

62. See Keith Bybee, *Mistaken Identity: The Supreme Court and the Politics of Minority Representation* (1998).

63. Shklar writes, "The deepest impulse for demanding the suffrage arises from the recognition that it is the characteristic, the identifying, feature of democratic citizenship in America, not a means to other ends." Shklar, *American Citizenship* (1991), 56. I am not disagreeing with Shklar here, but characterizing her focus.

64. See Alec C. Ewald, " 'Civil Death': The Ideological Paradox of Criminal Disenfranchisement Law in the United States," 2002 *Wisconsin Law Review* 1045 (2002).

65. In some respects this tracks what Timothy J. O'Neill described as one of the political effects of "law language." "Law language," writes O'Neill, "narrows the debate and helps to simplify complexities, but it may also impoverish public understanding of serious controversies." O'Neill, "The Language of Equality in a Constitutional Order," 75 *American Political Science Review* 626 (1981).

66. Samuel Issacharoff, Pamela S. Karlan, and Richard H. Pildes, *The Law of De-*

mocracy: Legal Structure of the Political Process, rev. 2d ed. (2002), 19. See also Daniel N. Hoffman, *Our Elusive Constitution* (1997), particularly chap. 2, "Representation and Constitutional Politics."

67. Richard H. Pildes, "What Kind of Right Is 'The Right to Vote'?" 93 *Virginia Law Review In Brief* 43, 44 (2007). Richard Fallon writes that "if the Court thought that the Constitution embodied a general theory of democracy, it could resolve election law cases under that theory. But the Justices have been unable to discern or develop such a theory." Richard Fallon, *The Dynamic Constitution* (2004), 210. For a celebration of the Court's lack of a theory of politics, see Daniel H. Lowenstein, "The Supreme Court Has No Theory of Politics—and Be Thankful for Small Favors," in Lee Epstein and David K. Ryden, eds., *The Supreme Court and the Electoral Process*, (2000), 245.

68. See Pamela S. Karlan, "Convictions and Doubts: Retribution, Representation, and the Debate over Felon Disenfranchisement," 56 *Stanford Law Review* 1147, 1156 (2004). Karlan identifies participation, aggregation, and governance as the most important elements of the constellation; her primary purpose is to explain why there is inevitably a group dimension to voting rights: "Courts, legislatures, and the public have come to see that any right to genuinely meaningful political participation implicates groups of voters, rather than atomistic individuals."

69. Neal Devins and Louis Fisher, *The Democratic Constitution* (2004), 5. As one perceptive author observed twenty years ago, the Constitution "involves a process in which many other formal and informal, authoritative and functional actors participate." W. Michael Reisman, "International Incidents: Introduction to a New Genre in the Study of International Law," 10 *Yale Journal of International Law* 1, 8n13 (1984). Today an emerging consensus holds that the Congress, the presidency, and political parties all help construct our constitutional order. See, for example, Mark Tushnet, *The New Constitutional Order* (2003). Tushnet writes, "Both institutions and principles constitute a constitutional order. On the institutional level, a constitutional order extends well beyond the Supreme Court and includes the national political parties, Congress, and the presidency." Ibid., 1.

70. Karl Llewellyn, "The Constitution as an Institution," 34 *Columbia Law Review* 1 (1934). Llewellyn wrote, "Wherever there are today established practices 'under' or 'in accordance with' the Document, *it is only the practice which can legitimize the words as being still part of our going Constitution. It is not the words which legitimize the practice.*" Ibid., 12; emphasis in original. Interestingly, the institutional example Llewellyn chose to explore was an electoral institution— the Electoral College. On the limited impact of *Engel v. Vitale*, see Kenneth M. Dolbeare and Phillip E. Hammond, *The School Prayer Decisions: From Court Policy to Local Practice* (1971); on *Brown*, see Gerald N. Rosenberg, *The Hollow Hope* (1991).

71. Albert Shaw, "The American State and the American Man," *Contemporary Re-*

view 1 (1887). I owe this quotation to William J. Novak, *The People's Welfare: Law and Regulation in Nineteenth-Century America* (1996), 237.

72.   For a particularly astute discussion of the ritual aspect of modern elections, see Graeme Orr, "The Ritual and Aesthetic in Electoral Law," 32 *Federal Law Review* 1, 3 (2004). As Orr writes, "We cannot fully grasp what the legal forms underlying balloting are about without exploring the ritual aspects of the voting system."

Chapter 1

Epigraph: Oath quoted in Cortlandt F. Bishop, *History of Elections in the American Colonies* (1893), Appendix, 268; An act to extend the right of suffrage in the Indiana Territory, March 3, 1811, 3 *U.S. Stat.* 670, Sec. 5.

1.   "History is not the past," Glassie wrote. "History is a map of the past drawn from a particular point of view to be useful to the modern traveler." Henry Glassie, *Passing the Time in Ballymenone: Culture and History of an Ulster Community* (1982), 621.
2.   Karen Orren and Stephen Skowronek, *The Search for American Political Development* (2004), 123, 127.
3.   Alexander Keyssar, *The Right to Vote: The Contested History of Democracy in the United States* (2000), 115.
4.   Orren and Skowronek, *Search for American Political Development*, 141–43.
5.   Marie Gottschalk, *The Prison and the Gallows: The Politics of Mass Incarceration in America* (2006), 236. See also David Brian Robertson, *The Constitution and America's Destiny* (2005), 6; David F. Ericson, "The Federal Government and Slavery: Following the Money Trail," 19 *Studies in American Political Development* 105, 107 (2005); Rogan Kersh, "The Growth of American Political Development: The View from the Classroom," 3 *Perspectives on Politics* 335, 340 (2005); Stephen Bragaw, "The Constitutional Dimension of American Indian Policy under the Federalists and Jefferson: Acceleration of Tragedy, or a Durable Shift in Governing Authority?" paper presented at the Annual Meetings of the American Political Science Association, Philadelphia, 2006; Jonathan Chausovsky, "State Regulation of Corporations in the Late Nineteenth Century: A Critique of the New Jersey Thesis," 21 *Studies in American Political Development* 30, 34 (2007); Justin Crowe, "The Forging of Judicial Autonomy: Political Entrepreneurship and the Reforms of William Howard Taft," 69 *Journal of Politics* 73, 74 (2007). A somewhat critical discussion of the implications of Orren and Skowronek's formulation is in Bartholomew H. Sparrow, "American Political Development, State-Building, and the 'Security State': Reviving a Research Agenda," 40 *Studies in American Political Development* 355, 357 (2008).
6.   Jack N. Rakove, "Introduction: Dangling Questions," in *The Unfinished Election of 2000* (2001), xv–xvi; Roy G. Saltman, *The History and Politics of Voting Technology* (2006), 1.

7.   Saltman, *History and Politics of Voting Technology*, xiv.
8.   Richard H. Pildes, "The Future of Voting Rights Policy: From Anti-discrimination to the Right to Vote," 49 *Howard Law Journal* 741, 742 (2006).
9.   Robert J. Dinkin, *Voting in Provincial America: A Study of Elections in the Thirteen Colonies, 1689–1776* (1977), 3.
10. Michael Schudson, *The Good Citizen: A History of American Civic Life* (1998), 4–5, 7; see also Don Herzog, *Happy Slaves: A Critique of Consent Theory* (1989).
11. Chilton Williamson, *American Suffrage: From Property to Democracy, 1760–1860* (1960), 55–56.
12. Williamson, *American Suffrage*, 68. Churches were less prominent in southern than northern elections, both in qualification and as polling places.
13. Perry Miller, ed., *The American Puritans: Their Prose and Poetry* (1982/1956), 108.
14. Charles Seymour and Donald Paige Frary, *How the World Votes: The Story of Democratic Development in Elections*, vol. 1 (1918), 208.
15. Spencer D. Albright, *The American Ballot* (1942), 14. Indeed, according to Albright, the relatively early American use of ballots may well have been linked with the "democratic and elective principles of the Congregational form of the Christian Church," among other intellectual precursors.
16. Dinkin, *Voting in Provincial America*, 133; see also Albright, *The American Ballot*, 15.
17. Dinkin, *Voting in Provincial America*, 133.
18. The regular use of paper ballots is illustrated by the vote-counter's oath of 1679–1680 contained in the Appendix to Cortlandt F. Bishop, *History of Elections in the American Colonies* (1893), and reproduced at the beginning of this chapter.
19. Dinkin, *Voting in Provincial America*, 136–43.
20. Edmund S. Morgan, *Inventing the People: The Rise of Popular Sovereignty in England and America* (1988), 183. See also Dinkin, *Voting in Provincial America*, 136–37.
21. George Frederick Miller, *Absentee Voters and Suffrage Laws* (1948), 25.
22. Dinkin, *Voting in Provincial America*, 133.
23. Williamson, *American Suffrage*, 41.
24. Ibid., 135.
25. Ibid., 77–78, 41–42.
26. Montesquieu held that the public pressure of open voting was needed to help the "lower classes" comport themselves correctly in elections, since they would feel "the gravity of eminent personages." Montesquieu, *The Spirit of the Laws* (1949/1748), vol. 1, 155.
27. Quoted in Williamson, *American Suffrage*, 12; emphasis added. On Montesquieu's influence on constitutional debates, see Bernard Bailyn, *The Ideological Origins of the American Revolution* (1967), 344–45.
28. Dudley O. McGovney, *The American Suffrage Medley: The Need for a National*

Uniform Suffrage (1949), 2. See generally Rosemary Zagarri, *The Politics of Size: Representation in the United States, 1776–1850* (1987).

29. James A. Morone, *The Democratic Wish: Popular Participation and the Limits of American Government*, rev. ed. (1998), 41.

30. Only three confined the vote explicitly to males, six required that voters be twenty-one, and four set no residency standard at all. Williamson, *American Suffrage*, 15–16.

31. Ibid., 16. Only Rhode Island drew no distinction between town and colony elections.

32. James H. Kettner, *The Development of American Citizenship, 1608–1870* (1978), 100, 100n31.

33. Williamson, *American Suffrage*, 52. This practice continued after independence, including in Maryland, where foreigners were frequently "naturalized just before elections in illegal fashion and allowed to vote." Ibid., 140.

34. Ibid., 60, 16.

35. As Joseph Harris writes, this was not a true voter-registration roll but was "probably the earliest forerunner in this country of an official registration system." Joseph Harris, *Registration of Voters in the United States* (1929), 66–67.

36. Saltman, *History and Politics of Voting Technology*, 41, 42–43; George W. McCrary, *A Treatise on the American Law of Elections* (1875), sec. 162.

37. "Enfranchisement," writes Alexander Keyssar, "varied greatly by location," with some newly settled, cheap-land communities allowing four-fifths of white men to vote, and others restricting the franchise to only about half. Keyssar, *The Right To Vote*, 7.

38. Orren and Skowronek, *Search for American Political Development*, 97.

39. See generally Stein Rokkan et al., *Citizens, Elections, and Parties: Approaches to the Comparative Study of the Processes of Development* (1970).

40. Stephen Skowronek, *Building a New American State: The Expansion of National Administrative Capacities, 1877–1920* (1982), 23.

41. Samuel Huntington, *Political Order in Changing Societies* (1968), 96. By "constitution," Huntington here reforms to institutions, norms, and practices—the "small-c constitution."

42. Ibid., 96, 98. That Huntington gives a remarkably flat account of the expansion of electoral rights in America (see ibid., 93–94) does not detract from the applicability here of his account of early American institutions.

43. Francis S. Philbrick, *The Rise of the West* (1965), 351n23, citing Charles Beard, "Centralization," in Andrew C. McLaughlin and Albert B. Hart, eds., *Cyclopedia of American Government* (New York, 1914), vol. 1, 238–39. Philbrick writes that "one reason democracy developed on the frontier was that Englishmen had acquired a devotion to local self-government." Ibid., 351. The governing principles of the founding period, writes Charles Lockhart, "honored to an extraordinary degree the limited and local government aspects" of the American experience, and decentralization in that era has had enduring consequences. Charles Lock-

hart, *The Roots of American Exceptionalism: Institutions, Culture and Policies* (2003), 160–61.

44. Robertson focuses on differences of land use and labor, the use of titles, indigenous peoples, revenue extraction and war, and the prominence of courts and lawyers. David Brian Robertson, *The Constitution and America's Destiny* (2005), 7–8.

45. Robert C. Lieberman, "Ideas, Institutions, and Political Order: Explaining Political Change," 96 *American Political Science Review* 697, 709 (2002). Stephen Skowronek writes that states change (or don't) "through political struggles rooted in and mediated by pre-established institutional arrangements." Skowronek, *Building a New American State*, ix. See also Pildes, "The Future of Voting Rights Policy." As Pildes writes, decentralized elections are "a path-dependent product of America's unique political history—including, ironically, the fact that American democracy was established over 200 years ago and has endured since." Ibid., 742.

46. Lieberman, "Ideas, Institutions, and Political Order," 709.

47. Saltman, *History and Politics of Voting Technology*, 40; Marc W. Kruman, *Between Authority and Liberty: State Constitution Making in Revolutionary America* (1997), 95, 88. Indeed, Kruman concludes that the revolutionaries "moved the suffrage to the center of American political thought and redefined the act of voting," holding the franchise to be "the most important of rights." Ibid., 103.

48. For a tally of state constitutions' suffrage qualifications both before and after independence, see Willi Paul Adams, *The First American Constitutions*, expanded ed. (Rowman and Littlefield, 2001), 315–27.

49. James Madison, *Federalist* 52, in Clinton Rossiter, ed., *The Federalist Papers* (1961), 323.

50. Jack N. Rakove, *Original Meanings: Politics and Ideas in the Making of the Constitution* (1997), 204.

51. Gordon S. Wood, *The American Revolution* (2002), 153.

52. U.S. Constitution, Article II, sec. 1; Article I, sec. 3; Article I, sec. 2, cl. 1. More than a century later, the Seventeenth Amendment, requiring direct election of U.S. senators and ratified in 1913, would repeat this language relating to qualifications verbatim. The Supreme Court has interpreted Article I, sec. 2, in an inclusionary way: "Far from being a device to limit the federal suffrage, the Qualifications Clause was intended by the Framers to prevent the mischief which would arise if state voters found themselves disqualified from participation in federal elections." *Tashjian v. Republican Party*, 479 U.S. 208, 229 (1986).

53. For a critical discussion, see Jeffrey Rosen, "Divided Suffrage," chap. 16 in William N. Eskridge Jr. and Sanford Levinson, eds., *Constitutional Stupidities, Constitutional Tragedies* (1998). Rosen calls this arrangement—together with the passages regarding voter qualifications and apportionment—the "stupidest" thing in the U.S. Constitution.

54. U.S. Const, Article I, sec. 4, cl. 1.

55. *United States v. Missouri*, U.S.D.C. Western Mo., Apr. 13, 2007, 23. As a federal Circuit Court of Appeals put it a few years earlier, the Constitution "confers on the states broad authority to regulate the conduct of elections, including federal ones." *Griffin v. Roupas*, 385 F.3d 1128, 1129 (Seventh Cir. 2004).

56. Daniel Tokaji and Thad Hall, "Money for Data: Funding the Oldest Unfunded Mandate," Commentary, Election Law Moritz weblog, June 5, 2007, *moritzlaw. osu.edu/electionlaw/*.

57. "Centinel," quoted in Saltman, *History and Politics of Voting Technology*, 48.

58. Quoted in Jonathan Elliott, ed., *The Debates in the Several State Conventions on the Adoption of the Federal Constitution*, vol. 3, 60 (1836).

59. Pamela S. Karlan, "Section 5 Squared: Congressional Power to Extend and Amend the Voting Rights Act," 44 *Houston Law Review* 1 (2007), 16.

60. *U.S. Term Limits v. Thornton*, 514 U.S. 779, 833–34 (1995).

61. U.S. Constitution, Article IV, sec. 3, empowers Congress to "make all needful Rules and Regulations respecting the Territory or other Property belonging to the United States."

62. "A freehold in fifty acres of land in the district, having been a citizen of one of the States, and being a resident in the district, or the like freehold and two years' residence in the district, shall be necessary to qualify a man as an elector of a representative." See "An Ordinance for the government of the territory of the United States Northwest of the river Ohio," Confederate Congress, July 13, 1787, sec. 9.

63. In the early national period, only Maryland, North Carolina, South Carolina, and Virginia required voters to own a fifty-acre freehold. Keyssar, *The Right to Vote*, table A.1.

64. An earlier draft of the Ordinance had spelled this out even more clearly, specifying "two years' residence *if a foreigner*." *Journals of the Continental Congress*, vol. 32 (May 10, 1787), 282; emphasis added.

65. "An Act extending the right of suffrage in the Indiana Territory," Feb. 26, 1808, 2 *U.S. Statutes* 469. In 1809, Congress declared that the Territory's voters would "also elect one delegate to the Congress of the United States." "An Act extending the right of suffrage in the Indiana Territory," Feb. 27, 1809, 2 *U.S. Statutes* 525, sec. 1.

66. "An act to extend the right of suffrage in the Indiana Territory," Mar. 3, 1811, 3 *U.S. Statutes* 659, sec. 1.

67. "An Act extending the right of suffrage in the Mississippi territory," Jan. 9, 1808, 2 *U.S. Statutes* 455, sec. 1 and 3. Interestingly, the statute appears to restrict suffrage to citizens—something few western states did at that time. See Leon E. Aylsworth, "The Passing of Alien Suffrage," 25 *American Political Science Review* 114 (1931); Jamin B. Raskin, "Legal Aliens, Local Citizens: The Historical, Constitutional and Theoretical Meanings of Alien Suffrage," 141 *University of Pennsylvania Law Review* 1391 (1993). When Congress created the Mississippi Territory by statute in 1798, it did not mention suffrage rules. "An Act for an

amicable settlement of limits with the state of Georgia, and authorizing the establishment of a government in the Mississippi Territory," Apr. 7, 1798, 2 *U.S.
Statutes* 549, sec. 3.

68. "An act further to extend the right of suffrage ... in the Mississippi territory,"
Oct. 25, 1814, 3 *U.S. Statutes* 143, sec. 1.

69. In April 1812, the House formally received a petition from "sundry inhabitants
of the Territory of Illinois, praying that the right of suffrage may be extended to
the inhabitants of that territory." A committee was formed, but no further action
was taken on the matter. Annals of Congress, House of Reps., 12th Cong., 1st
sess., 1326 (Apr. 9, 1812). On April 9, 1812, the House formed a committee to
consider extending the suffrage in Illinois; the bill was presented the following
week, though the Annals record only that the bill would "extend the right of suffrage." Annals of Congress, House of Reps., 12th Cong., 1st sess. (Apr. 9, 1812),
1278, 1321.

70. Act of Feb. 27, 1809, 2 *U.S. Statutes* 525, sec. 2.

71. 3 *U.S. Statutes* 670, sec. 5.

72. "An act concerning the District of Columbia," Feb. 27, 1801, 2 *U.S. Statutes* 103,
chap. 15. There is an explicit constitutional warrant for the district's creation.
U.S. Constitution, Article I, sec. 8, cl. 17.

73. Charles W. Harris, "District of Columbia," in Donald C. Bacon et al., eds., *The
Encyclopedia of the United States Congress* (1995), vol. 2, 646–47.

74. Peter Raven-Hansen, "Congressional Representation for the District of Columbia: A Constitutional Analysis," 12 *Harvard Journal on Legislation* 167, 175
(1975).

75. Ibid., 176–77, quoting Rep. Dennis.

76. Ibid., 177.

77. Certainly Illinois' 1812 request for an expanded franchise implies that territorial
residents accepted national authority in this area. Regarding later congressional suffrage rules for the Nebraska and Colorado territories, one historian has
written that "these measures were noncontroversial, since they were based on
explicit provisions for congressional authority over the District of Columbia
and federal territories." Robert M. Goldman, *Reconstruction and Black Suffrage:
Losing the Vote in* Reese *and* Cruikshank (2001), 12.

78. Jimmy Carter et al., *To Assure Pride and Confidence in the Electoral Process: Report
of the National Commission on Federal Election Reform* (2002), 26–27.

79. Keyssar, *The Right to Vote*, appendixes A.1 and A.2. For an authoritative account
of the limited extent of state taxation in early America, see *Pollock v. Farmers'
Loan and Trust Co.*, 158 U.S. 601, 607–11 (1895).

80. Williamson, *American Suffrage*, 136, 205.

81. Morgan, *Inventing the People*, 184, 185. As one participant described an election for a U.S. House seat in 1790s South Carolina, the Greenville courthouse
became "a scene of noise, blab, and confusion," with "much drinking, swearing,
cursing, and threatening ... clamor and confusion and disgrace." Ibid., quot-

ing from the diary of Edward Hooker. The "disgrace" here was probably the intimidation and physical force sometimes used to keep one's opponents from the polls, occasionally with official acquiescence. Ibid., 186–88.

82. Peter H. Argersinger, *Structure, Process, and Party: Essays in American Political History* (1992), 34–68.

83. State law required paper ballots in 1891. Albright, *The American Ballot*, 15–19.

84. For Ohio law, see Salmon P. Chase, *Statutes of Ohio* (1794), chap. 102, 241.

85. Dinkin, *Voting in Provincial America*, 133.

86. Albright, *The American Ballot*, 19, 19n39.

87. Williamson, *American Suffrage*, 122, 108, 121, 104, 110, 101. In 1788, New Jersey would increase the number of counties employing the ballot.

88. Ibid., 140, 160, 164.

89. *Luther v. Borden*, 48 U.S. (7 How.) 1 (1849).

90. The Jacksonian party system "derived considerable strength from the capability of parties to emphasize national, state, or local issues as their situation dictated." William E. Gienapp, "Politics Seem to Enter into Everything," in Stephen E. Maizlish and John J. Kushma, eds., *Essays on American Antebellum Politics, 1840–1860* (1982), 49, 50.

91. Argersinger, *Structure, Process, and Party*, 45, 46.

92. Ibid., 124.

93. Glenn C. Altschuler and Stuart M. Blumin, *Rude Republic: Americans and Their Politics in the Nineteenth Century* (2000), 265.

94. Saltman, *History and Politics of Voting Technology*, 64.

95. A. J. Reichley, *The Life of the Parties: A History of American Political Parties* (1992), 72.

96. Quoted in Williamson, *American Suffrage*, 121, 141, 179–80.

97. Ibid., 123.

98. Argersinger, *Structure, Process, and Party*, 43–44.

99. Some contemporary critics believe district elections damage American democracy as much as any other structural characteristic. See, for example, Lani Guinier, "The Representation of Minority Interests: The Question of Single-Member Districts," 14 *Cardozo Law Review* 1135 (1993). I discuss simultaneity further in Chapter 4.

100. "Developments in the Law: Voting and Democracy," 119 *Harvard Law Review* 1165, 1166 (2006).

101. Steven J. Mulroy, "The Way Out: A Legal Standard for Imposing Alternative Electoral Systems as Voting Rights Remedies," 33 *Harvard Civil Rights–Civil Liberties Law Review* 333, 380n12 (1998).

102. Act of June 25, 1842, 5 *U.S. Statutes* 491, sec. 2. "Slow to interfere" is the judgment of David Butler and Bruce Cain, *Congressional Redistricting: Comparative and Theoretical Perspectives* (1992), 24.

103. Emanuel Celler, "Congressional Apportionment—Past, Present, and Future," 17 *Law and Contemporary Problems* 268.

104. Celler, "Congressional Apportionment," 272.
105. *Congressional Globe*, 27th Cong., 2d sess., 104. For an excellent summary of state resistance to and rejections of federal legal authority in this period, see Leslie Friedman Goldstein, *Constituting Popular Sovereignty* (2001), table 3, 24–29.
106. *Congressional Globe*, 27th Cong., 2d sess. (Appendix), 391; emphasis added. Other speakers agreed, describing apportionment and districting decisions as "organic and fundamental." *Congressional Globe*, 27th Cong., 2d sess. (Appendix), 402 (Speech of Mr. Benton of Missouri).
107. Chester H. Rowell, *A Historical and Legal Digest of All the Contested Election Cases in the House of Representatives* (Washington: Government Printing Office, 1901), 117–20.
108. Celler, "Congressional Apportionment," 272.
109. The Court would point approvingly to the 1842 law in *Ex parte Siebold*, 100 U.S. 371, 384 (1880), but no pre–Civil War decisions of the Court did so. Mark A. Graber, "Resolving Political Questions into Judicial Questions: Tocqueville's Thesis Revisited," 21 *Constitutional Commentary* 485, 520 (2004). Writing thirty years after these events, George W. McCrary concluded that at least as far as the weight of congressional authority was concerned, the 1842 district-election requirement may have exceeded Congress's power. McCrary, *Treatise on the American Law of Elections*, 107. Justice Harlan's *Wesberry* dissent points out that Congress *had* purposefully enacted legislation regulating congressional districts; the *Wesberry* majority, he argued, operated on the "unstated premise" that Congress "has not dealt" with such matters. *Wesberry v. Sanders*, 376 U.S. 1, 42 (1964) (Harlan, J., dissenting). In Harlan's eyes, Congress clearly possessed this authority, despite not having stood consistently behind it.
110. The figure from 1820 is compiled from Saltman, *History and Politics of Voting Technology*, table 2.1, 57; Svend Petersen, *A Statistical History of the American Presidential Elections* (1981/1968), 18.
111. 1 *U.S. Statutes* 239, 2d Cong., 1st sess., chap. 8 (Mar. 1, 1792).
112. Peter H. Argersinger, "Electoral Processes," in Jack P. Greene, ed., *Encyclopedia of American Political History* (1984), 496.
113. "An act to establish a uniform time for holding elections for electors of the President and Vice President in all the States of the Union," Jan. 23, 1845, 2 *U.S. Statutes* 721. In Congress, one speaker commented that "the object of the bill was to prevent frauds at the ballot box." *Congressional Globe*, 28th Cong., 2d sess. (1844), 14.
114. *Congressional Globe*, 28th Cong., 2d sess. (1844), 15. Representative Hale, meanwhile, explained that under New Hampshire law, a majority of votes rather than a plurality was required, so any national simultaneity requirement should allow room for repeat elections or runoffs in any states that needed them. *Congressional Globe*, 28th Cong., 2d sess. (1844), 14.
115. *Congressional Globe*, 28th Cong., 2d sess. (1844), 15.
116. "An act to establish a uniform time for holding elections for electors of the

President and Vice President in all the States of the Union," Jan. 23, 1845, 2 *U.S. Statutes* 721. For current law, see U.S.Code, Title 3, chap. 1, sec. 2.

117. Quoted in Manning J. Dauer, *The Adams Federalists* (1953), 103.

118. Little has been written about this incident, but it seems the rumors were wrong. Vermont's presidential-elector law appears flawless. The 1791 compilation of Vermont's *Acts and Laws* includes "An act directing the mode of appointing electors to elect the president and vice president of the United States," and the statute is written in exactly the same language as those preceding and following it. See *Acts and Laws Passed by the State of Vermont* (Windsor, Vermont, 1791), 37–38. Manning Dauer concludes that the whole thing may have been Hamilton's doing, a disinformation campaign meant to help Thomas Pinckney. See Dauer, *The Adams Federalists*, 103–5.

119. Letter from Madison to Jefferson, Dec. 25, 1796, quoted in Dauer, *The Adams Federalists*, 105.

120. Bruce Ackerman and David Fontana, "Thomas Jefferson Counts Himself into the Presidency," 90 *Virginia Law Review* 551, 553 (2004).

121. Under the rules set up by the founders, that meant Jefferson and his own vice-presidential candidate, Aaron Burr, tied with seventy-three electoral votes each. Because that was a majority of the votes cast, the election went into the House of Representatives as a runoff between Jefferson and Burr—a runoff Jefferson won only on the thirty-sixth ballot. Had Georgia's votes not been counted, *no* candidate would have received a majority, and the Constitution would have required that the House decide among all *five* vote-receiving candidates, adding John Adams, Charles Pinckney, and John Jay. That would have badly hurt Jefferson's chances. Ackerman and Fontana conclude that Jefferson probably understood all of this and took advantage of his position as president of the Senate in order to make sure Georgia's electoral votes counted. Ackerman and Fontana, "Thomas Jefferson Counts Himself into the Presidency," 552.

122. Morgan Kousser explored contested elections in the setting of the post-Reconstruction South in *The Shaping of Southern Politics: Suffrage, Restriction, and the Establishment of the One-Party South* (1974). More recently, Richard Bensel delved deep into records from 1850 to 1868 in his exploration of the physical and sociological context in which Americans voted. Richard F. Bensel, *The American Ballot Box in the Mid-Nineteenth Century* (2004). Altschuler and Blumin relied on contested-election records in their revisionist account of nineteenth-century voting behavior. Altschuler and Blumin, *Rude Republic*. Jeffery Jenkins explores the role of partisanship in determining the outcome of contested elections in "Partisanship and Contested Elections in the House of Representatives, 1789–2002," 18 *Studies in American Political Development* 112 (2004), and "Partisanship and Contested Elections in the Senate, 1789–2002," 19 *Studies in American Political Development* 53 (2005).

123. These figures are derived from data generously shared with the author by Jeffery Jenkins.

124. Rowell, *A Historical and Legal Digest*, 3.
125. I derive these totals from Bensel, *American Ballot Box*, table 1.1, 6.
126. Nelson W. Polsby, "The Institutionalization of the U.S. House of Representatives," 62 *American Political Science Review* 164 (1968).
127. Jenkins, "Partisanship and Contested Elections in the House of Representatives," 120; Jenkins, "Partisanship and Contested Elections in the Senate," 60. There are further important differences between how the two chambers hear contests: the House has enacted statutory guidance for itself, while the Senate has not adopted any formal rules or procedures governing contests. Federal Contested Election Act of 1969, 83 *U.S. Statutes* 284; Charles T. Howell, "Contested Elections," in Donald C. Bacon et al., eds., *The Encyclopedia of the United States Congress* (1995), vol. 2, 570–71.
128. Rowell, *A Historical and Legal Digest*, 39.
129. Rowell, *A Historical and Legal Digest*, 41–43.
130. Morgan, *Inventing the People*, 166–88.
131. Rowell, *A Historical and Legal Digest*, 45–47.
132. Ibid., 53, 54.
133. Ibid., 60, 65, 67, 76, 83.
134. Ibid., 62.
135. Ibid., 63.
136. Ibid., 87, 88, 98–99, 105.
137. See generally Jenkins, "Partisanship and Contested Elections in the House of Representatives" and "Partisanship and Contested Elections in the Senate."
138. Jenkins, "Partisanship and Contested Elections in the House of Representatives," table 1, 117; Jenkins, "Partisanship and Contested Elections in the Senate," table 1, 58.
139. Rowell, *A Historical and Legal Digest*, 76.
140. Howell, "Contested Elections," 572.
141. White men did gain from reduced or eliminated property qualifications. But in New York, free blacks had to meet a new property test, while other states lengthened residency requirements or required that voters be citizens. And apportionment remained deeply flawed, with wealthy rural landowners holding disproportionate power at the expense of growing city populations. Still, the conventions certainly played an important role in American political development. In many states, suffrage reformers argued for an "unfiltered, unbalanced, unchecked will of the greatest number" that was new in American theories of self-rule, as Daniel T. Rodgers writes. Rodgers, *Contested Truths: Keywords in American Politics since Independence* (1998), 83.
142. This set mirrors the cases chosen by previous students of the period, for these states—and very few others—left some records of their convention. See Laura J. Scalia, *America's Jeffersonian Experiment: Remaking State Constitutions, 1820–1850* (1999) (which includes Ohio and Louisiana as well); Merrill D. Peterson, *Democracy, Liberty, and Property: The State Constitutional Conventions of the 1820s*

(1966) (an edited collection of excerpts from the conventions of Massachusetts in 1820–1821, New York in 1821, and Virginia in 1829–1830); and G. Alan Tarr, *Understanding State Constitutions* (1998). John Dinan accomplished a much more comprehensive assessment in *The American State Constitutional Tradition* (2006), but his discussions of suffrage focus on these states. The convention records do present challenges to the reader. At one point in North Carolina's 1836 convention, a Mr. Gaston of Craven prefaced a disquisition on electoral districts by pledging to make his case "with the utmost brevity, consistent with perspicuity." *Proceedings and Debates of the Convention of North-Carolina, Called to Amend the Constitution of the State, 1835* (1836), 358. Thousands of words later, his motion failed. The unrelenting "perspecuity" of delegates means the reader encounters scores of pages of tiny, hand-set debates over the suffrage, supported by only a rudimentary index or none at all.

143. *Journal of Debates and Proceedings in the Convention of Delegates, Chosen to Revise the Constitution of Massachusetts, 1820–1821* (1853), 246.

144. Ibid., 246.

145. Ibid., 252.

146. Ibid., 256.

147. Williamson, *American Suffrage*, 193.

148. *Journal of Debates and Proceedings*, 257; emphasis added. Later, another delegate moved an amendment requiring that "the tax be assessed in some town in the Commonwealth." Ibid., 521. One delegate argued that the tax rolls were an inaccurate and inadequate measure of the citizenry. Surely we all know, he said, "that there are persons in every town, who are never put into a tax bill, because the town officers know very well that no tax could be collected from them." *Journal of Debates and Proceedings*, 256.

149. Ibid., 553.

150. Ibid., 553.

151. Ibid., 553, 618.

152. *Reports of the Proceedings and Debates of the New York Constitutional Convention of 1821* (1821/1970), 286.

153. *Journal of Debates and Proceedings*, 554.

154. Ibid., 555.

155. Ibid.

156. Constitution of New York, Article II, sec. 1, reprinted in *Reports of the Proceedings and Debates*, 661.

157. *Reports of the Proceedings and Debates*, 284.

158. For example, a Colonel Young argued against allowing black men to vote, contending that the ballot would be "unsafe in their hands," since "their vote would be at the call of the richest purchaser." *Reports of the Proceedings and Debates*, 191. For similar comments, see ibid., 243, 280–81.

159. Ibid., 205.

160. Ibid., 203.

161. Ibid., 180.
162. Ibid., 203.
163. *Proceedings and Debates of the Virginia State Convention, of 1829–1830* (1830). Only in the state's next constitutional convention, that of 1850–1851, did western political power finally increase. Scalia, *America's Jeffersonian Experiment*, 12–13. Merrill Peterson estimates that when the 1830 constitution was ratified, two-thirds of the state's white men could vote, a "modest expansion of the franchise [which] had no significant effect on the politics and government of the Old Dominion." Peterson, *Democracy, Liberty, and Property*, 281.
164. See, for example, Peterson, *Democracy, Liberty, and Property*, 363 (where one speaker refers to the "ancient republic of Athens, and some of the other Grecian states"), 54 (on Locke); and 157 (on "the days of Solon [and] those of George Washington").
165. *Proceedings and Debates of the Virginia State Convention*, 533.
166. See, for example, ibid., 156, 158, 167, 664, 665, and on "bondage," 318.
167. Ibid., 532. For the debate on the County Courts, see 526–30, 532–35.
168. See, for example, ibid., 845–47.
169. Ibid., 366.
170. Ibid., 180; see *Hylton v. United States*, 3 Dall. 171 (1796). Another debate, however, made clear that the apportionment of state levies was more contentious, particularly in terms of slaves, which were of course some of the most valuable "property" in the state. Peterson, *Democracy, Liberty, and Property*, 169.
171. Reprinted in *Proceedings and Debates of the Virginia State Convention*, 900.
172. "Now the introduction of the ballot . . . is a plain distinct acknowledgement, that the Right of Suffrage is extended too far—extended to men who cannot be expected to give an independent vote, openly, in the face of day—to men liable to the influence of others, and desirous to conciliate their favour." Ibid., 406; see also 417.
173. *Proceedings and Debates of the Convention of North-Carolina*. New systems of representation did slightly increase western power. Scalia, *America's Jeffersonian Experiment*, 13.
174. See, for example, *Proceedings and Debates of the Convention of North-Carolina*, 358, 359, 362–63.
175. For example, one delegate argued that a county's senatorial representation should be determined by the *average* of a county's tax contribution over a period rather than by its taxes in a given year. Otherwise, "a few wealthy men in a small county, in order to obtain a Senator, might join together and put up a Billiard Table or two." A colleague took the remark quite seriously, agreeing that more "permanent" sources of revenue like the "land-tax and poll-tax" ought to determine Senatorial representation, rather than what was raised "from Billiard Tables [and] Natural Curiosities." *Proceedings and Debates of the Convention of North-Carolina*, 181.
176. Ibid., 179, 181.

177. Benjamin F. Shambaugh, ed., *Fragments of the Debates of the Iowa Constitutional Conventions of 1844 and 1846* (1900), 260–66, 276–313. For discussion of the two conventions more generally, see Scalia, *America's Jeffersonian Experiment*, 17. As the Iowa political scientist Shambaugh explained in introducing his edited collection on the conventions, participants kept no official records, and no "Madison's Journal" has come to light. Shambaugh, *Fragments of the Debates*, iii. Shambaugh's excerpts are long and detailed, stylistically and rhetorically indistinguishable from the more official records of other states. Shambaugh chooses selections from the *Iowa Standard* and the *Iowa Capital Reporter* for both the 1844 and 1846 conventions.

178. Shambaugh, *Fragments of the Debates*, 214.

179. Ibid., 44. By "poll tax," O'Brien meant a "head tax," or a tax not linked to property value. In Iowa, as in other states, discussion of the advisability of "poll taxes" was frequently not linked at all to voting.

180. Ibid., 44–47. Nevertheless, two years later one newspaper praised the convention simply for debating the measure, calling it "progress [for] the principle of universal suffrage." Ibid., 341–42.

181. Ibid., 56.

182. Ibid., 153.

183. Ibid., 299; emphasis in original.

184. This speaker said the question before the assembly comes down to "*shall this Legislature give them the opportunity of voting on this change, by causing polls to be opened in each township or precinct throughout the Territory?*" Ibid., 306; emphasis in original. The territorial governor's official proclamation of Iowa's entry into the Union referred to "the general election held . . . in all the organized counties." Ibid., 371.

Chapter 2

Epigraph: "Purity of the Ballot Box," *New York Times*, March 26, 1870; *United States v. Reese*, 92 U.S. 214, 219 (1876).

1. For example, see "Viewpoint: A Dose of Honesty for Florida 13," AEI-Brookings Election Reform Project weblog, Jan. 10, 2007, *www.electionreformproject.org/Resources*, which states that HAVA's passage marked "the first real public discussion about voting administration in United States history."

2. For an outstanding example of scholarship consciously aiming to "recover" "old institutional language" (and examining this same time period), see Pamela Brandwein, "The *Civil Rights Cases* and the Lost Language of State Neglect," in Ronald Kahn and Ken I. Kersch, eds., *The Supreme Court and American Political Development* (2006).

3. *United States v. Reese*, 92 U.S. 214, 219 (1876).

4. Richard F. Bensel, *The American Ballot Box in the Mid-Nineteenth Century*

(2004), 217–19. For a full exploration of the dynamics of voting during the Civil War, see chapter 6 of *The American Ballot Box*, "Loyalty Oaths, Troops, and Elections during the Civil War."

5.   Peter H. Argersinger, *Structure, Process, and Party: Essays in American Political History* (1992), 47, 48. Argersinger lists Virginia, West Virginia, Arkansas, and Missouri in the latter category. Later, some Radical Republicans would unsuccessfully push to require southern states to abandon viva voce voting as a condition of readmission to the Union. Paul Bourke and Donald DeBats, *Washington County: Politics and Community in Antebellum America* (1995), 9.

6.   Akhil Amar, *America's Constitution: A Biography* (2005), 380. Amar is talking here about the change from militias to a national army, but the point applies well to suffrage rules.

7.   Scholars today generally agree that as a historical matter, the "civil" rights granted in the Fourteenth Amendment omitted the "political" right to vote. Amar, *America's Constitution*, 351. For a summary of recent literature on this question, see Michael J. Perry, *We the People: The Fourteenth Amendment and the Supreme Court* (1999), 217n69.

8.   U.S. Constitution, Amend. XIV, sec. 2.

9.   For an argument that in fact the Fifteenth Amendment *repealed* section 2 of the Fourteenth Amendment, see Jack Chin, "Reconstruction, Felon Disenfranchisement, and the Right to Vote: Did the Fifteenth Amendment Repeal Section 2 of the Fourteenth Amendment?" 92 *Georgetown Law Journal* 259 (2004).

10.   *Richardson v. Ramirez*, 418 U.S. 24 (1974).

11.   Sen. Dixon of Connecticut, *Congressional Globe*, Jan. 29, 1869, 705. I first encountered this quotation in Alexander Keyssar, *The Right to Vote: The Contested History of Democracy in the United States* (2000).

12.   Karen Orren and Stephen Skowronek, *The Search for American Political Development* (2004), 134.

13.   For an authoritative explanation both of this general point and of the Fifteenth Amendment's limited initial effects, see Richard Valelly, *The Two Reconstructions: The Struggle for Black Enfranchisement* (2004).

14.   "Troops at polls," Act of Feb. 25, 1865, 18 U.S.C.A. 592.

15.   *Revised Statutes*, sec. 25; Mar. 3, 1875, 18 *U.S. Statutes* 400, chap. 130, sec. 6; derived from Act of Feb. 2, 1872, 17 *U.S. Statutes* 28, chap. 11, sec. 3. See also Act of June 5, 1934, 48 *U.S. Statutes* 879, chap. 390, sec. 2.
       Congress enacted many statutes relating to the suffrage during this time, as shown in George W. McCrary's 1875 book *A Treatise on the American Law of Elections*. The book deals with scores of topics in election law, and though most of its sections detail the creation of a common law of elections in state courts, federal law and cases are described in numerous sections, and statutes are tallied in the appendixes. See ibid., 405–31.

16.   *Ex parte Yarbrough*, 110 U.S. 651, 661 (1884).

17.   *Foster v. Love*, 522 U.S. 67, 73 (1997).

18. "At the regular election held in any State next preceding the expiration of the term for which any Senator was elected to represent such State in Congress, at which election a Representative to Congress is regularly by law to be chosen, a United States Senator from said State shall be elected by the people thereof for the term commencing on the 3d day of January next thereafter." Act of June 4, 1914, 38 *U.S. Statutes* 384, chap. 103, sec. 1.

19. "The Census and the Election Law," *New York Times,* June 2, 1870. See "Enforcement Act of May 31, 1870," reproduced in the best account of the period: Xi Wang, *The Trial of Democracy: Black Suffrage and Northern Republicans, 1860–1910* (1997), 267–74.

20. *United States v. Reese,* 219; emphasis added. The closing sentence hints at the Court's reluctance to enforce the act, and, indeed, in this case the Court struck down part of the 1870 Act. In a companion case, *United States v. Cruikshank,* the Court further limited enforcement of the 1870 Act, voiding federal indictments and suggesting that any punishment for the white men who perpetrated the Easter 1873 Colfax Massacre should come from the state of Louisiana. Scholars differ as to whether *Cruikshank* is best understood as a limited, technical decision on the bills of indictment (and thus *not* a threat to the substance of the present statute or congressional enforcement powers under the Reconstruction amendments) or a serious undermining of the federal law, weakening Congress's power to prevent racial discrimination in southern elections. Leslie Friedman Goldstein concludes that while the core of *Cruikshank* may be merely the voiding of indictments "on legal technicalities," the decision also "accepted the *U.S. v. Reese* ruling that voided two sections of the Enforcement Act of May 1870." Leslie Friedman Goldstein, "The Specter of the Second Amendment: Rereading *Slaughterhouse* and *Cruikshank,*" *Studies in American Political Development* 21 (2007): 131, 134, 141. Another authority writes that these decisions interpreted the 1870 Act in a "cramped, technical" way that "crippled the [Enforcement] acts for practical purposes." Ward E. Y. Elliott, "*U.S. v. Reese,*" in Kermit L. Hall, ed., *The Oxford Companion to the Supreme Court of the United States* (1992), 714.

21. Albie Burke, "Federal Regulation of Congressional Elections in Northern Cities, 1871–94," 14 *American Journal of Legislative History* 17, 25 (1970).

22. Wang, *The Trial of Democracy,* 57. Argersinger writes that the act "constituted the largest federal attempt to regulate elections" up to that time. Argersinger, *Structure, Process, and Party,* 50. Another study says the 1871 law established "a system of national supervision over state-administered election laws." Scott C. James and Brian L. Lawson, "The Political Economy of Voting Rights Enforcement in America's Gilded Age," 93 *American Political Science Review* 115 (1999). See also U.S. Dept. of Justice, Civil Rights Division, Voting Section, "Before the Voting Rights Act," *www.usdoj.gov/crt/voting/intro/intro_a.htm.*

23. Robert M. Goldman, *Reconstruction and Black Suffrage: Losing the Vote in* Reese *and* Cruikshank (2001), 20. Ronald Hayduk writes that events in New York

"led to the passage of the federal election laws of 1870–1871." Ronald Hayduk, *Gatekeepers to the Franchise: Shaping Election Administration in New York* (2005), 42. Albie Burke writes that "the record fraud vote the Tweed Ring produced in the New York election of 1868" precipitated the act. Burke, "Federal Regulation," 21.

24. Wang, *The Trial of Democracy*, 65, 64n77.

25. Ibid., 58, 62; citing *Congressional Globe*, 41st Cong., 2d sess. (1870), pt. 4: 3569–70.

26. Wang, *The Trial of Democracy*, 60–61.

27. Argersinger, *Structure, Process, and Party*, 51.

28. Ibid., 51–52. At least once, the marshals arrested the federally appointed Democratic supervisor himself.

29. Burke, "Federal Regulation," table 1, 27. For a more detailed accounting, broken out by region and specific offices, see James and Lawson, "Political Economy of Voting Rights Enforcement," 121–26.

30. *Ex parte Siebold*, 100 U.S. 371 (1880); *Ex parte Clark*, 100 U.S. 399 (1880).

31. Richard M. Valelly, "Partisan Entrepreneurship and Policy Windows: George Frisbie Hoar and the 1890 Federal Elections Bill," in Stephen Skowronek and Matthew Glassman, eds., *Formative Acts: American Politics in the Making* (2007), 126.

32. Bourke and DeBats, *Washington County*, 9. The U.S. Code still requires that "all votes for Representatives in Congress must be by written or printed ballot, or voting machine the use of which has been duly authorized by the State law." Act of Feb. 14, 1899, 30 *U.S. Statutes* 836, derived from the acts of Feb. 28, 1871, 16 *U.S. Statutes* 440, chap. 99, sec. 19, and May 30, 1872, 17 *U.S. Statutes* 192, chap. 239.

33. Wang, *The Trial of Democracy*, 57. Another authority agrees that the acts constituted "nothing less than the first national criminal code." Goldman, *Reconstruction and Black Suffrage*, 23.

34. Though the language of section 19 of the statute does not restrict its application to cities, this is the interpretation of one authoritative history. Bourke and DeBats, *Washington County*, 9.

35. Woodrow Wilson, *Congressional Government*, 2d ed. (1885), 27. I learned of this quotation in Richard Valelly, *The Two Reconstructions*, 244.

36. Richard A. Posner, *Breaking the Deadlock: The 2000 Election, the Constitution, and the Courts* (2001), 207.

37. *Giles v. Harris*, 189 U.S. 475, 488 (1903). For a full-length interrogation of *Giles* and an argument that it belongs in the "canon" of constitutional law—precisely because its analysis is so "fascinatingly repellant"—see Richard H. Pildes, "Democracy, Anti-democracy, and the Canon," 17 *Constitutional Commentary* 295, 298 (2000). I will have more to say about *Giles* in Chapter 4, on localism's relationship with exclusion and inequality.

38. *United States v. Reese*, 219.

39. *Reese* and *Cruikshank* were actually the endpoints of prosecutions initiated under the statutes *before* those statutes were integrated into the Code. As Richard Valelly explains, congressional Republicans led by George Boutwell strategically scattered the revised statutes all around the U.S. Code. Valelly, *The Two Reconstructions* (2004), 243.

40. *United States v. Munford*, 16 F. 223, 227 (1883); emphasis added.

41. Ibid., 228. "There is little regarding an election that is not included in the terms, time, place, and manner of holding it." Ibid.

42. Congress "has general powers of legislation concerning federal elections, but can legislate concerning state and municipal elections solely for the purpose of preventing discriminations on account of race." Ibid., 230. This quotation comes from Judge Hughes, who concurred with the opinion of Judge Bond in *Munford* (quoted above), and also wrote a separate opinion.

43. *United States v. Goldman*, 25 F. Cas. 1350, 1353 (1878). Implying that Congress might regulate the process quite broadly, the *Goldman* court said, "An election is not simply the depositing of a ballot in a box." Ibid.

44. *Ex parte Siebold*, 100 U.S. 371 (1880); *Ex parte Clark*, 100 U.S. 399 (1880); *Ex parte Yarbrough*, 110 U.S. 651 (1884).

45. *Ex parte Siebold*, 396. In an 1883 case, the Court would cite *Siebold* and *Clark* and again uphold a prosecution for vote fraud under the federal statute. *United States v. Gale*, 109 U.S. 65 (1883).

46. *Ex parte Siebold*, 396.

47. *Ex parte Yarbrough*, 662, 665, 666.

48. Ibid., 660.

49. Valelly, "Partisan Entrepreneurship and Policy Windows," 131.

50. *Mills v. Green*, 159 U.S. 651 (1895). The phrase "disingenuous nonsense" is in Charles A. Heckman, "Keeping Legal History 'Legal' and Judicial Activism in Perspective: A Reply to Richard Pildes," 19 *Constitutional Commentary* 625, 634 (2002). Heckman argues that *Mills v. Green* was the most important decision of this era.

51. *Ratliff v. Beale*, 20 So. 865 (Miss. 1896).

52. *Williams v. Mississippi*, 170 U.S. 213, 223 (1898).

53. *James v. Bowman*, 190 U.S. 127 (1903).

54. *Giles v. Harris*, 491.

55. Ibid.

56. *In re Coy*, 127 U.S. 731, 751 (1888).

57. Ibid., 752.

58. *Wiley v. Sinkler*, 179 U.S. 58 (1900); *Swafford v. Templeton*, 185 U.S. 487 (1902).

59. *Wiley v. Sinkler*, 62. After affirming federal jurisdiction, however, the *Wiley* court rejected the plaintiff's claim, because he had not been registered to vote under South Carolina law. Ibid., 65–67.

60. *Swafford v. Templeton*, 493, 494.

61. Ibid., 492, quoting *Ex parte Yarbrough*, 664.
62. *Swafford v. Templeton*, 493; emphasis added.
63. Justice Clifford asserted that antipathy between blacks and whites was "in the nature of things" in an 1877 case; the Court also employed the phrase in the 1883 *Civil Rights Cases*, and *Plessy v. Ferguson* would rest on that discriminatory premise as well. See Mark Weiner, *Black Trials: Citizenship from the Beginnings of Slavery to the End of Caste* (2004), 235–37; *Hall v. DeCuir*, 95 U.S. 485, 503 (1877); *Plessy v. Ferguson*, 163 U.S. 544, 552 (1896). Weiner does not note here the *Civil Rights Cases*, in which the Court said that "the personal rights and immunities recognized in the prohibitive clauses of the [Fourteenth] amendment were, prior to its adoption, under the protection, primarily, of the States, while rights, created by or derived from the United States, have always been, and, *in the nature of things*, should always be, primarily, under the protection of the general government." *Civil Rights Cases*, 109 U.S. 3, 56 (1883); emphasis added.
64. It had appeared repeatedly in at least one John Marshall opinion on contracts, as well. *Sturges v. Crowninshield*, 17 U.S. 122 (1819).
65. *Minor v. Happersett* states baldly that "the Constitution of the United States does not confer the right of suffrage upon any one." *Happersett* is not the only gender-related case that aroused such statements from federal judges. Consider this passage from a federal decision of 1873: "If the state of New York should provide that no person should vote until he had reached the age of thirty years, or after he had reached the age of fifty, or that no person having gray hair, or who had not the use of all his limbs, should be entitled to vote, I do not see how it could be held to be a violation of any right derived or held under the constitution of the United States." *United States v. Anthony*, 24 F. Cas. 829, 830 (N.D. New York, 1873). The case involved a person who voted in an 1872 congressional election and was now being prosecuted for voting without having a lawful right to vote because, as the Court said of Susan B. Anthony, "she is a woman." Some of these decisions, together with their robust reading of the Elections Clause, would surface in Justice Hugo Black's opinion upholding most of the 1970 amendments to the Voting Rights Act for a fractured five-justice majority in *Oregon v. Mitchell*. That opinion cites *Siebold*, *Yarbrough*, *Swafford*, and *Wiley*. See *Oregon v. Mitchell*, 400 U.S. 112, 121 (1970).
66. *Wiley v. Sinkler*, 59, 66.
67. *In re Coy*, 751, 745, 748.
68. *Swafford v. Templeton*, 489.
69. *Mills v. Green*, 652. *Williams v. Mississippi* is the exception that proves the rule, as it includes virtually no close attention to actual administrative practice. In *Williams* the Court acted with willful blindness toward voting conditions—a crucial reason why that decision is such a poor one.
70. Valelly, *The Two Reconstructions*, 246–48.
71. Morgan Kousser, *The Shaping of Southern Politics: Suffrage, Restriction, and the Establishment of the One-Party South* (1974), 263.

72. Richard Pildes, "Democracy, Anti-democracy, and the Canon," 308–9 (2000).
73. Quoted in Pildes, "Democracy, Anti-democracy, and the Canon," 310.
74. *Ex parte Yarbrough*, 662.
75. Ibid.
76. *In re Coy*, 755.
77. Burke, "Federal Regulation," 34.
78. Bourke and DeBats, *Washington County*, 6.
79. Eldon Cobb Evans, *A History of the Australian Ballot System in the United States* (1917), 24.
80. William H. Glasson, "The Australian Voting System: A Sketch of Its History and Principles—Why North Carolina, South Carolina, and Georgia Should Adopt It," *South Atlantic Quarterly* (1909), 8.
81. Quoted in L. E. Fredman, *The Australian Ballot: The Story of an American Reform* (1968), 20.
82. Evans, *History of the Australian Ballot System*, 11.
83. Robert Goldberg, "Election Fraud: An American Vice," in A. James Reichley, ed., *Elections American Style* (1987), 182.
84. Roy G. Saltman, *The History and Politics of Voting Technology* (2006), 89–96.
85. On this function of parties, see, for example, Fredman, *The Australian Ballot*, 27–28; Evans, *History of the Australian Ballot System*, 22n3; Glasson, "The Australian Voting System," 6–8; Brad Smith, "Judicial Protection of Ballot Access Rights: Third Parties Need Not Apply," 28 *Harvard Journal of Legislation* 167 (1991). These expenses could be considerable. One account of the costs borne by a candidate in 1882 included "about $25,000 for manning the polls and supplying booths, $10,000 for printing the tickets, and $8,000 for their distribution, besides other expenses of the campaign." Evans, *History of the Australian Ballot System*, 14.
86. Fredman, *The Australian Ballot*, ix; Saltman, *History and Politics of Voting Technology*, 96. The French had apparently experimented with secrecy as early as 1789, but the practice had not stuck. Stein Rokkan et al., *Citizens, Elections, and Parties: Approaches to the Comparative Study of the Processes of Development* (1970), 152–53.
87. Among other early adopters, this was the case in Minnesota, Missouri, Tennessee, and Wisconsin, as well as Kentucky. North Carolina adopted the Australian ballot in one county in 1909, extending it to the entire state two decades later; in 1922, Georgia authorized counties to adopt reform on their own if they wished. Spencer D. Albright, *The American Ballot* (1942), 27.
88. Saltman, *History and Politics of Voting Technology*, 131. Texas, Connecticut, and New Jersey did not adopt mandatory secret-voting laws until 1905, 1909, and 1911, respectively. Georgia passed legislation allowing counties to adopt the Australian ballot in 1922, but not all counties did so immediately. South Carolina did not adopt the secret ballot until 1950. And Delaware actually *abandoned* the requirement in 1913, permitting parties to distribute ballots before elections,

so that voters could mark them before election day; the state eventually adopted lever machines in 1953.

89. Glasson, "The Australian Voting System," 10.

90. Abram Flexner, *The New Ballot Law of Louisville, Kentucky at work and compared with the Massachusetts Law* (1889), 9, 5.

91. Thos. E. Hill, *Hill's Political History of the United States* (1894), 121. Defenders of public voting raised to no avail the old argument that secrecy was no guarantee of virtue. As one Englishman put it in arguing against the Australian system, "Nothing was supposed to prevent misconduct and robbery at night so effectually as gas lamps." Quoted in Evans, *History of the Australian Ballot System*, 21–22n4. And one American opponent of reform argued that there would be *more* corruption under the new system, since "it would be easier, safer, and would require less money to corrupt [ballot clerks and inspectors] than to bribe so many electors." Evans, *History of the Australian Ballot System*, 21.

92. Glasson, "The Australian Voting System," 9.

93. Quoted in Mark McKenna, "Building 'a Closet of Prayer' in the New World: The Story of the Australian Ballot," *London Papers in Australian Studies*, No. 6 (2002), 2–3. For a summary of nineteenth-century voting reforms in various countries, see generally John H. Wigmore, *The Australian Ballot System as Embodied in the Legislation of Various Countries*, 2d ed. (1889).

94. Massachusetts Governor Oliver Ames, quoted in Glasson, "The Australian Voting System," 6.

95. Matthew A. Crenson and Benjamin Ginsberg, *Downsizing Democracy: How America Sidelined Its Citizens and Privatized Its Public* (2002), 46.

96. Rokkan et al., *Citizens, Elections, and Parties*, 35.

97. *Wiley v. Sinkler*, 62–63.

98. *In re Coy*, 737.

99. Guy Ward Mallon, *The Ohio Election Law: A Manual for the Guidance of Electors and Election Officers* (1892), 7, 9, 10, 11–12.

100. "The Australian Ballot Act and other acts constituting the Election Laws of North Dakota" (1891), 3, 7.

101. Massachusetts Statute 1888, chap. 436, as Amended by Stat. 1889, chap. 413; reprinted in Wigmore, *Australian Ballot System*, 54–65, 66, 73.

102. Public Act No. 9 of 1890, "An Act to Promote Purity of Elections, Secure Secrecy of the Ballot, and to Provide for the Printing and Distribution of Ballots at Public Expense," sec. 25.

103. Hill, *Hill's Political History*, 123–24. Unfortunately, Hill does not state what jurisdiction this provision comes from.

104. "The Australian Ballot Act and other acts constituting the Election Laws of North Dakota" (1891), 16.

105. Evans, *History of the Australian Ballot System*, 25, 23. Another contemporary advocate spoke of "ballots printed at public expense." Glasson, "The Australian Voting System," 3.

106. Reprinted in Flexner, *New Ballot Law of Louisville, Kentucky*, 11.

107. "The Australian Ballot Act and other acts constituting the Election Laws of North Dakota," 3.

108. Public Act No. 9 of 1890, "An Act to Promote Purity of Elections," sec. 2, sec. 3, sec. 25.

109. James H. Blodgett, "Suffrage and Its Mechanism in Great Britain and the United States," *American Anthropologist*, Jan. 1889, 70, 71.

110. Saltman, *History and Politics of Voting Technology*, 108.

111. See generally William J. Novak, *The People's Welfare: Law and Regulation in Nineteenth-Century America* (1996), and particularly 237–38.

112. Ibid., 237.

113. See Fredman, *The Australian Ballot*, 119–30. Fredman notes that fraud survived, major parties retained a great deal of power, the "long ballot" confused many voters, registration rules contributed to disenfranchisement, and "frequent allegations of miscounting, repeating and other abuses" persisted. This is not to mention racist disenfranchisement in the South.

114. Argersinger, *Structure, Process, and Party*, 53.

115. Richard Henry Dana, *The Australian Ballot System of Massachusetts: Some Fallacious Questions Answered* (1911), 22. One scholar tallied rough records of ballot-reform votes in state legislatures in the late 1880s and found that in most states, no party lines were clearly apparent, though Democrats were slightly more likely to favor reform. Wigmore, *Australian Ballot System As Embodied in the Legislation of Various Countries*, Appendix VI.

116. Peter H. Argersinger, " 'A Place on the Ballot': Fusion Politics and Antifusion Laws," 85 *American Historical Review* 287, 295 (1980).

117. Argersinger, *Structure, Process, and Party*, 142.

118. Lisa Jane Disch, *The Tyranny of the Two-Party System* (2002), 13. As Argersinger writes, the new laws "permitted the politicians in power to use state authority to promote self-serving conditions to order." Argersinger, *Structure, Process, and Party*, 146. In some areas, new rules and partisan maneuvering led to confusing county-level variation in ballot design that made it virtually impossible for state-wide fusion to work. One satisfied Oregon Republican described the resulting inconsistencies as "a very pretty jungle." Argersinger, *Structure, Process, and Party*, 293–94. As one prominent reformer noted, while "the system undoubtedly favors independent voting, it has by no means broken up parties." Dana, *Australian Ballot System of Massachusetts*, 8.

119. Party scholar Leon D. Epstein writes that the Australian ballot "may well have been a necessary condition" for the modern American belief in "treating our parties as public utilities." Epstein, *Political Parties in the American Mold* (1986), 163. See also Disch, *Tyranny of the Two-Party System*, 44.

120. Saltman, *History and Politics of Voting Technology*, 108–18.

121. Act of February 14, 1899, 55th Cong., 3d sess., chap. 154. For a brief discussion, see Saltman, *History and Politics of Voting Technology*, 117–18.

Chapter 3

Epigraph: Joseph Harris, *Registration of Voters in the United States* (1929), 1; V. O. Key, *Southern Politics in State and Nation* (1949), 445; "Findings and Purposes," National Voter Registration Act (1993).

1. Jimmy Carter et al., *To Assure Pride and Confidence in the Electoral Process: Report of the National Commission on Federal Election Reform* (2002), 27; emphasis added.
2. As Tocqueville observed in his study of Massachusetts law, registration was "compulsory" for local officials as well as for voters, since Massachusetts selectmen who failed to draw up a list of township voters "were guilty of a misdemeanor." But there is little evidence that this law was enforced, much less that state officials checked the accuracy of town lists. Alexis de Tocqueville, *Democracy in America*, vol. 1 (1990/1835), 63.
3. James H. Blodgett, "Suffrage and Its Mechanism in Great Britain and the United States," *American Anthropologist*, Jan. 1889, 73. Here three different scholars attest either to experiencing this rule themselves or to hearing of its use. Richard Bensel shows this to have been an old tradition: a Kentucky laborer involved in an 1859 contested-election hearing "claimed [the precinct of] Wolf Creek as his residence, as he had his washing done there." Richard F. Bensel, *The American Ballot Box in the Mid-Nineteenth Century* (2004), 92. As Bensel explains, unmarried, unpropertied transient workers regularly relied on the fact that their washing was done in a specific place as proof that they had some connection to that community and so were eligible to vote there. Ibid., 90.
4. Joseph Harris, *Registration of Voters in the United States* (1929), 312–13.
5. Ibid., 65.
6. In-person registration was not initially required by most laws, and local officials were often authorized to "prepare lists of qualified electors from their knowledge," so party machines had little trouble corrupting the new system. Typically, party precinct captains would simply hand in long lists of names, including those of people who had moved away, had died, or were altogether fictional. Harris, *Registration of Voters*, 66. See also National Municipal League, Committee on Election Administration, *A Model Registration System* (1927), 48–49.
7. Harris, *Registration of Voters*, 66.
8. National Municipal League, *A Model Registration System*, 45. As the report observed, "It is impossible even to estimate the cost in time and bother to the mass of citizens to keep registered under existing inconvenient registration systems. In a number of states they must register every year, and are permitted to register only on two or three specified days when sessions are held in the precinct."
9. Harris, *Registration of Voters*, 15–16.
10. An excellent general introduction to Australian election law is Graeme Orr, Bryan Mercurio, and George Williams, eds., *Realising Democracy: Electoral Law in Australia* (2003).

11. For a summary of the history and current role of Canada's Chief Electoral Officer, see "The Administration of Canada's Independent, Non-Partisan Approach," 3 *Election Law Journal* 406 (2004).

12. As Walter Dean Burnham points out, centralization "presupposed the existence of a bureaucracy for administering such enrollment laws or a consensus that such a bureaucracy should be created." Burnham, "The System of 1896: An Analysis," in Paul Kleppner et al., *The Evolution of American Electoral Systems* (1981), 167.

13. National Municipal League, *A Model Registration System*, 52.

14. Harris, *Registration of Voters*, 1.

15. The league's Committee on Election Administration, headed by political scientists like Charles E. Merriam and Joseph Harris, appears to have been heavily populated by city and state elections officials. Thus its call for centralization was quite muted, as statements like this one indicate: "The registration law for any city or state should be drafted with careful attention to the local election law and organization, as well as any peculiar local problems, and should be prepared by a competent person who has a thorough knowledge of registration administration." Ibid., 48. This connection had not been general until the twentieth century, since partisans in many states purposefully kept elections separate lest national issues overwhelm their ability to focus voter attention on matters closer to home. Peter H. Argersinger, *Structure, Process, and Party: Essays in American Political History* (1992), 45.

16. Daniel McCool, Susan M. Olson, and Jennifer L. Robinson, *Native Vote: American Indians, the Voting Rights Act, and the Right to Vote* (2007), 9.

17. Ibid, 11–19, 96–97. The case was *Allen v. Merrell*, 6 Utah 2d 32 (1956).

18. *United States v. Mosley*, 238 U.S. 383, 386 (1915).

19. *United States v. Gradwell*, 243 U.S. 476 (1917); *United States v. Bathgate* (1918). A good discussion of these and other cases is Richard Claude, *The Supreme Court and the Electoral Process* (1970), 30–32.

20. *Smiley v. Holm*, 285 U.S. 355, 366 (1932).

21. *Cook v. Gralike et al.*, 531 U.S. 510 (2001).

22. *United States v. Classic*, 313 U.S. 299 (1941).

23. Ibid., 320.

24. Claude, *Supreme Court and the Electoral Process*, 33, quoting Alpheus T. Mason, *Harlan Fiske Stone, Pillar of the Law* (1956), 589; emphasis added.

25. V. O. Key, *Southern Politics in State and Nation* (1949), 201. Probably because Key identified as a southerner himself, and because he knew he had evidence to support his judgments, the Texan was not afraid to use chapter titles like "Louisiana: The Seamy Side of Democracy."

26. While one-party areas were the worst offenders, Key concluded that the check theoretically offered by two-party politics was "vastly overrated." Ibid., 443, 460, 444, 454.

27. Public voting practices were unsuccessfully challenged by the state Republican

Party in *Gardner v. Blackwell*, 167 S.C. 313 (1932), and *Smith v. Blackwell*, 115 F. 2d 186 (1940). Key, *Southern Politics in State and Nation*, 457.

28. In Texas, Key explained, the number alongside a voter's name on the voting list was written on the ballot; this policy was also used in those Georgia counties that failed to adopt secrecy rules. In Arkansas, the voter had to make a carbon copy of his ballot, sign the copy, and deposit it in a box used for formal contests of election results. Alabama used ballot numbering until 1939, then began covering the numbers with a black seal. Ibid., 458. Recall that a 1922 Georgia state law had allowed county grand juries to adopt secrecy as they wished.

29. Ibid., 458.

30. Ibid., 460.

31. *Davis v. Schnell*, 81 F. Supp. 872 (1949). "To state it even more plainly, the board, by the use of the words 'understand and explain,' is given the arbitrary power to accept or reject any prospective elector that may apply. . . . Such arbitrary power amounts to a denial of equal protection of the law within the meaning of the Fourteenth Amendment to the Constitution, and is condemned by the *Yick Wo* [*v. Hopkins* (1886)] and many other decisions of the Supreme Court." Ibid., 878.

32. *Voting Integrity Project, Inc., et al., v. Oregon*, 259 F.3d 1169, 1175 (2001).

33. George Frederick Miller, *Absentee Voters and Suffrage Laws* (1948), 21.

34. Roy G. Saltman, *The History and Politics of Voting Technology* (2006), 141; Ira Michael Heyman, "Federal Remedies for Voteless Negroes," 48 *California Law Review* 190, 192 (1960).

35. *United States v. Raines*, 362 U.S. 17 (1960).

36. Laughlin McDonald, *A Voting Rights Odyssey: Black Enfranchisement in Georgia* (2003), 71–72.

37. Civil Rights Act of 1960, Title VI, sec. 601; see also Heyman, "Federal Remedies for Voteless Negroes," 207. The Lodge bill of 1890 would have allowed federal officials to do even more, but it failed to pass.

38. Civil Rights Act of 1960, Title III, sec. 301; see also Saltman, *History and Politics of Voting Technology*, 141.

39. Statement of Roy Wilkins, Hearings before the Subcommittee on Constitutional Rights, Committee on the Judiciary, U.S. Senate, 87th Cong., 2d sess. (1962), 489.

40. See Civil Rights Act of 1964, Preamble and Title I; Brian K. Landsberg, *Free at Last to Vote: The Alabama Origins of the 1965 Voting Rights Act* (2007), 149. For an excellent summary of the antecedents of the "freezing doctrine," see Landsberg, *Free at Last to Vote*, 104–7.

41. Landsberg, *Free at Last to Vote*, 149.

42. Neal Devins and Louis Fisher, *The Democratic Constitution* (2004), 158.

43. Landsberg, *Free at Last to Vote*, 167–68.

44. Quoted in Landsberg, *Free at Last to Vote*, 156.

45. Excerpted in David M. O'Brien, *Constitutional Law and Politics*, vol. 1 (2003), 774–75.

46. Howard Ball, Dale Krane, and Thomas Lauth, *Compromised Compliance: Implementation of the 1965 Voting Rights Act* (1982), 193. The VRA was enacted for the purpose of "ridding the country of racial discrimination in voting" and ending southern states' "unremitting and ingenious defiance of the Constitution," as the Supreme Court put it when it upheld the law in 1966. *South Carolina v. Katzenbach*, 383 U.S. 301, 315, 309 (1966).

47. An excellent summary of the first two decades of litigation under the act and its amendments is Daniel Tokaji, "The New Vote Denial: Where Election Reform Meets the Voting Rights Act," 57 *South Carolina Law Review* 689, 702–9 (2006).

48. Charles V. Hamilton, *The Bench and the Ballot: Southern Federal Judges and Black Voters* (1973).

49. See, for example, Barbara Y. Phillips, *How to Use Section 5 of the Voting Rights Act* (1983), 43–47.

50. Ruth Morgan, *Governance by Decree: The Impact of the Voting Rights Act in Dallas* (2004), 32. Generally, Morgan's is a cautionary analysis, which urges us to "recognize the limitations of legislation to effect complex political change." Ibid., 11.

51. Landsberg, *Free at Last to Vote*, 148–49.

52. Ibid., table 7.1. Alexander Keyssar goes further, concluding that the VRA was essentially the failed Lodge Force Bill of 1890 "reincarnated." Keyssar, *The Right to Vote: The Contested History of Democracy in the United States* (2000), 111. That metaphor flattens out the history of twentieth-century election law too much, but certainly the VRA was constructed in a layered, cumulative process.

53. Spencer Overton, "The Coverage Curve: Identifying States at the Bottom of the Class," in David L. Epstein et al., eds., *The Future of the Voting Rights Act* (2006), 243.

54. Richard M. Valelly, *The Two Reconstructions* (2004), table 9.6 ("The Extended Voting Rights Act in 2004"), 222.

55. Penn Kimball, *The Disconnected* (1972); Frances Fox Piven and Richard A. Cloward, *Why Americans Still Don't Vote and Why Politicians Want It That Way* (1988).

56. Richard H. Pildes, "The Future of Voting Rights Policy: From Anti-discrimination to the Right to Vote," 49 *Howard Law Journal* 741, 742 (2006).

57. On the 1965 VRA, see H.R. Rep. No. 89-439 (1965), 1, stating that the VRA "is also designed to enforce the 14th Amendment and article 1, section 4." For the 1982 amendments, see S. Rep. No. 97-417 (1982), 39, stating that "the proposed amendment modifying a results test to Section 2 is a clearly constitutional exercise of Congressional power under Article I and the Fourteenth and Fifteenth Amendment." I owe these citations to Daniel Katz. In constitutional terms, the Equal Protection Clause has dominated cases interpreting the VRA and its de-

scendants. But the Elections Clause has surfaced, notably in *Oregon v. Mitchell* (1970), where it anchored Justice Hugo Black's opinion ruling that Congress could lower the voting age in federal elections. *Oregon v. Mitchell*, 400 U.S. 112 (1970).

58. Bernard Grofman, Lisa Handley, and Richard G. Niemi, *Minority Representation and the Quest for Voting Equality* (1992), 137; Keyssar, *The Right to Vote*, 264. Landsberg seconds this judgment, using Keyssar's phrase as a chapter subtitle. Landsberg, *Free at Last to Vote*, 148.

59. Nathaniel Persily, "The Promise and Pitfalls of the New Voting Rights Act," 115 *Yale Law Journal* 101, 103 (2007).

60. Carol M. Swain, "Focus on the Voting Rights Act: Reauthorization of the Voting Rights Act: How Politics and Symbolism Failed America," 5 *Georgetown Journal of Law and Public Policy* 29 (2007); Charles S. Bullock III and Ronald Keith Gaddie, "Focus on the Voting Rights Act: Good Intentions and Bad Social Science Meet in the Renewal of the Voting Rights Act," 5 *Georgetown Journal of Law and Public Policy* 1 (2007).

61. Persily, "Promise and Pitfalls," 135, quoting the Fannie Lou Hamer, Rosa Parks, and Coretta Scott King Voting Rights Act Reauthorization and Amendments Act of 2006, Pub. L. No. 109-246, 120 *U.S. Statutes* 577 (2006), sec. 5, 120 Stat. 580–81. The overridden decisions are *Reno v. Bossier Parish School Board* (*Bossier Parish II*), 528 U.S. 320 (2000), and *Georgia v. Ashcroft*, 539 U.S. 461 (2003).

62. Having already voted unanimously in favor of the bill, the Senate Judiciary Committee later issued a post-enactment committee interpretation of the measure supported only by Senators from one party (Republicans). As Persily points out, such *post hoc* interpretation had never happened before in congressional history, and appears to have been directed at courts that might later investigate the law: a "self-conscious manipulation of legislative history for partisan ends." Persily, "Promise and Pitfalls," 104, 113.

63. *N.A.M.U.D.N.O. v. Mukasey*, U.S.D.C. for the District of Columbia (May 30, 2008).

64. John D. Skrentny, *The Minority Rights Revolution* (2002), 21.

65. George H. W. Bush, "Message to the Senate Returning without Approval the National Voter Registration Act of 1992," July 2, 1992.

66. William J. Clinton, "Remarks on Signing the National Voter Registration Act of 1993," May 20, 1993.

67. U.S. Code, sec. 1973gg-5(B)(i).

68. Carter et al., *To Assure Pride and Confidence*, 22.

69. U.S. Code, sec. 1973gg(b), "Purposes."

70. U.S. Code, sec. 1973gg(a), "Findings"; emphasis added. See also sec. 1973gg-6(j), which defines "Registrar's jurisdiction" as including counties, cities, towns, parishes, and any "other form of municipality."

71. U.S. Election Assistance Commission, "The Impact of the National Voter Reg-

istration Act," Report to the 110th Congress, June 30, 2007, 5, 6; paraphrasing U.S. Code, sec. 1973gg-6.

72. U.S. Code, sec. 1973gg-6, "Requirements with Respect to Administration of Voter Registration."

73. U.S. Code, sec. 1973gg-6(g), "Conviction in Federal Court."

74. "U.S. Sues 3 States to Force Them to Obey Voter Registration Law," *New York Times*, Jan. 24, 1995; "Albany Seeks Repeal of Law on New Voters," *New York Times*, Mar. 23, 1995.

75. As states implement HAVA and write new election laws of their own, partisanship continues to exert heavy influence. One study of election reform between 2000 and 2004 concludes that self-interested politicians at the state level obstruct change that they are not sure will benefit them and their constituents. If one party is dominant, it is more likely to support the status quo than reform. Donald Edward Greco, "Election 2000 and the Future of Election Administration," in Christopher Banks et al., eds., *The Final Arbiter: The Consequences of Bush v. Gore for Law and Politics* (2005).

76. *Association of Community Organizations for Reform Now [ACORN] v. Edgar*, 56 F.3d 791 (Seventh Cir. 1995); *Voting Rights Coalition v. Wilson*, 60 F.3d 1411 (Ninth Cir. 1995).

77. *ACORN v. Edgar*, 796. More recent federal-court decisions also rest the NVRA squarely on the Elections Clause. See *United States v. Missouri*, 2007 U.S. Dist. LEXIS 27640 (Apr. 13, 2007), 1.

78. *ACORN v. Edgar*, 794.

79. For a review of the literature on this question, see Daniel Hays Lowenstein, Richard L. Hasen, and Daniel P. Tokaji, *Election Law*, 4th ed. (2008), 341–42.

80. Douglas R. Hess and Scott Novakowski, "Unequal Access: Neglecting the National Voter Registration Act, 1995–2007," Project Vote, Feb. 2008, 3.

81. Ibid., 1, 5, 9.

82. U.S. Election Assistance Commission, "The Impact of the National Voter Registration Act," Report to the 110th Congress, June 30, 2007, 4.

83. See Cass Sunstein, *One Case at a Time: Judicial Minimalism on the Supreme Court* (2001), 267n5. Sunstein writes, "My argument . . . finds its foundations in the aspiration to deliberative democracy, with an insistence that the principal vehicle is the legislature, not the judiciary; the judiciary is to play a catalytic and supplementary role." See also Devins and Fisher, *The Democratic Constitution*, 149. Devins and Fisher argue that while the Court "occasionally serves as a catalyst in a national conversation about race," elected officials have been more important to civil rights.

84. *Bush v. Gore*, 531 U.S. 98, 104 (2000).

85. Pildes, "The Future of Voting Rights Policy," 743.

86. See 42 USC 15483(a)(2)(A). For excellent summaries of the act, see Leonard M. Shambon, "Implementing the Help America Vote Act," 3 *Election Law Journal* 424 (2004); Brian Kim, "Help America Vote Act," 40 *Harvard Journal on*

Legislation 579 (2003); and Sarah F. Liebschutz and Daniel J. Palazzolo, "HAVA and the States," 35 *Publius* 497 (2005).

87. "The Help America Vote Act at 5," *Electionline.org*, Nov. 2007, pp. 2–4, *www.pewcenteronthestates.org/uploadedFiles/HAVA.At.5.pdf*.

88. Sarah F. Liebschutz and Daniel J. Palazzolo, "Complying with the Help America Vote Act (HAVA): Variations among the States," in Andrew Rachlin, ed., *Making Every Vote Count* (2006), 90–91.

89. Eric A. Fischer and Kevin J. Coleman, "Election Reform and Local Elections Officials: Results of Two National Surveys," CRS Report for Congress, Congressional Research Service, Feb. 7, 2008, 27.

90. For example, as of January 2004, forty-one states had requested waivers allowing them more time to complete their new voter rolls. "What's Changed, What Hasn't, and Why," *Electionline.org*, Jan. 2004, 4.

91. Dan Seligson, "NASS to EAC: Three Years Is Enough," *Electionline.org Weekly Briefing*, Feb. 10, 2005.

92. Jeffrey Toobin, "Fraud Alert," *New Yorker*, Jan. 14, 2008, 28; Heather Gerken, "How Does Your State Rank on 'The Democracy Index'?" *Legal Times*, Jan. 1, 2007; Miles Rapoport, "The Democracy We Deserve," *American Prospect*, Jan. 2005, A10.

93. David Nather, "Election Board Facing Votes of No Confidence," *CQ Weekly*, Apr. 23, 2007; Christopher Elmendorf, "Representation Reinforcement through Advisory Commissions: The Case of Election Law," 80 *N.Y.U. Law Review* 1366, 1443 (2005).

94. See U.S. Election Assistance Commission, "Register to Vote in Your State by Using This Postcard Form and Guide," p. 1, *www.eac.gov/files/voter/nvra_update.pdf*.

95. Brian Kim, "Help America Vote Act," 40 *Harvard Journal on Legislation* 579, 601 (2003). HAVA itself explicitly anticipates that county and municipal authorities will continue to administer U.S. elections.

96. Tova Wang et al., "Voting in 2008: Ten Swing States," co-sponsored by the Century Foundation and Common Cause, Oct. 2008, 6–7.

97. *State ex. Rel Skaggs et al. v. Brunner*, U.S.D.C. So. Ohio, Nov. 20, 2008.

98. Fischer and Coleman, "Election Reform and Local Elections Officials," 27.

99. Ibid., 29, 31.

100. Pildes, "The Future of Voting Rights Policy."

101. Pildes laments that despite this progress, we seem to be further postponing the day when "the United States works itself out of a voting regime that remains excessively dependent, even for national elections, on the rules and institutions, not to mention the competence and whims, of elections officials, of the more than 3,000 counties in the oldest and one of the largest democracies in the world." Richard Pildes, "The Future of Voting Rights Policy," in Andrew Rachlin, ed., *Making Every Vote Count* (2006), 69.

102. Richard B. Saphire and Paul Moke, "Litigating *Bush v. Gore* in the States: Dual

Voting Systems and the Fourteenth Amendment," 51 *Villanova L. Rev.* 229, 245 (2006).

103. U.S. Code, sec. 1973aa-6, "Voting Assistance for Blind, Disabled, or Illiterate Persons."

104. U.S. Code, sec. 1973ee-1, "Selection of Polling Facilities." Note that this statute clearly enlarges federal authority, yet simultaneously reinforces the place of those "subdivisions" within federal election law. The statute also provides for the possibility of enforcement by requiring each state's chief elections officer to report to the Federal Election Commission every even-numbered year on "the number of accessible and inaccessible polling places" in the state. Notably, this part of the law would "only be effective for a period of ten years" following the fall of 1984. See ibid., sec. c.

105. Hollister Bundy, "Election Reform, Polling Place Accessibility, and the Voting Rights of the Disabled," 2 *Election Law Journal* 217, 226 (2003).

106. Bundy, "Election Reform, Polling Place Accessibility," 228, quoting a 1996 publication of the Federal Election Commission.

107. *Tennessee v. Lane*, 541 U.S. 509 (2004).

108. Cheryl Wittenauer, "Lawyers Debate Alleged Ban on Voting Rights for Mentally Ill," Associated Press, Feb. 13, 2007.

109. *MOPAS et al. v. Carnahan*, U.S.C.A. Eighth Cir., Aug. 23, 2007, 11, 14.

110. Jim Abrams, "Congress Looks to Paper, Again, to Guarantee Honest Elections," Associated Press, Sept. 7, 2007.

111. Mark Tushnet, *The New Constitutional Order* (2003), 1, 9. Tushnet defines a constitutional order as "a reasonably stable set of institutions through which a nation's fundamental decisions are made over a sustained period, and the principles that guide those decisions. These institutions and principles provide the structure within which ordinary political contention occurs, which is why I call them *constitutional* rather than merely political." Ibid., 1.

Chapter 4

Epigraph: Don Herzog, *Happy Slaves: A Critique of Consent Theory* (1989), 23; Barbara Swann, interview with the author, Apr. 7, 2003; Kathy Dent, quoted in Dan Seligson, "Florida Preview: The End of an Error?" *Electionline Weekly*, Jan. 24, 2008.

1. Abby Goodnough, "Reassurance for the Florida Voters Made Wary by the Electoral Chaos of 2000," *New York Times*, May 24, 2004, A18. One county commissioner said, "Every population has gotten the feel of that machine. Sometimes it's a little awkward when Shirley shows up at these events, but people say, 'If she's taking it way out here then there must not be anything to hide.' "

2. Barbara Swann, interview with the author, Apr. 7, 2003.

3. Stephen Ansolabehere and Charles Stewart III, "Residual Votes Attributable to Technology," 67 *Journal of Politics* 365, 366 (2005); Stephen Knack and Mar-

tha Kropf, "Who Uses Inferior Voting Technology?" 35 *PS: Political Science and Politics* 541 (2002).

4.   R. Michael Alvarez, Morgan Llewellyn, and Thad E. Hall, "Are Americans Confident Their Ballots Are Counted?" CalTech/MIT Voting Technology Project, July 2006, 4.

5.   This is the title of an initiative launched by the Pew Center for the States and the Jeht Foundation, aiming to improve accuracy, convenience, efficiency, and security for voters. The Make Voting Work Initiative awarded $2.5 million in funding to sixteen projects in 2008.

6.   Donald S. Lutz, *Principles of Constitutional Design* (2006), 67.

7.   See Arend Lijphart, *Democracies* (1984); Richard Katz, *Democracy and Elections* (1997). Katz provides an intriguing analysis of how theory and institutions meet in his typology of fourteen different kinds of electoral democracy. Katz, *Democracy and Elections*, 280–96.

8.   Ansolabehere writes, "The election of 2000 has made the technical perfection of the voting system into the voting rights [issue] of the twentieth century." Stephen Ansolabehere, "Election Administration and Voting Rights," in David L. Epstein et al., eds., *The Future of the Voting Rights Act* (2006), 219.

9.   Steven Schier, *You Call This an Election?* (2001), 115.

10. Wendy M. Rahm, John Brehm, and Neil Carlson, "National Elections as Institutions for Generating Social Capital," in Theda Skocpol and Morris Fiorina, eds., *Civic Engagement in American Democracies* (1999).

11. G. Bingham Powell Jr., *Elections as Instruments of Democracy: Majoritarian and Proportional Visions* (2000), 4.

12. *Burdick v. Takushi*, 504 U.S. 428 (1992).

13. Hannah Pitkin, *The Concept of Representation* (1967), 234.

14. Dennis F. Thompson, *The Democratic Citizen: Social Science and Democratic Theory in the Twentieth Century* (1970), 140. As one political-science text concludes, voting is best understood not as an act of rational calculation but rather as "an act of social participation or civic involvement." Nelson Polsby and Aaron Wildavsky, *Presidential Elections* (2000), 9.

15. Quoted in Kenneth L. Karst, *Belonging to America: Equal Citizenship and the Constitution* (1989), 93.

16. John Mark Hansen makes this point in "The Majoritarian Impulse and the Declining Significance of Place," in Gerald M. Pomper and Marc D. Weiner, eds., *The Future of American Democratic Politics* (2003), 43–44.

17. Jørgen Elklit and Andrew Reynolds, "The Impact of Election Administration on the Legitimacy of Emerging Democracies: A New Comparative Politics Research Agenda," 40 *Commonwealth and Comparative Politics* 86 (2002), 113–16.

18. Dan Seligson, "Florida Preview: The End of an Error?" *Electionline Weekly*, Jan. 24, 2008.

19. *Purcell v. Gonzales*, 127 S. Ct. 5 (2006).

20. Ibid., 7.
21. This point is made particularly well in Richard Hasen, "The Untimely Death of *Bush v. Gore*," 60 *Stanford Law Review* 1, 36 (2007).
22. *Purcell v. Gonzales*, 7.
23. *Webster's Ninth New Collegiate Dictionary* (1988), 628.
24. Robert Dahl, *How Democratic Is the American Constitution?* (2003); Sanford Levinson, *Our Undemocratic Constitution* (2006).
25. Levinson, *Our Undemocratic Constitution*, 51.
26. Ibid., 88–89.
27. Meanwhile, states decide how to apportion their Electoral College votes, so if our former New Yorker were to leave Vermont and move further east, across the White Mountains of New Hampshire and into Maine, her individual instrumental capacity to shape a presidential election would be enlarged, because Maine allots its Electoral College votes by congressional district rather than winner-take-all.
28. Ronald Keith Gaddie made this point in a post to the Election Law e-mail list moderated by Rick Hasen and Dan Lowenstein. See Gaddie, "Re: D.C. representation bill may pass House this week," Mar. 21, 2007.
29. Thus, if our friend from Vermont moved her legal residence to the District of Columbia or Puerto Rico, she would not forfeit her U.S. citizenship, but she would essentially lose much of her right to vote.
30. Lisa Rein, "Gansler Supports Voting at Age 17," *Washington Post*, Dec. 20, 2007; Colin Poitras, "Plan to Let Some 17-Year-Olds Vote in Primaries Fails in House," *Hartford Courant*, May 4, 2007.
31. John C. Fortier, *Absentee and Early Voting: Trends, Promises, and Perils* (2006), 1.
32. Brian Lundy, quoted in Jo Becker, "Voters May Have Their Say before Election Day," *Washington Post*, Aug. 26, 2004.
33. *Voting Integrity Project, Inc., et al., v. Oregon*, 259 F.3d 1169, 1176 (2001).
34. See the Early Voting Information Center at Reed College, "Absentee and Early Voting Laws," *www.earlyvoting.net/states/abslaws.php*.
35. Hawaii, Nevada, Oklahoma, and South Dakota ban write-in votes altogether. Issacharoff, Karlan, and Pildes, *The Law of Democracy*, 3rd ed. (2007), 233.
36. Richard L. Morrill, "Representation, Law, and Redistricting in the United States," in Clive Barnett and Murray Low, *Spaces of Democracy: Geographical Perspectives on Citizenship, Participation, and Representation* (2004), 70. See also Edmund S. Morgan, *Inventing the People: The Rise of Popular Sovereignty in England and America* (1988); Daniel N. Hoffman, *Our Elusive Constitution* (1997). Hoffman writes, "Places, in the Whig-republican view, had objective interests which elected members were to discover and represent. In so doing, they served all their constituents, regardless of whether or how those constituents might have voted." Hoffman, *Our Elusive Constitution*, 64.

37. Rosemary Zagarri, *The Politics of Size: Representation in the United States, 1776–1850* (1987), 148.

38. *Reynolds v. Sims*, 377 U.S. 533, 562 (1964).

39. Levinson, *Our Undemocratic Constitution* (2006), 147; emphasis in original. Levinson is critical of this "bias towards localism."

40. James A. Gardner, "What Is 'Fair' Partisan Representation, and How Can It Be Constitutionalized? The Case for a Return to Fixed Election Districts." 90 *Marquette Law Review* 555, 558, 573 (2007).

41. Levinson, *Our Undemocratic Constitution*, 30.

42. James G. Gimpel and Jason E. Schuknecht, *Patchwork Nation* (2003), 1.

43. Madison was concerned about designing institutions to channel and control the effects of self-interested instrumental conduct, and he concluded that extending government authority over a vast territory and varied population would protect worthy minorities by forcing government to achieve consensus rather than a simple majority. See *Federalist* 10, on factions, and 51, on federalism and the separation of powers; a particularly good concise analysis is A. J. Reichley, *The Life of the Parties* (1992), 27.

44. Michael Kammen, *Sovereignty and Liberty: Constitutional Discourse in American Culture* (1988), 3.

45. Robert A. Dahl, *A Preface to Democratic Theory* (1956). Gerald Leonard, like others, calls those traditions "Madisonian" and "Jeffersonian." Gerald Leonard, *The Invention of Party Politics: Federalism, Popular Sovereignty, and Constitutional Development in Jacksonian Illinois* (2002).

46. *Voting Rights Coalition et al. v. Wilson*, 60 F.3d 1411, 1415 (Ninth Cir. 1995).

47. Daniel T. Rodgers, *Contested Truths: Keywords in American Politics since Independence* (1998), 86.

48. Katz, *Democracy and Elections*, 291.

49. Max Farrand, ed., *The Records of the Federal Convention of 1787*, rev. ed. (1966), vol. 2, 240–41.

50. Ibid., 241; Hamilton, *Federalist* 59, in Garry Wills, ed., *The Federalist Papers* (1982/1787–1788), 299.

51. My interpretation here may be somewhat at odds with that of Justice Black's reading in *Oregon v. Mitchell* of a different statement of Madison's. Black quoted Madison stating that "it was thought that the regulation of time, place, and manner of electing the representatives, should be uniform throughout the continent. Some States might regulate the elections on the principles of equality, and others might regulate them otherwise. This diversity would be obviously unjust." See *Oregon v. Mitchell*, 400 U.S. 112, n. 5 (1970), citing J. Elliott's *Debates on the Constitution*, vol. 3, 367 (1876). Justice Black cited this passage in support of a strong federal role in governing voting qualifications. Putting aside the question of why Madison used such passive and anonymous phrasing ("it was thought"), I think it is correct to conclude that Madison likely believed both in locally

varying voting practices and in a strong latent federal power to regulate suffrage, when it was necessary to prevent corruption and distorted election results.

52. Hamilton, *Federalist* 59, in Wills, *The Federalist Papers*, 300. Continuing, Hamilton raised what he thought was a farfetched rhetorical specter: "Suppose an article had been introduced into the Constitution, empowering the United States to regulate the elections for the particular States, would any man have hesitated to condemn it?" Ibid., 301. Hamilton's point seems to be that leaving election management *completely* under state control would be an equivalent catastrophe.

53. Today, one scholar refers to this passage in articulating what he calls the "Hamiltonian proviso": localities and states control elections as long as they do not impair representation at the national level. Dennis F. Thompson, *Just Elections: Creating a Fair Electoral Process in the United States* (2002), 135.

54. Joseph Story, *Commentaries on the Constitution of the United States* (1987/1833), 291.

55. Ibid., 292. Story's language here matches Hamilton's in *Federalist* 59 almost verbatim.

56. Ibid., 291.

57. We do need to note a tension between Madison's apparent views about decentralized voting practices and his ideas about representation, which were explicitly *anti*-local, in the context of the time. A "spirit of locality," Madison argued, was destroying "the aggregate interests of the community." Madison, quoted in Gordon S. Wood, *The American Revolution* (2002), 141. Madison saw corruption and intrigue in the towns and small districts that selected state legislators; enlarging those units to encompass thirty thousand people in national electoral politics, he hoped, "would eliminate the local pressures and locally oriented candidates that had made the state governments a disgrace." Garry Wills, "Introduction," in Wills, *The Federalist Papers*, at xxii. When Anti-Federalists charged that the national government would swallow up the smaller units, Federalists like Madison and Hamilton assured them it would not. Their reasoning, writes Edmund Morgan, was that "the people would be more attached to their familiar, local representatives in the state legislatures than they would be to their more remote national representatives." Morgan, *Inventing the People*, 280.

58. Levinson, for example, not only is critical of American electoral structures but offers them as evidence that the American constitutional order is excessively consensual and insufficiently majoritarian, and that this grave flaw is to blame for some of our most serious national problems. Levinson, *Our Undemocratic Constitution*.

59. Thompson, *Just Elections*, 180.

60. Stephen Macedo, "School Reform and Equal Opportunity in America's Geography of Inequality," 1 *Perspectives on Politics* 743 (2003) (quoting Tocqueville, *Democracy in America*, trans. George Lawrence, 69).

61. Tocqueville, *Democracy in America*, vol. 1 (1990/1835), 59, 60.
62. Ibid., 61.
63. Ibid., 62, 64, 68, 67. As always, Tocqueville finds a tension and paradox here, noting that local power is "an infrequent and fragile thing," because a "highly civilized community can hardly tolerate a local independence, is disgusted at its numerous blunders, and is apt to despair of success before the experiment is completed." Ibid., 60. Later, he acknowledges that in some cases Americans have "overstepped the limits of sound policy" by allowing localities too much independence. Ibid., 88–89.
64. Robert T. Gannett Jr., "Bowling Ninepins in Tocqueville's Township," 97 *American Political Science Review* 1, 7 (2003). Gannett links a close reading of Tocqueville to current debates within political science over civic culture and democratic citizenship.
65. Gianfranco Poggi, *The State: Its Nature, Development, and Prospects* (1990), 138.
66. Matthew A. Crenson and Benjamin Ginsberg, *Downsizing Democracy: How America Sidelined Its Citizens and Privatized Its Public* (2002), 45.
67. Ibid., 45–46.
68. Michael Schudson, *The Good Citizen: A History of American Civic Life* (1998), 1–3.
69. Ibid., 1. "The labor required to run an election is substantial: with more than 25,000 precincts in California alone, each employing three to five poll workers, the outpouring of volunteer labor is enormous and their organization and training no mean feat." Ibid.
70. "Helping Americans Vote: Poll Workers," *Electionline.org*, Sept. 2007, 1.
71. Spencer Overton, *Stealing Democracy: The New Politics of Voter Suppression* (2006), 57. Despite this passage, Overton remains concerned about the inequities local administration permits.
72. Thompson, *Just Elections*, 56. Such benefits, Thompson argues, "may be worth the sacrifice of uniformity not only because they may outweigh the costs of unequal treatment, but because the unequal treatment is not so objectionable." In Thompson's view, a resident of a Florida county that did not count hanging chads was unlucky but did not have her "civic dignity" insulted and was not really discriminated against. Moreover, she has the ability to change her county's counting standard, if she can persuade her neighbors to do so. Ibid., 56.
73. Paul Krugman, "Faith in America," *New York Times*, Nov. 2, 2004, A27.
74. David M. Shribman, "More Than a Vote," *Boston Globe*, Oct. 29, 2002. Shribman writes, "I miss the ritual of giving my name to the clerk who knows very well who I am because I have lived here for years. I miss being ushered into the polling booth. I miss being given one of those I Voted stickers. . . . I miss the people standing outside with the placards and their cups of coffee and the most tempting piece of American food there is—the jelly doughnut."
75. Paul Gronke, "Electing to Change How We Vote," *Los Angeles Times*, Oct. 16,

2003, 17; Thompson, *Just Elections*, 34–35. Political scientist Michael Schudson describes his participation in the 1996 elections as "a small ritual of neighborly cheer." Schudson, *The Good Citizen*, 3.

76. Brian Kim, "Help America Vote Act," 40 *Harvard Journal on Legislation* 579, 601 (2003).

77. Hansen, "The Majoritarian Impulse," 44.

78. Alvarez, Llewellyn, and Hall, "Are Americans Confident Their Ballots Are Counted?" 26, 25.

79. Lonna Rae Atkeson and Kyle Saunders, "The Effect of Election Administration on Voter Confidence: A Local Matter?" 40 *PS: Political Science and Politics* 655 (2007). Atkeson and Saunders emphasized that partisanship also exerts strong influence.

80. Thad Hall, J. Quin Monson, and Kelly D. Patterson, "Poll Workers and the Vitality of Democracy: An Assessment," 40 *PS: Political Science and Politics* 647 (2007).

81. Robert M. Stein et al., "Voting Technology, Election Administration, and Voter Performance," 7 *Election Law Journal* 123, 131, 134 (2008). See also Stephen Ansolabehere and Charles Stewart III, "Residual Votes Attributable to Technology," 67 *Journal of Politics* 365 (2005).

82. R. Michael Alvarez and Thad E. Hall, "Controlling Democracy: The Principal-Agent Problems in Election Administration," 34 *Policy Studies Journal* 491 (2006).

83. James H. Blodgett, "Suffrage and Its Mechanism in Great Britain and the United States," *American Anthropologist*, vol. 2 (Jan. 1889), 73. Blodgett was referring to the administration of state and national elections as well as to local government proper. While the focus of this book is on the benefits of local administration in national elections, a rich and growing interdisciplinary literature develops a kind of cognate argument, emphasizing the importance of experimentation and variation in the institutions of local governance itself. For examples in the U.S. setting, see Richard Briffault, "Our Localism: Part I—The Structure of Local Government Law," 90 *Columbia Law Review* 1 (1990), and "Our Localism: Part II—Localism and Legal Theory," 90 *Columbia Law Review* 346 (1990); Frank L. Bryan, *Real Democracy: The Vermont Town Meeting and How It Works* (2003); Shaun Bowler, Todd Donovan, and David Brockington, *Electoral Reform and Minority Representation: Local Experiments with Alternative Elections* (2003); Dorothy Holland et al., *Local Democracy under Siege* (2007). On the international front, in *Going Local: Decentralization, Democratization, and the Promise of Good Governance* (2007), Merilee S. Grindle explores ways decentralization can lead to better government in Mexico.

84. Brian Kim, "Help America Vote Act," 40 *Harvard Journal on Legislation* 579, 601 (2003). For a typical "laboratories of democracy" argument, see "Don't Standardize Election Systems" (unsigned editorial), *Rocky Mountain News*, Oct. 5, 2005.

85. Mitch Stacy, "Panel Votes to End Fla. Election Probe," Associated Press, Feb. 8, 2008.

86. Leonard M. Shambon, "Implementing the Help America Vote Act," 3 *Election Law Journal* 424, 442 (2004).

87. Christopher Drew, "Overhaul Plan for Vote System Will Be Delayed," *New York Times,* July 20, 2007.

88. See Daniel Tokaji and Thad Hall, "Money for Data: Funding the Oldest Unfunded Mandate," Commentary, Election Law Moritz weblog, June 5, 2007, *moritzlaw.osu.edu/electionlaw/.*

89. Gary Fineout and Mary Ellen Klas, "Florida Election Chiefs: Get Rid of Election Day," *Miami Herald,* Dec. 1, 2004.

90. See Dan Seligson, "New Data Suggests Vote Centers Boost Turnout," *Electionline Weekly,* Aug. 18, 2005.

91. M. Mindy Moretti, "In Focus This Week: Bigger Is Not Always Better: Voting Centers, Consolidation Draw Complaints," *Electionline.org's Electionline Weekly,* Jan. 26, 2006.

92. Christopher Conkey, "States Rush In to Spur Voters," *Wall Street Journal,* Oct. 13, 2004.

93. For evidence on voter turnout, see, for example, Thad Kousser and Megan Mullin, "Vote-by-Mail Doesn't Deliver Voters," *San Diego Union-Tribune,* Apr. 19, 2007.

94. Quoted in John M. Broder, "Growing Absentee Voting Is Reshaping Campaigns," *New York Times,* Oct. 21, 2006. Norman Ornstein of the American Enterprise Institute is also among those who worries that voting by mail and online can "lead to alienation from the community." Ann McFeatters, "Americans Want Voting Practices to Change, Poll Reveals," *Pittsburgh Post-Gazette,* Nov. 8, 2005.

95. Dennis F. Thompson, "Election Time," 98 *American Political Science Review* 51 (2004).

96. W. J. M. Mackenzie, *Free Elections: An Elementary Textbook* (1958), 103.

97. Representative Bob Ney, quoted in Brian Kim, "Help America Vote Act," 40 *Harvard Journal on Legislation* 579, 601 (2003).

98. *Siegel v. LePore,* 120 F. Supp. 2d 1041, 1052 (S.D. Fla.) (2000). Abner Greene has emphasized this passage in *Understanding the 2000 Election* (2001).

99. Jonah Berger, Marc Meredith, and S. Christian Wheeler, "Can Where People Vote Influence How They Vote?" Stanford Research Paper Series No. 1926, Feb. 2006.

100. Jo Becker, "Voters May Have Their Say."

101. Joe Stinebaker, "Officials Manipulate Elections with Polling Location," Associated Press, Feb. 14, 2007.

102. Elizabeth M. Addonizio, Donald Green, and James M. Glaser, "Putting the Party Back into Politics: An Experiment Testing Whether Election Day Festi-

vals Increase Voter Turnout," 40 *PS: Political Science and Politics* 721, 723, 725 (2007).

103. Alan S. Gerber, Donald Green, and Christopher W. Larimer, "Social Pressure and Voter Turnout: Evidence from a Large-Scale Field Experiment," 102 *American Political Science Review* 33, 42 (2008).

104. Patricia Funk, "Theory and Evidence on the Role of Social Norms in Voting," paper presented at the annual meetings of the Midwest Political Science Association, Chicago, Apr. 20, 2006, discussed in Stephen J. Dubner and Steven D. Levitt, "Why Vote?" *New York Times*, Nov. 6, 2005.

105. Richard F. Bensel, *The American Ballot Box in the Mid-Nineteenth Century* (2004), 289. Studying early American elections, Edmund S. Morgan makes this point in colorful fashion, finding that turnout in the "sober elections" of democratic New England "was smaller than in the aristocratic South's drunken ones." Morgan, *Inventing The People*, 207. To be sure, Morgan also describes southern elections as characterized by violence and corruption, as well as excitement; Rhode Island was an exception to New England's probity. New England may have been the cradle of American democracy, but if elections and electoral campaigns "give plausibility to the fiction of popular government, southerners knew a good deal more about engaging the public in elections than New Englanders did." Ibid., 208.

106. Hansen, "The Majoritarian Impulse," 46; Robert Huckfeldt, "Political Participation and Neighborhood Social Context," 23 *American Journal of Political Science* 579 (1979), asserting that the political process does not operate in isolation and that, in fact, participation has effects beyond the casting of a vote; Scott D. McClurg, "Social Networks and Political Participation: The Role of Social Interaction in Explaining Political Participation," 56 *Political Research Quarterly* 449 (2003), noting influence of social networks on political participation.

107. Studying Maryland, James Gimpel and Jason Schuknecht found a positive, nonlinear relationship between proximity of the polling place and turnout. Gimpel and Schuknecht, "Political Participation and the Accessibility of the Ballot Box," 22 *Political Geography* 471 (2003). Studying Atlanta, Haspel and Knotts concluded that small differences in distance from the polls can have significant impact on turnout. Moshe Haspel and H. Gibbs Knotts, "Location, Location, Location: Precinct Placement and the Costs of Voting," 67 *Journal of Politics* 560 (2005). Henry Brady and John McNulty found a "transportation effect" diminishing turnout when California polling places were moved. Brady and McNulty, "The Costs of Voting: Evidence from a Natural Experiment," paper prepared for the 2005 Annual Meeting of the Western Political Science Association, Oakland. But Robert M. Stein and Greg Vonnahme concluded that turnout increased when a Colorado county switched to larger "vote centers." Stein and Vonnahme, "Engaging the Unengaged Voter: Vote Centers and Voter Turnout," 70 *Journal of Politics* 487 (2008).

108. James A. Morone, *The Democratic Wish: Popular Participation and the Limits of American Government,* rev. ed. (1998), 1, 5.
109. Tocqueville, *Democracy in America,* vol. 1, 70, 404, 71, 271. Listing the "CAUSES WHICH MITIGATE THE TYRANNY OF THE MAJORITY IN THE UNITED STATES," Tocqueville placed the "absence of centralized administration" first in line. Ibid., 271. And Tocqueville wrote that "the townships, municipal bodies, and counties form so many concealed breakwaters, which check or part the tide of popular determination." Ibid., 272.
110. John A. Rohr, *Civil Servants and Their Constitutions* (2002), 147.
111. Quoted in George Grayson, "Registering and Identifying Voters: What the United States Can Learn from Mexico," 3 *Election Law Journal* 513, 518 (2004). Recall the 1885 statement of Woodrow Wilson, quoted in Chapter 2: "The federal supervisor who oversees the balloting for congressmen represents the very ugliest side of federal supremacy." Woodrow Wilson, *Congressional Government,* 2d ed. (1885), 27.
112. Ronald Hayduk, *Gatekeepers to the Franchise: Shaping Election Administration in New York* (2005), 9.
113. Edward B. Foley, "The Analysis and Mitigation of Electoral Errors: Theory, Practice, Policy," 18 *Stanford Law and Policy Review* 350 (2007).
114. Richard H. Pildes, "Democracy, Anti-democracy, and the Canon," 17 *Constitutional Commentary* 295 (2000).

Chapter 5

Epigraph: Steven F. Huefner, Daniel Tokaji, and Edward B. Foley, *Registration to Recounts* (2007), 174; *Griffin v. Roupas,* 385 F. 3d 1128, 1132 (2004); Louisiana parish elections official, interview with the author, 2005.

1. Michael Powell and Peter Slevin, "Several Factors Contributed to 'Lost' Voters in Ohio," *Washington Post,* Dec. 15, 2004.
2. Richard L. Hasen, "Beyond the Margin of Litigation: Reforming U.S. Election Administration to Avoid Electoral Meltdown," 62 *Washington and Lee Law Review* 937 (2005).
3. Henry E. Brady, "Equal Protection for Votes," reprinted in Arthur J. Jacobson and Michel Rosenfeld, eds., *The Longest Night: Polemics and Perspectives on Election 2000* (2001), 47; emphasis added.
4. *Bush v. Gore,* 531 U.S. 98, 109 (2000). Critics have assailed that limitation, some quoting Justice Scalia: "The Supreme Court of the United States does not sit to announce 'unique' dispositions." Antonin Scalia, dissenting in *United States v. Virginia,* 518 U.S. 515, 596 (1996). Quoted in Alan Dershowitz, *Supreme Injustice* (2001), 122–23.
5. A rehabilitationist account is Steven J. Mulroy, "Lemonade from Lemons: Can Advocates Convert *Bush v. Gore* into a Vehicle for Reform?" 9 *Georgetown Jour-*

nal of Poverty Law and Policy 357 (2002). The Sixth Circuit Court of Appeals relied on *Bush v. Gore* in *Stewart et al. v. Blackwell et al.*, No. 05-3044, Sixth Cir. C.A. (Apr. 21, 2006). For a review of post–*Bush v. Gore* cases as of 2006, see Clifford A. Jones, "Out of Guatemala?" 5 *Election Law Journal* 121, 136 (2006).

6.   *Stewart et al. v. Blackwell et al.*

7.   Richard Fallon, *Our Dynamic Constitution* (2004), 217.

8.   *West Virginia Board of Education v. Barnette*, 319 U.S. 624 (1943).

9.   Quoted in E. J. Dionne, "When Did Voting Get So Intimidating?" *Washington Post*, Oct. 31, 2004.

10. Stephen Ansolabehere and Charles Stewart III, "Residual Votes Attributable to Technology," 67 *Journal of Politics* 365, 385 (2005).

11. Lisa Disch, *The Tyranny of the Two-Party System* (2002), 131.

12. Richard Niemi and Paul Herrnson, "Beyond the Butterfly: The Complexity of U.S. Ballots." 1 *Perspectives on Politics* 317, 318 (2003). Niemi and Herrnson, said editor Jennifer Hochschild, "dissect a surprisingly simple and effective way of ensuring that some voters remain political losers." Variation in balloting procedures, she wrote, "almost always [acts] to the detriment of those with the least education and resources and the most need of gaining political influence." Jennifer Hochschild, "Introduction and Comments," 1 *Perspectives on Politics* 247, 247–48 (2003).

13. Ronald Hayduk, *Gatekeepers to the Franchise: Shaping Election Administration in New York* (2005), 7. Election practices and technologies, Hayduk writes, "can function to disenfranchise eligible citizens at every stage: before an election, on election day, and during vote tabulation/certification. This is especially true for low-income individuals, minorities, newly naturalized citizens, people with disabilities, and first-time voters—groups that have disproportionately low turnout rates." Ibid., 5.

14. Steven F. Huefner, Daniel Tokaji, and Edward B. Foley, *From Registration to Recounts* (2007), viii.

15. Ansolabehere and Stewart, "Residual Votes Attributable to Technology," 386.

16. Charles Seymour and Donald Paige Frary, *How the World Votes: The Story of Democratic Development in Elections*, vol. 1 (1918), 242.

17. Quoted in Kirk Harold Porter, *A History of Suffrage in the United States* (1971/1918), 218. "The Mississippi version" of the test, William Riker writes, "*adapted to local circumstances*, required that electors be able to read from the state constitution *or* to understand it *or* to interpret it reasonably. The alternatives were, of course, intended to allow registration of wholly illiterate whites while the test itself was to be administered to exclude all Negroes, whether literate or not." William Riker, *Democracy in the United States* (1965), 53; emphasis added. Alex Keyssar writes that "many of the disfranchising laws were designed expressly to be administered in a discriminatory fashion, permitting whites to vote while barring blacks. Small errors in registration procedures or marking ballots might or might not be ignored at the whim of election officials; taxes

might be paid easily or only with difficulty; tax receipts might or might not be issued." Keyssar, *The Right to Vote: The Contested History of Democracy in the United States* (2000), 112.

18.   *Louisiana v. United States*, 380 U.S. 145 (1965). Note that while literacy and "understanding" tests were not the same thing, they shared common exclusionary purposes.

19.   Keyssar, *The Right to Vote*, 86; Riker, *Democracy in the United States*, 53. "This plan of popular suffrage," said Glass, will "eliminate the darkey as a political factor in this State in less than five years, so that in no single county of the Commonwealth will there be the least concern felt for the complete supremacy of the white race in the affairs of government." Paul Lewinson, *Race, Class, and Party: A History of Negro Suffrage and White Politics in the South* (1932), 84–86.

20.   Rogers M. Smith, *Civic Ideals: Conflicting Visions of Citizenship in U.S. History* (1997), 383; Laughlin McDonald, *A Voting Rights Odyssey: Black Enfranchisement in Georgia* (2003), 2–3. Morgan Kousser has written that "cross-fertilization and coordination" between southern states in adopting reforms "amounted to a public conspiracy." Kousser, *The Shaping of Southern Politics: Suffrage, Restriction, and the Establishment of the One-Party South* (1974), 39. Confusing election announcements and the deceptive use of multiple ballot boxes for multiple-office elections were also widely employed to keep black votes from counting. Seymour and Frary, *How the World Votes*, 243.

21.   Joseph Harris, *Registration of Voters in the United States* (1929), 312.

22.   Riker, *Democracy in the United States*, 53.

23.   Kousser, *Shaping of Southern Politics*, 2–3n4.

24.   Kenneth Karst, *Belonging to America: Equal Citizenship and the Constitution* (1989), 3.

25.   *Monroe v. Collins*, 17 Oh. St. 665 (1867); see also Harris, *Registration of Voters*, 311.

26.   *United States v. Reese*, 92 U.S. 214 (1876). At this time the right to vote itself was more likely to be defined as a privilege than a right. *Yick Wo v. Hopkins* (1886) offers a good example. Speaking of "the political franchise of voting," the Court said, "Though not regarded strictly as a natural right, but *as a privilege merely conceded by society according to its will, under certain conditions, nevertheless it is regarded as a fundamental right*, because preservative of all rights." *Yick Wo v. Hopkins*, 118 U.S. 356, 370 (1886); emphasis added.

27.   *Williams v. Mississippi*, 170 U.S. 213 (1898).

28.   Justice Oliver Wendell Holmes wrote that the Court "cannot undertake now, any more than it has in the past, to enforce political rights." Noting the allegation that "the great mass of the white population intends to keep the blacks from voting," Holmes declared that "a name on a piece of paper will not defeat them." *Giles v. Harris*, 189 U.S. 475, 486, 488 (1903). Into the 1950s, *Giles* stood as a "seemingly insurmountable" obstacle in the path of those who would chal-

lenge discriminatory administration of registration rules. Brian K. Landsberg, *Free at Last to Vote: The Alabama Origins of the Voting Rights Act* (2007), 1.

29. Landsberg, *Free at Last to Vote*, 2, 4.

30. Steven Hill, "Will Your Vote Count in 2006?" Think Tank Town, *Washington Post*, Aug. 1, 2006, *www.washingtonpost.com*.

31. Michael Schudson, *The Good Citizen: A History of American Civic Life* (1998), 137; Herbert Croly, *The Promise of American Life* (1965/1909), 271.

32. On Brandeis, see Melvin I. Urofsky, *Louis D. Brandeis and the Progressive Tradition* (1981). On "Decentralist" and "Nationalist" strands in Progressive political economy, see Michael Sandel, *Democracy's Discontent: America in Search of a Public Philosophy* (1996), 211–21.

33. Jimmy Carter et al., *To Assure Pride and Confidence in the Electoral Process: Report of the National Commission on Federal Election Reform* (2002), 27; emphasis added.

34. Daniel T. Rodgers, *Contested Truths: Keywords in American Politics since Independence* (1998), 174. The Progressive model of citizenship "helped free people from parties, but it also provided new means to exclude some people from voting altogether." Schudson, *The Good Citizen*, 183. For a contrasting view, see Paul Kleppner, "Defining Citizenship: Immigration and the Struggle for Voting Rights in Antebellum America," in Donald W. Rogers, ed., *Voting and the Spirit of American Democracy* (1992), 45.

35. Robert Wiebe, *Self-Rule: A Cultural History of American Democracy*, 135.

36. Keyssar, *The Right to Vote*, table A.13 ("Literacy Requirements for Suffrage: 1870–1924").

37. Matthew A. Crenson and Benjamin Ginsberg, *Downsizing Democracy: How America Sidelined Its Citizens and Privatized Its Public* (2002), 56. Historically, American registration rules have been so variable and fine-grained that it is all but impossible to summarize state-by-state policies. Alexander Keyssar writes that "a preliminary attempt to produce such a tabular presentation [of state registration rules] yielded an incomplete document more than fifty pages long." Keyssar, *The Right to Vote*, 325. One authority calculates that around 1900, about 30 percent of counties outside the South required some kind of personal registration, while about 24 percent used state-compiled lists. By 1920, the corresponding figures were 45 percent and 22 percent of counties, respectively. A. J. Reichley, *The Life of the Parties* (1992), 208.

38. William E. Gienapp, "Politics Seem to Enter into Everything," in Stephen E. Maizlish and John J. Kushma, eds., *Essays on American Antebellum Politics, 1840–1860* (1982), 24.

39. National Municipal League, Committee on Election Administration, *A Model Registration System* (1927), 51, 62.

40. Crenson and Ginsberg, *Downsizing Democracy*, 55–56. Indeed, Crenson and Ginsberg conclude that the Progressives "regarded mass mobilization as an impediment to effective government."

41. Reichley, *The Life of the Parties*, 208–9. Progressive reforms, Reichley writes, aimed to get rid of this corruption, happily paying the price in "some contraction of democracy." Ibid., 207.
42. Rodgers, *Contested Truths*, 174.
43. Kevin Phillips and Paul H. Blackman, *Electoral Reform and Voter Participation* (1975), 5. G. Alan Tarr notes that registration requirements and a ninety-day waiting period for naturalized citizens were also part of a nationwide "late-century movement to restrict the franchise." Tarr, *Understanding State Constitutions* (1998), 108.
44. Keyssar, *The Right to Vote*, 159–62.
45. Ibid., 158. Crenson and Ginsberg also conclude that together with ballot-design reform, voter registration "disfranchised millions of immigrants and working-class voters." Crenson and Ginsberg, *Downsizing Democracy*, 55–56.
46. Frances Fox Piven and Richard A. Cloward, *Why Americans Still Don't Vote and Why Politicians Want It That Way* (2000), 45–46. Fox Piven and Cloward argue that elites purposefully put such obstructions in place because they feared the increasing ability of lower-income voters to affect government policy. Large chunks of the electorate were "demobilized" in what amounted to "something like a democratic counterrevolution" *because* of the increasing power of lower-strata voters to shape elections and policy. Ibid. Robert Wiebe, however, concludes that what he calls "the mechanics of exclusion" made only "a contribution" to shrinking turnout: "the sinking of the lower class" was its ultimate cause. Wiebe, *Self-Rule*, 136.
47. Keyssar, *The Right to Vote*, 158–59.
48. Richard F. Bensel, *The American Ballot Box in the Mid-Nineteenth Century* (2004), chap. 6, "Loyalty Oaths, Troops, and Elections during the Civil War."
49. Eric Foner, *The Story of American Freedom* (1998), 119.
50. Kousser, *Shaping of Southern Politics*, 250–51. Daniel T. Rodgers notes that the new discipline of political science displayed "an extraordinary fertility of imagination" in developing new arguments demonstrating "that suffrage was not a right, but a gift of the state." Rodgers, *Contested Truths*, 174.
51. Schudson, *The Good Citizen*, 184.
52. Robert J. Dinkin, *Voting in Provincial America* (1977), 47.
53. James H. Kettner, *The Development of American Citizenship, 1608–1870* (1978), 122. Maryland and Pennsylvania had similar experiences, Kettner writes.
54. Kettner, *Development of American Citizenship*, 9. A letter sent back to London in 1664 by Massachusetts Governor Endicott seems to indicate that the Americans believed in qualifications—perhaps just not the formal ones: "Such as vote in elections should be orthodox in religion, virtuous (and not vicious) in conversation, and all those that according to the orders and the customs of the colony, here established, agreeable to the liberties of the charter, having proved themselves to be such in the places where they live, have from time to time been admitted in our elections." Quoted in Richard C. Simmons, *Stud-

ies in the Massachusetts Franchise, 1631–1691 (1989), 67. What is striking about this list—orthodox, virtuous, agreeable, "in the places where they live"—is that as exclusionary and moralistic as they sound to modern ears, these criteria are mostly informal, and judgments would virtually all have been local. This is not to say that *anything* was permissible: in 1664, Edward Hutchinson was fined ten pounds for voting in Boston, because he was not a freeman but a merchant. Ibid.

55. Kenneth A. Lockridge, *A New England Town: The First Hundred Years* (1985/1970), 47–48. Similarly, the Connecticut General Court required in 1679 that only those adult white men holding fifty shillings of assessed property could participate in town meetings. This requirement stayed on the books for at least a century, but it "was never enforced after the 1720s and became a dead letter." Bruce C. Daniels, *The Connecticut Town: Growth and Development, 1635–1790* (1979), 67.

56. Chilton Williamson, *American Suffrage: From Property to Democracy* (1960), 49.

57. For example, when an Anglican stood for office in Puritan Boston, the people cried that "popery had come upon them like a scarlet whore," and the election moderator carefully accepted virtually all voters who weighed in against the Anglican candidate, while rejecting many of those who were for him. Dinkin, *Voting in Provincial America*, 47.

58. Ibid., 100.

59. Williamson, *American Suffrage*, 103. Elsewhere, local elections helped broaden the franchise in cities from New Haven to Charleston. Ibid., 123.

60. Marchette Chute, *The First Liberty: A History of the Right to Vote in America, 1619–1850* (1969), 289.

61. Williamson, *American Suffrage*, 152–53.

62. Ibid., 230.

63. John Dinan, *The American State Constitutional Tradition* (2006), 148–49. Some scholars have concluded that taxpayer tests were merely slightly more inclusionary versions of the property tests they replaced. Willi Paul Adams, for example, wrote that the property qualification was taken for granted in drafting early state constitutions, and the only question was "what kind of property qualification was suitable, whether, for instance, tax paying was suitable." Adams, *The First American Constitutions*, expanded ed. (2001), 194. But Marc Kruman persuasively shows that the taxpayer tests were about consent, rather than qualification, and were built on the new idea that the suffrage was "a defensive device capable of protecting popular liberty against potentially rapacious legislators." Marc W. Kruman, *Between Authority and Liberty: State Constitution Making in Revolutionary America* (1997), 94.

64. Williamson, *American Suffrage*, 134, 171.

65. Ibid., 198–99.

66. *Journal of the Debates and Proceedings in the Convention of Delegates, Chosen to Revise the Constitution of Massachusetts, 1820–1821* (1853), 249.

67. Ibid., 254.

68. Bensel, *American Ballot Box*, 139.

69. Williamson, *American Suffrage*, 177. "The country was more democratic than its institutions," he writes. Ibid., 181.

70. Bensel, *American Ballot Box*, 22.

71. Quoted in Kruman, *Between Authority and Liberty*, 105.

72. Quoted in Lawrence Tribe, *American Constitutional Law* (1988), 1559n2; emphasis added.

73. Marian Thompson Wright, "Negro Suffrage in New Jersey, 1776–1875," 33 *Journal of Negro History* 168, 173 (1948). One study has concluded that New Jersey's de facto enfranchisement of property-owning single women was very likely purposeful. Kruman, *Between Authority and Liberty*, 106.

74. Chute, *The First Liberty*, 289–90.

75. See generally Sandra F. VanBurkleo, *Belonging to the World: Women's Rights and American Constitutional Culture* (2001); Aileen Kraditor, *The Ideas of the Woman Suffrage Movement, 1890–1920* (1971); Keyssar, *The Right to Vote*. See Akhil Amar, *America's Constitution: A Biography* (2005), 366, 605–6n49, for an intriguing discussion of how men justified enfranchising black men, but not women, during Reconstruction.

76. VanBurkleo, *Belonging to the World*, 182–83.

77. Keyssar, *The Right to Vote*, 167. In some cases, this flexibility led to restrictions—for example, only taxpayers or property owners could vote on a bond question. A history of home rule in 1916 noted this variation and faulted women suffragettes for failing to capitalize on it adequately. Howard Lee McBain commented that "it would seem . . . that the protagonists in the cause of woman's suffrage have been somewhat derelict in their failure to institute campaigns for an extension of the voting right through the medium of freeholders' charters or amendments in the cities" of states where charters had such authority. McBain, *The Law and the Practice of Municipal Home Rule* (1916), 582–83.

78. Holly J. McCammon et al., "How Movements Win: Gendered Opportunity Structures and U.S. Women's Suffrage Movements, 1866 to 1919," 66 *American Sociological Review* 49 (2001); Holly J. McCammon and Karen E. Campbell, "Winning the Vote in the West: The Political Successes of the Women's Suffrage Movements, 1866–1919," 15 *Gender and Society* 55, 56 (2001); Keyssar, *The Right to Vote*, tables A.20, A.18, and A.17. Twenty territories and states fully enfranchised women between 1869 (Wyoming) and 1918 (South Dakota).

79. Keyssar, *The Right to Vote*, 186.

80. VanBurkleo, *Belonging to the World*, 182. Presumably, women were then understood to have legitimate expertise and interests in local issues—a stake they lacked in state and national politics. John J. Dinan, *Keeping the People's Liberties: Legislators, Citizens, and Judges as Guardians of Rights* (1998), 107.

81. Maude Wood Park, "Campaigning State by State," in *Victory! How Women Won It*, National American Woman Suffrage Association (1940), 74.

82. Suzanne M. Marilley, *Woman Suffrage and the Origins of Liberal Feminism in the United States, 1820–1920* (1996), 207.

83. Holly J. McCammon et al., "How Movements Win," 54.

84. Ibid., 61.

85. Andrea Moore Kerr, "White Women's Rights, Black Men's Wrongs," in Marjorie Spruill Wheeler, ed., *One Woman, One Vote* (1995), 73; Marjorie Spruill Wheeler, "A Brief History of the Woman Suffrage Movement in America," in Wheeler, *One Woman, One Vote*, 17; Mari Jo and Paul Buhle, "Introduction," in *The Concise History of Woman Suffrage* (1978), 25.

86. William F. Ogburn and Inez Goltra, "How Women Vote," 34 *Political Science Quarterly* 413 (1919).

87. Nancy F. Cott, "Across the Great Divide," in Wheeler, *One Woman, One Vote*, 358.

88. VanBurkleo, *Belonging to the World*, 183. There is even fragmentary evidence that some advocates thought local suffrage held the potential to dissolve the lingering racial divides within the movement. After black as well as white women in Tennessee won municipal suffrage in 1919, one white woman wrote that the record of black women voters in Nashville "was one of which every southern suffragist may not only feel proud but hopeful for the future," since the black women had "voted with the best white women thereby eliminating any political prejudice." Catherine Kenny, quoted in Anastatia Sims, "Armageddon in Tennessee," in Wheeler, *One Woman, One Vote*, 344, 345.

89. Some new states required that voters be citizens, but Vermont, Tennessee, and Ohio did not; these states did not exclude noncitizens from suffrage until 1828, 1834, and 1852, respectively. New Hampshire was first to require voters to be citizens, in 1814; Connecticut and Virginia followed a few years later, and half a dozen other states excluded noncitizens in the next two decades. Paul Kleppner, "Defining Citizenship: Immigration and the Struggle for Voting Rights in Antebellum America," in Donald W. Rogers, ed., *Voting and the Spirit of American Democracy* (1992), 45. The most comprehensive analysis of historical, legal, and political issues connected to voting by noncitizens is in Jamin B. Raskin, "Legal Aliens, Local Citizens: The Historical, Constitutional and Theoretical Meanings of Alien Suffrage," 141 *University of Pennsylvania Law Review* 1391 (1993).

90. *Lanz v. Randall et al.*, 14 F. Cas. 1131, 1133 (1876).

91. Keyssar, *The Right to Vote*, 33.

92. Leon E. Aylsworth, "The Passing of Alien Suffrage," 25 *American Political Science Review* 114, 1931.

93. *Shelton v. Tiffin*, 6 How. 163, 185 (1848). The federal courts did not reach unanimity on these questions—a Minnesota federal court ruled in 1876 that "there is no necessary or uniform relation between citizenship and the right to vote." *Lanz v. Randall et al.*, 1133.

94. *Trop v. Dulles*, 356 U.S. 86, 102 (1958).

95. See Ronald Hayduk, *Democracy for All: Restoring Immigrant Voting Rights in the United States* (2006). Chicago and New York long allowed noncitizens to vote in school board elections, and Takoma Park, Maryland, has voted to permit resident aliens to vote in local elections. John McIlhenny, "Amherst [Massachusetts] Tries to Allow Its Aliens to Vote," Associated Press, Sept. 4, 2001. San Francisco has considered allowing noncitizens to vote in school board elections. Jessie Mangaliman, "San Francisco Considers School Board Voting Rights for Noncitizens," *San Jose Mercury News*, June 21, 2004.

96. Leonard Shambon and Keith Abouchar, "Trapped by Precincts? The Help America Vote Act's Provisional Ballots and the Problem of Precincts," 10 *New York University Journal of Law and Public Policy* 133, 137 (2006).

97. Stephen Knack and Martha Kropf, "Who Uses Inferior Voting Technology?" *PS: Political Science and Politics*, Sept. 2002, 541–48 (2002). Other studies have shown a relationship between error rates in predominantly African American communities and the use of punch-card technology. Ibid., 547, 541.

98. Richard Posner, *Breaking the Deadlock: The 2000 Election, the Constitution, and the Courts* (2001), 259. Posner goes further, calling punch-card voting technology "a de facto literacy test" for people who are "poorly educated." Indeed, Posner argues that the same is true of other ballot types "when the votes are counted at the county rather than the precinct level." Ibid., 259.

99. Stephen Knack and Martha Kropf, "Voided Ballots in the 1996 Presidential Election: A County Level Analysis," 65 *Journal of Politics* 881, 887 (2003).

100. Michael Tomz and Robert Van Houweling, "How Does Voting Equipment Affect the Racial Gap in Voided Ballots," 47 *American Journal of Political Science* 46, 47 (2003). On this issue, see also Paul Moke and Richard B. Saphire, "The Voting Rights Act and the Racial Gap in Lost Votes," 58 *Hastings Law Journal* 1 (2006); Stephen Ansolabehere, "Voting Machines, Race, and Equal Protection," 1 *Election Law Journal* 61 (2002). For a strong argument that locally varying election machinery has discriminatory effects, see Richard B. Saphire and Paul Moke, "Litigating *Bush v. Gore* in the States: Dual Voting Systems and the Fourteenth Amendment," 51 *Villanova Law Review* 229 (2006).

101. For an authoritative review of recent history and arguments over voter ID, see Spencer Overton, "Voter Identification," 105 *Michigan Law Review* 631 (2007).

102. *Crawford et al. v. Marion County Election Board et al.*, 128 S.Ct. 1610 (2008).

103. Linda Greenhouse, "In a 6–3 Vote, Justices Uphold a Voter ID Law," *New York Times*, Apr. 29, 2008.

104. Stephen Ansolabehere and Nathaniel Persily, "Vote Fraud in the Eye of the Beholder: The Role of Public Opinion in the Challenge to Voter Identification Requirements," 121 *Harvard Law Review* 1738, 1739 (2008). For a comprehensive critical examination of recent voter fraud allegations, see Lorraine Minnite, "The Politics of Voter Fraud," Project Vote (2008).

105. Greenhouse, "In a 6–3 Vote, Justices Uphold a Voter ID Law"; Peter Wallsten, "Parties Battle over New Voter ID Laws," *Los Angeles Times*, Sept. 12, 2006.

106. Deborah Hastings, "Indiana Nuns Lacking ID Denied at Poll by Fellow Sister," Associated Press, May 7, 2008.

107. "Making Votes Count" (editorial), *New York Times*, Sept. 7, 2004.

108. Steven Rosenfeld, "Election Day 2007: New ID Laws Disenfranchise Voters," *AlterNet.org*, Nov. 7, 2007.

109. Stephen Ansolabehere, "Ballot Bonanza," *Slate*, Mar. 16, 2007; Ansolabehere, "Access versus Integrity in Voter Identification Requirements," paper presented at the New York University Law School's Election Law Symposium for the Annual Survey of American Law, 2007.

110. "In Search of Accurate Vote Totals" (editorial), *New York Times*, Sept. 5, 2006; Daniel Tokaji, "Ohio Voter ID Lawsuit," Equal Vote weblog, Oct. 24, 2006, *moritzlaw.osu.edu/blogs/tokaji/*.

111. Asian American Legal Defense and Education Fund, "Asian American Access to Democracy in the 2006 Elections" (2008), 17–18.

112. One study of the 2004 election found that turnout was lower where more ID was required—that is, in states where voters had to provide some form of ID instead of just swearing or signing in. Timothy Vercellotti and David Andersen, "Protecting the Franchise, or Restricting It? The Effects of Voter Identification Requirements on Turnout." Paper prepared for the 2006 annual meetings of the American Political Science Association, Philadelphia. But another survey found that in 2006, virtually no one was turned away from the polls for failure to provide ID. Stephen Ansolabehere, "Ballot Bonanza," *Slate*, Mar. 16, 2007. Of course, these two findings are not incompatible: more demanding ID requirements may *deter* voters from even showing up, something the 2006 study would not have detected.

113. Adam Cohen, "American Elections and the Grand Old Tradition of Disenfranchisement," *New York Times*, Oct. 8, 2006.

114. Art Levine, "Lesson from Voting Rights Activists' Big Win in Missouri," *AlterNet.org*, June 10, 2008.

115. Though this seems very unlikely today, voter-ID laws could also lead American election administration to take a very different shape in the years ahead. If Americans and their representatives decide that voter ID is critically important *and* that varying implementation is unacceptable, the obvious solution would be a governmentally provided voter-ID card. While several election-law specialists have already recommended such a policy, that kind of centralization seems quite unlikely given broad American skepticism toward governmental databases.

116. See, for example, Jeff Manza and Chris Uggen, *Locked Out: Felon Disfranchisement and American Politics* (2005); Sasha Abramsky, *Conned: How Millions Went to Prison, Lost the Vote, and Helped Send George W. Bush to the White House* (2006); Elizabeth A. Hull, *The Disenfranchisement of Ex-felons* (2006). On his-

tory, see John Dinan, "The Adoption of Criminal Disenfranchisement Provisions in the United States: Lessons from the State Constitutional Convention Debates," 19 *Journal of Policy History* 282 (2007). On public opinion, see Brian Pinaire, M. Heumann, and L. Bilotta, "Barred from the Vote: Public Attitudes toward the Disenfranchisement of Felons," 30 *Fordham Urban Law Journal* 1519 (2003). On recent changes, see Ryan King, "Expanding the Vote: State Felony Disenfranchisement Reform, 1997–2008," Sentencing Project (2008).

117. Relatively little academic work has looked directly at local variation in the administration of criminal disenfranchisement law. Two outstanding exceptions are Guy Stuart, "Databases, Felons, and Voting: Bias and Partisanship of the Florida Felons List in the 2000 Elections," 119 *Political Science Quarterly* 453 (2004); and Anna Bassi, Rebecca Morton, and Jessica Trounstine, "Delegating Disenfranchisement Decisions" (unpublished manuscript on file with the author).

118. U.S. Department of Justice, Office of the Pardon Attorney, *Civil Disabilities of Convicted Felons: A State-by-State Survey* (1996), 1.

119. See 42 USC 15483(a)(2)(A).

120. On removal from the rolls, see the American Civil Liberties Union, Demos, and the Right to Vote Campaign, "Purged! How a Patchwork of Flawed and Inconsistent Voting Systems Could Deprive Millions of Americans of the Right to Vote," Oct. 2004.

121. Jeff Manza and Christopher Uggen, "Punishment and Democracy: Disenfranchisement of Nonincarcerated Felons in the United States," 2 *Perspectives on Politics* 491 (2004), 495.

122. "Denying the Vote" (unsigned editorial), *New York Times*, Sept. 11, 2006.

123. "Felon-Voting Laws Confusing, Ignored," *Seattle Times*, May 22, 2005.

124. *Richardson v. Ramirez*, 418 U.S. 24, 34n2 (1974).

125. *Hunter v. Underwood*, 471 U.S. 222, 226 (1985).

126. Gary Fields, "U.S. News: Felons' Voting Requests Pile Up; Florida's Process to Restore Suffrage Illustrates Haze," *Wall Street Journal*, Mar. 31, 2008; Morgan Kousser, "Disfranchisement Modernized," 6 *Election Law Journal* 104 (2007), 112.

127. See Alec C. Ewald, *A Crazy-Quilt of Tiny Pieces: State and Local Administration of American Criminal Disenfranchisement Law* (Sentencing Project, 2005), 16 and appendix A.

128. I summarize this research in more detail in *Crazy-Quilt of Tiny Pieces*. The local-interview states were Connecticut, Delaware, Georgia, Illinois, Indiana, Louisiana, Maryland, Nebraska, Tennessee, and Wyoming. In each state, online lists of counties or town elections officials were used; typically, seven or eight localities were chosen randomly, usually from the beginning or the end of the alphabet, and then a few large population centers were selected. State maps were consulted to avoid having the chosen localities cluster in one part of the state.

129. Unless otherwise indicated, quotations in this chapter are from interviews conducted by the author.

130. The remaining officials gave an answer that did not indicate a clear "direction"— stating, for example, that they did not know whether someone on parole should be allowed to register.

131. For analysis and criticism of this decision, see Alec C. Ewald, " 'Civil Death': The Ideological Paradox of Criminal Disenfranchisement Law in the United States," 2002 *Wisconsin Law Review* 1045, 1064–71 (2002).

132. "Felony Disenfranchisement Laws in the United States" (online document), Sentencing Project, 2008, *www.sentencingproject.org*.

133. State officials in Colorado, Illinois, Indiana, Michigan, and South Carolina indicated that misdemeanants in jail could not vote. Until state law changed in 2007, Maryland disqualified people convicted of those misdemeanors deemed "infamous crimes" by the attorney general.

134. *Jarrard v. Clayton County Board of Registrars*, 425 S.E. 2d 874 (Ga. 1993).

135. Maryland Code, sec. 3-102(b)(1); Office of the Attorney General, Maryland, "July 2006 Infamous Crimes List" (copy on file with the author).

136. Louisiana Constitution, Article I, sec. 10; emphasis added. See also Louisiana Rev'd Statutes, sec. 18:102(1) and 18:171.1A(1).

137. Louisiana HB 1017 (Act 136), effective date June 6, 2008; HB 1011 (Act 604), effective date Aug. 15, 2008.

138. To the state's credit, Tennessee explains the statutes and time periods online. See the web document "Restoration of Voting Rights," the web pages of the Tennessee Department of State, and the links therein. The rights-restoration form for use by most convicts is also now posted online by the Department of State.

139. Author Sasha Abramsky shows that Tennessee lawyers have to avoid concentrating their vote-restoration appeals with any one judge, lest a judge catch "political heat." Abramsky, *Conned*, 170.

140. Alabama attempted to streamline restoration procedures in 2003, but it did so by creating different eligibility and restoration rules for different categories of offenses. See King, "Expanding the Vote," 5. What Erika Wood calls this "tangled bureaucratic web" may have resulted in thousands of potential voters failing to secure their eligibility, including some who were wrongly turned away by elections officials. Erika Wood, "Restoring the Right to Vote," Brennan Center for Justice, New York University (2008), 15.

141. Shaila Dewan, "In Alabama, a Fight to Regain Voting Rights Some Felons Never Lost," *New York Times*, Mar. 2, 2008.

142. Jake Armstrong, "Felon Voting Ban Questioned," *Florida Times-Union*, May 30, 2008.

143. Code of Alabama, Title 17, chap. 3, sec. 6 ("judicial officers"), sec. 55 (appeal process).

144. Danza Johnson, "Groups Debate Whether Felons Should Regain the Right to Vote," *Northeast Mississippi Daily Journal*, May 28, 2008. For a glimpse at the politics behind these "suffrage bills," see Abramsky, *Conned*, 201.

145. Ben Piper, "Sec. of State Pushes to Further Restrict Felons' Voting Rights," *Hattiesburg American*, Mar. 4, 2008.

146. *Cotton v. Fordice*, 157 F.3d 388 (1998). Burglary, however, is not a disqualifying offense according to the attorney general, since it does not necessarily entail the "wrongful taking of property."

147. See "Attorney General's Opinions," available through the Mississippi secretary of state's web page, at *www.sos.state.ms.us/elections/2004/Handbook/AGOpinions. pdf*.

148. Piper, "Sec. of State Pushes to Further Restrict Felons' Voting Rights."

149. U.S. Census Bureau, "Migration by Race and Hispanic Origin: 1995 to 2000," table 1, 3.

150. Brendan Riley, "Dispute Delays Rule on Ex-felon Voting in Nevada," Associated Press, Dec. 4, 2007.

151. See generally "Election Crimes: An Initial Review and Recommendations for Further Study," U.S. Election Assistance Commission, Dec. 2006. This issue featured prominently in litigation in the Washington State recount controversy, where lawyers for Republican candidate Dino Rossi argued that hundreds of ineligible felons voted. "Rossi Team Issues List of 'Felon' Voters," *Seattle Times*, Mar. 4, 2005. Thomas J. Miles reviews media accounts showing that "at least in some jurisdictions, ineligible ex-felons have little trouble registering to vote and casting ballots." Thomas J. Miles, "Felon Disenfranchisement and Voter Turnout," 33 *Journal of Legal Studies* 85, 120 (2004), 116–17nn50–52.

152. Erika Wood and Rachel Bloom, "De Facto Disenfranchisement," American Civil Liberties Union and the Brennan Center for Justice, 2008.

153. Michael Pinard, "Broadening the Holistic Mindset: Incorporating Collateral Consequences and Reentry into Criminal Defense Lawyering," 31 *Fordham Urban Law Journal* 1067 (2004). Courts and lawmakers have long struggled with whether the sanction is a way of punishing people or a way of protecting the ballot box. Disenfranchisement clearly has punitive effects: in 1995 a federal judge described disenfranchisement as "the harshest civil sanction imposed by a democratic society," an "axe" by which a person is "severed from the body politic and condemned to the lowest form of citizenship." *McLaughlin v. City of Canton*, 947 F. Supp. 954, 971 (S.D. Miss. 1995). Yet the Supreme Court in the 1958 case *Trop v. Dulles* said disenfranchisement "is not a punishment but rather a nonpenal exercise of the power to regulate the franchise." *Trop v. Dulles*, 96–97.

154. Nora V. Demleitner, "Continuing Payment on One's Debt to Society: The German Model of Felon Disenfranchisement as an Alternative," 84 *Minnesota Law Review* 753, 755–56 (2000).

155. See Richard A. Posner, *Law, Pragmatism, and Democracy* (2003), 234–35. First,

Judge Posner calls the idea that disenfranchisement is a deterrent "ludicrous," notes that "felons have interests like everybody else," and mocks the idea that felons can be denied the vote because they are "bad people." But then Posner blithely and tacitly appears to endorse the "bad people" argument by advocating a five-year post-sentence "cooling off" period, and argues that allowing inmates to vote would be "inimical to prison discipline." Posner does not offer empirical support for that claim, and indeed there is none: where inmates of jails and prisons vote in the United States and in many other countries, "prison discipline" is unaffected. One suspects that on no other core voting-rights question would a sitting federal judge meander back and forth on key questions, ultimately resting an argument for a rights-restricting policy on what amounts to a hunch.

156. I explore these ideas in some detail in " 'Civil Death': The Ideological Paradox of Criminal Disenfranchisement Law in the United States," 2002 *Wisconsin Law Review* 1045 (2002). For analysis of the presence of these and related ideas in state constitutional deliberations, see John Dinan, "The Adoption of Criminal Disenfranchisement Provisions in the United States: Lessons from the State Constitutional Convention Debates."

157. Keyssar, *The Right to Vote*, 308.

158. As the Brennan Center put it in a 2008 publication, laws disenfranchising people after release from prison "often lead to widespread confusion among both elections officials and people with criminal records." Wood, "Restoring the Right to Vote," 15.

159. William H. Riker, *Democracy in the United States* (1965), 25, 35. Daniel N. Hoffman has also made this point well, noting that "our constitutional history contains a deep transformative impulse—even a transformative mandate—toward democratic empowerment, equal dignity, and a more equitable system of representation." Hoffman, *Our Elusive Constitution* (1997), 77.

160. Dennis F. Thompson, *Just Elections: Creating a Fair Electoral Process in the United States* (2002), 28.

Conclusion

Epigraph: W. J. M. Mackenzie, *Free Elections: An Elementary Textbook* (1958), 170; *Storer v. Brown*, 415 U.S. 724, 730 (1974).

1. Barry Friedman and Scott B. Smith, "The Sedimentary Constitution," 147 *University of Pennsylvania Law Review* 1 (1998).

2. Stephen Skowronek, *Building a New American State: The Expansion of National Administrative Capacities, 1877–1920* (1982), viii.

3. In my view, Karen Orren and Stephen Skowronek's exacting definition of "development" as a zero-sum durable shift does not provide a useful guide to the history of American suffrage. Moreover, I do not find support for Orren and Skowronek's suggestion that the plenary nature of authority means that a

polity should be motivated to *resolve* conflicts created by the interplay of different governing orders. Orren and Skowronek, *The Search for American Political Development* (2004), 116. But other elements of the theoretical framework laid out in *The Search for American Political Development* find perfect illustration in the evolution of our voting practices. Understood in their institutional setting, American voting rights illustrate nicely the "intercurrence" created by coexisting political orders, the "multiplicity of authorities" common in several U.S. policy arenas, and "the fragmented, uneven quality of change that . . . political development regularly produces and that constructs politics through time." American suffrage rules have always been "an arrangement of authority riddled with uncertainty." Orren and Skowronek, *Search for American Political Development*, 114, 143, 118–19. As the authors write elsewhere, "Any realistic depiction of politics in time will include multiple orders, as well as the conflict and irresolution built into their reciprocal interactions." Ibid., 17. In more recent work, Skowronek and Glassman have accurately described American political development as "always to some degree imminent, unsettled, in the making." This expectation seems more accurate than the zero-sum, durable-shift conception. Stephen Skowronek and Matthew Glassman, "Formative Acts," in Skowronek and Glassman, eds., *Formative Acts: American Politics in the Making* (2007), 1.

4. Adam Cohen, "Voting Rights Are Too Important to Leave to the States," *New York Times*, May 2, 2008.

5. Alexander Mooney, "Senator Calls for Sweeping Election Overhaul," *CNN.com*, Mar. 28, 2008.

6. Alexis de Tocqueville, *Democracy in America*, vol. 2 (1990/1835), 2.

7. Assessing the mixed motives behind the high-turnout, high-partisanship, high-corruption elections of the mid-nineteenth century, Bensel writes that the electoral rituals that helped construct nineteenth-century communal identity "were of a kind that we might not want to celebrate, at least not without serious qualification." Richard F. Bensel, *The American Ballot Box in the Mid-Nineteenth Century* (2004), 288.

8. See Daniel Tokaji and Thad Hall, "Money for Data: Funding the Oldest Unfunded Mandate," Commentary, Election Law Moritz weblog, June 5, 2007, *moritzlaw.osu.edu/electionlaw/*.

9. Heather Gerken, "How Does Your State Rank on 'The Democracy Index'?" *Legal Times*, Jan. 1, 2007. In a weblog commentary after the 2008 election, Chris Elmendorf called for a "recruit the states" approach, through which federal agencies distribute funds and, as necessary, waivers allowing states to experiment with new ways of improving electoral performance. See "Elmendorf: Two Models for Building Public Confidence in the Electoral Process," Election Law Blog, Nov. 9, 2008, *electionlawblog.org*. The Election Assistance Commission seems to be moving in this direction; in May 2008 it announced that five states will receive a total of $10 million to improve election data collection. U.S. Elec-

tion Assistance Commission, "EAC Awards Five States $10 Million to Improve Election Data Collection," press release, May 29, 2008.

10. Ian Urbina, "V.A. Ban on Voter Drives Is Criticized," *New York Times*, June 13, 2008; Ian Urbina, "V.A. to Allow Voter Signup for Veterans at Facilities," *New York Times*, Sept. 9, 2008.

11. While by no means comprehensive, the following list highlights a few typical publications from among the excellent recent works manifesting an ironic approach to election law. One prime example is William Poundstone's 2008 book *Gaming the Vote*. Poundstone shows with levity and wit that every electoral system ever imagined has profound strengths and weaknesses, and that none of them are guaranteed to produce a perfectly fair or accurate reflection of the voters' will. (Poundstone concludes by recommending the adoption of "range" voting.) Poundstone, *Gaming the Vote: Why Elections Aren't Fair (and What We Can Do About It)* (2008). Others arrive at less optimistic conclusions. For example, economist Bryan Caplan believes that understanding voter ignorance is "the key to a realistic picture of democracy," and argues in *The Myth of the Rational Voter* that modern democracies fail to adopt good economic policies ultimately because voters are irrational. Caplan, *The Myth of the Rational Voter: Why Democracies Choose Bad Policies* (2007), 3. Caplan qualifies as an ironist in large part because he delivers that dark conclusion in an amusing style, punctuating almost every section of every chapter with pungent and often hilarious quotations. And an ironic sensibility has characterized much of the rational-choice literature to which Caplan responds, such as work exploring "rational ignorance" and "low-income rationality." See, for example, Arthur Lupia and Mathew D. McCubbins, *The Democratic Dilemma: Can Citizens Learn What They Need to Know?* (1998); Samuel L. Popkin, *The Reasoning Voter: Communication and Persuasion in Presidential Campaigning* (1991); Arthur Lupia, Mathew D. McCubbins, and Samuel L. Popkin, eds., *Elements of Reason: Cognition, Choice, and the Bounds of Rationality* (2000). Other projects are more earnestly pragmatic. For example, Ned Foley eschews the goal of electoral "perfection" and attempts to work out a quantitative standard that legislators and judges may use to define just how much error a good election can actually stand. Edward B. Foley, "The Analysis and Mitigation of Electoral Errors: Theory, Practice, Policy," 18 *Stanford Law and Policy Review* 350 (2007). Challenging another element of contemporary conventional wisdom, Justin Buchler argues that close elections are not necessarily good for democracy: "there is nothing beneficial about competitive elections as a social choice mechanism," either in terms of their outcomes or their procedural characteristics. Justin Buchler, "The Social Sub-optimality of Competitive Elections," 133 *Public Choice* 439, 454 (2007). And in one of the most fascinating studies of American voting behavior published in years, Richard Lau and David Redlawsk demonstrate in their careful, data-driven, non-normative exploration of voter cognition that almost a third

of voters may vote "incorrectly": not in terms of how their votes are tabulated or what an external observer thinks they should want, but in terms of *their own preferences*, given more time and more information about the candidates. Richard R. Lau and David P. Redlawsk, *How Voters Decide: Information Processing during Election Campaigns* (2006), 81.

12.   The full passage merits reproduction here: "This is like the unhappy persons who live, if they can be said to live, in the statical chair—who are ever feeling their pulse, and who do not judge of health by the aptitude of the body to perform its functions, but by their ideas of what ought to be the true balance between the several secretions." Edmund Burke, "Speech on the State of the Representation," quoted in Hannah F. Pitkin, *The Concept of Representation*, 155. The "statical chair" was a device invented by the Venetian physician Sanctorious for weighing people and determining the amount of "insensible perspiration" lost by the body, such as after certain foods were eaten. Ibid., 283.

13.   Adam Berinsky, "The Perverse Consequences of Electoral Reform in the United States," 33 *American Politics Research* 471, 484 (2005).

14.   Todd Donovan, "A Goal for Reform: Make Elections Worth Stealing," 40 *PS: Political Science and Politics* 681, 685 (2007); emphasis added. Similarly, Lani Guinier asked rhetorically in 1992, "Have we focused exclusively on the electoral process without any sustained exploration of the governance process?" Guinier, "Development of the Franchise: 1982 Voting Rights Amendments," in Karen McGill Arrington and William L. Taylor, eds., *Voting Rights in America: Continuing the Quest for Full Participation* (1992), 107.

15.   Mark N. Franklin, "Electoral Participation," in Lawrence LeDuc et al., eds., *Comparing Democracies* (1996), 227.

Index